ON THIS DAY IN THE CHURCH

ON THIS DAY IN THE CHURCH

An Illustrated Almanac of the Latter-day Saints

Richard Neitzel Holzapfel

Alexander L. Baugh

Robert C. Freeman

Andrew H. Hedges

EAGLE GATE

Salt Lake City, Utah

Library of Congress Cataloging-in-Publication Data

On this day in the church: an illustrated almanac of the Latter-day Saints / Richard Neitzel Holzapfel . . . [et al.].
   p. cm.
  ISBN 1-57345-579-2
  1. Church of Jesus Christ of Latter-day Saints—History Chronology. 2. Church of Jesus Christ of Latter-day Saints—History Pictorial works. I. Holzapfel, Richard Neitzel.
BX8611.057 1999
289.3'32'09—dc21   99-17001

                                                  CIP

Printed in the United States of America   72082-6521

10 9 8 7 6 5 4 3 2 1

❧❧❧ CONTENTS ❧❧❧

❧❧❧ PREFACE ❧❧❧

Between sessions of the organizational meeting of the Church on Tuesday, 6 April 1830, at Fayette, New York, the Lord spoke to the young Prophet Joseph at Peter Whitmer's farmhouse: "Behold, there shall be a record kept among you" (Doctrine and Covenants 21:1). The Prophet also charged others to keep a record, and, as a result, the Latter-day Saints have become a record-keeping people—a boon to historians interested in source material for their research. The rich collections of diaries, letters, minutes, reminiscences, artifacts, and photographs produced and preserved by the Latter-day Saints make our history a "field already to harvest."

Beginning in 1832, the Prophet began to record and compile a history of his ministry and the rise of the Church. This effort, eventually identified as the "History of Joseph Smith," contained extracts from his personal record and other sources. This record is the basis of the multivolume *History of The Church of Jesus Christ of Latter-day Saints* (Salt Lake City: The Church of Jesus Christ of Latter-day Saints, 1932–51). After Joseph Smith's death in 1844, the effort to complete this project continued, and a manuscript history of the administration of Brigham Young, under the title "History of Brigham Young," was begun. The project was completed three years after the death of Brigham Young in 1877.

In 1896 the First Presidency of the Church asked former *Deseret News* editor Charles W. Penrose to continue the effort to provide a daily account of events in the history of the Church. Eventually, that record became known as the "Journal History of The Church of Jesus Christ of Latter-day Saints." It included material from diaries, letters, minutes, and newspaper clippings, highlighting events in the institutional Church and in the lives of numerous individuals. Assistant Church historian Andrew Jenson assumed supervision of the project in 1906 and not only continued the day-by-day record but also created the same type of daily record for the years previous to 1896. By 1922 the "Journal History" stretched back to the organization of the Church. The record for the nineteenth century alone consisted of 385 legal-size binders, some containing more that two hundred pages. Eventually, the story of the Church's first one hundred years (1830–1930) filled some 800 binders.

A day-by-day chronology, as provided in these sources, is one important way to view Church history. For this project we decided to look at Church history by reviewing events by the calendar day on which they took place—thus the title *On This Day in the Church.* Since this project is date specific and records do not always provide the dates for important events (such as the First Vision and the restoration of the Melchizedek Priesthood), we sometimes struggled to find enough appropriate information for certain dates. Other dates, such as 24 July and general conference weekends in early April and October, could alone supply enough information to fill an entire volume. Therefore it was necessary to select only a few significant events occurring on such dates and stretch to find information for less-eventful days in the calendar year.

In recording the lives of significant Church leaders and members, we set out to provide a representative sample of their accomplishments and life's events rather than a comprehensive chronology of their lives. Furthermore, it was impossible to identify every accomplishment of individual Latter-day Saints, so we have chosen to highlight a variety of people as examples of our culture, society, and world. We did, however, include entries listing the birth dates and dates of ordinations or setting apart of all General Authorities and general auxiliary presidents, with the exception of the Area Authorities, who are too numerous to include in this volume. Throughout the text, the reader should assume that the principal actors in each entry or those receiving recognition are Latter-day Saints, unless otherwise noted.

Our efforts to write, edit, and compile the data rest upon several primary and secondary sources. Foremost among the numerous books consulted are *History of The Church of Jesus*

Christ of Latter-day Saints, 2d edition revised (ed. B. H. Roberts, Salt Lake City: The Church of Jesus Christ of Latter-day Saints, 1932–51), Andrew Jenson's *Church Chronology,* 2d edition revised and enlarged with two supplements and index (Salt Lake City: Deseret News Press, 1914), B. H. Roberts, *A Comprehensive History of The Church of Jesus Christ of Latter-day Saints, Century One* (6 vols., Salt Lake City: The Church of Jesus Christ of Latter-day Saints, 1930), *Church History in the Fulness of Times: Religion 341–43* (Salt Lake City: The Church of Jesus Christ of Latter-day Saints, 1989), *Church News,* and several editions of the *Deseret News Church Almanac* series. Many other books dealing with various aspects of the Church and its members added depth and breadth to the project, especially detailed studies of people, places, and periods of Church history. Dates and events have been drawn from all these sources. Despite our best efforts, descriptions of some events may still be verbatim.

Although this book is not an interpretive history of the rise of Mormonism, we hope *On This Day in the Church: An Illustrated Almanac of the Latter-day Saints* will furnish those interested in this story with an opportunity to identify events from the past for particular days. We hope, too, that the images reproduced throughout the book will not only illustrate aspects of the story but also provide another source of information about "the kingdom, set up by the God of heaven, that would never be destroyed nor superseded, and the stone cut out of the mountain without hands that would become a great mountain and would fill the whole earth" (Spencer W. Kimball, in Conference Report, April 1976, 10).

ACKNOWLEDGMENTS

We appreciate the training, encouragement, and help of our colleagues in Latter-day Saint history and especially those in the Brigham Young University Department of Church History and Doctrine, including Susan Easton Black, Donald Q. Cannon, Richard O. Cowan, and Larry C. Porter. Of particular note, Donald Q. Cannon allowed us access to his wonderful and comprehensive library for use during the final stages of editing, and Richard O. Cowan provided us with an extensive twentieth-century chronology compiled over a number of years to help fill in gaps. We also thank Ja Neal Freeman, who offered valuable help in editing an early draft.

The following student secretaries and research assistants from Brigham Young University helped tremendously with this project: Leah Abbott, Wendy Agle, Amy Bucker, Julie DuVall, Katherine G. Garrett, Matthew J. Grey, Laurel Hogge, Keith Leonard, Hyrum Lewis, Kirsten Reid, Shelly Spencer, and James T. Stallings.

Additionally, we appreciate the support and assistance of the many at the Church Office Building: W. Randall Dixon, Matthew Heiss, Michael Landon, Veneese Nelson, Larry Skidmore, William W. Slaughter, and April Williamson (Library and Archives Division of the Church Historical Department); Bruce Pearson (Visual Resource Library); and Ronald Read (Museum of Church History and Art). And we thank Deseret Book Company, especially Sheri L. Dew, Kent Ware, Jana Erickson, Richard Erickson, Shauna Gibby, Laurie Cook, and Peter Gardner, for seeing this work through to publication.

JANUARY 1

1842 George Reynolds, later one of the First Seven Presidents of the Seventy and secretary to five Church Presidents, is born in London, England.

1846 In the Nauvoo Temple President Brigham Young performs the first marriage sealing for "time and all eternity" in a temple in this dispensation.

1849 John Smith, uncle of the Prophet Joseph Smith, is ordained Patriarch to the Church.

1866 The *Juvenile Instructor,* the official publication of the Sunday School, is first published.

1869 Karl G. Maeser begins publishing *Der Stern,* a monthly German-language Church periodical, in Zurich, Switzerland.

1877 With more than twelve hundred Saints present, President Brigham Young dedicates the lower portion of the St. George Temple (later the St. George Utah Temple), the first temple to be used since the Nauvoo era.

1898 The New Zealand Mission is organized.

1900 Martha LaVern Watts (Parmley), later the fifth general president of the Primary Association, is born in Murray, Utah.

1901 President Lorenzo Snow addresses a special New Year's Day congregation in the Tabernacle: "I hope and look for grand events to occur in the twentieth century. At its auspicious dawn, I lift my hands and invoke the blessings of heaven upon the inhabitants of the earth" (*Deseret Evening News,* January 1, 1901, 5).

1902 The *Children's Friend,* the official publication of the Primary Association, is first published.

1903 Alvin R. Dyer, later an Apostle and an additional member of the First Presidency, is born in Salt Lake City, Utah.

1909 The Presiding Bishopric instructs local priesthood leaders to ordain worthy young men as deacons at the age of twelve, as teachers at fifteen, and as priests at eighteen; this is the first policy regarding the ages to ordain young men to offices in the Aaronic Priesthood.

1910 The first number of the *Utah Genealogical and Historical Magazine* is released under the editorship of Anthon H. Lund.

1938 The West German and the East German Missions are organized.

1940 Amy Brown Lyman is called as the eighth general president of the Relief Society, with Marcia Knowlton Howells and Donna Durrant Sorensen as counselors.

1940 May Green Hinckley is called as the third general president of the Primary Association, with Adele Cannon Howells and Janet Murdock Thompson as counselors.

1968 The Pacific Northwest Mission is organized.

1968 Swedish convert Hilda Anderson Erickson, the last of the pioneers who made the trek west before the coming of the railroad to Utah in 1869, dies at the age of 108.

1971 The first issue of the *Ensign* magazine, which replaces the *Improvement Era,* is made available to English-speaking Saints.

1977 The First Presidency announces that general conferences will be held on the first Sundays of each April and October and on the preceding Saturdays.

1977 The Chile Santiago North and the Peru Lima North Missions are organized.

1979 The Alabama Birmingham Mission is organized.

1980 The Singapore Mission is organized.

1981 The Dominican Republic Santo Domingo Mission is organized.

1987 The Mexico Mexico City East Mission is organized.

1988 The Guatemala Guatemala City North Mission is organized.

1989 The Utah Provo Mission is organized.

1991 The Church announces that the contributions necessary to cover the expenses of single missionaries from the United States and Canada will be equalized.

1992 The Philippines Cabanatuan Mission is organized.

1993 The India Bangalore and the Australia Sydney North Missions are organized.

1994 The First Presidency endorses the United Nations' designation of 1994 as the International Year of the Family.

1996 Elder Merrill J. Bateman of the First Quorum of the Seventy begins his term as the eleventh president of Brigham Young University.

1997 The BYU football team defeats Kansas State University in the Cotton Bowl, in Dallas, Texas. The victory in BYU's first New Year's Day bowl appearance caps a 14–1 season.

1998 The Melchizedek Priesthood and Relief Society classes begin study of the *Teachings of Brigham Young,* the first manual in the series *Teachings of the Presidents of the Church.*

2000 For the first time, all forty-two language editions of the Church's International Magazine are entitled *Liahona.*

2000 The First Presidency and Quorum of the Twelve issue "The Living Christ: The Testimony of the Apostles," an official declaration reaffirming their personal testimonies of the Savior.

JANUARY 2

1830 Abner Cole, editor of *The Reflector,* begins publishing pirated extracts from the Book of Mormon, which is in the process of being printed at the Grandin press building, the same building used by Cole to print his newspaper. This marks the first time Book of Mormon text appears in print.

The Reflector, *containing pirated extracts of the Book of Mormon, 2 January 1830.*

1831 During the third conference of the Church, held at Fayette, New York, the Prophet receives Doctrine and Covenants 38, which reiterates the instruction for Church members to move to Ohio and promises them that they will receive the law and will "be endowed with power from on high" (v. 32).

1837 The Kirtland Safety Society is reorganized into a joint stock company under the title of the Kirtland Safety Society Anti-Banking Company.

1868 Alice Merrill Horne, later the second woman to serve in the Utah House of Representatives (1896–98) and a contributor to the arts, is born in Fillmore, Utah.

1882 President John Taylor moves into the Gardo House, the official residence of the President of the Church built but never lived in by Brigham Young.

1942 The Northern California Mission is organized.

1954 President David O. McKay leaves New York City for London en route to the South African, South American, and Central American Missions, making him the first Church President to visit these regions.

1985 BYU's football team is voted number one in the United States for the 1984 season by every major poll and is named national champion, having finished the season with a perfect 13–0 record.

1999 Church leaders announce that, commencing in June, the Mormon Youth Chorus will be reorganized and renamed the Temple Square Chorale, and its symphony orchestra will be renamed the Orchestra at Temple Square.

JANUARY 3

1876 Warren N. Dusenberry begins his term as the first principal (president) of Brigham Young Academy, the predecessor of Brigham Young University.

1885 President John Taylor, along with several other Church leaders, begins touring the Saints' southern settlements. On this trip they explore sites in northern Mexico for possible settlements, leading to the establishment of several Mormon colonies.

1929 Paul Alexander Yost Jr., later the first LDS commander of the U.S. Coast Guard (1986–90), is born in St. Petersburg, Florida.

1949 Brian Crane, later creator of the successful daily comic strip *Pickles* (first syndicated in 1990), is born in Twin Falls, Idaho.

1960 Via direct telephone wire transmission, President David O. McKay addresses some two hundred thousand youth in 290 stake centers across the United States (including Hawaii) and in western Canada. This is the first of a three-month Sunday-evening fireside series for youth.

1976 Because of increasing numbers of missionaries, those called to foreign language missions begin reporting directly to the Language Training Mission in Provo, Utah, instead of going to the Missionary Home in Salt Lake City.

1982 Professional golfer Johnny Miller receives $500,000 for winning a tournament in South Africa. The sum is the largest awarded in a golf tournament to date.

1833 "By commandment of God," Joseph Smith writes to a New York newspaper editor and provides information about the rise of the Church, stating: "I step forth into the field to tell you what the Lord is doing, and what you must do to enjoy the smiles of your Savior in these last days" (*History of the Church,* 1:313).

1852 The first branch of the Church in Australia is organized in Sydney with twelve members.

1879 Elder Hugh Findlay, the first missionary to the Shetland Islands, begins preaching the gospel.

1892 President George Q. Cannon of the First Presidency dedicates the Brigham Young Academy building at Provo, Utah, and installs Benjamin Cluff Jr. as the successor to Principal Karl G. Maeser.

1893 U.S. president Benjamin Harrison issues a proclamation of amnesty to all who entered plural marriage before 1 November 1890 (the Manifesto was issued in October 1890), protecting them from antipolygamy legislation.

1896 U.S. president Grover Cleveland signs the proclamation making Utah the forty-fifth state in the Union; the Saints had unsuccessfully tried to achieve statehood for nearly fifty years.

1905 In Salt Lake City, President Joseph F. Smith dedicates the Dr. Groves Latter-day Saint Hospital, the first in what would become an important health care network in the Intermountain West.

1916 Emil Feter, later the Church architect (1965–86), is born in Salt Lake City.

1933 Norman H. Bangerter, later the governor of Utah (1985–93), is born in Granger, Utah.

Documents related to the admission of Utah to the Union (see 1896).

1995 For the second time in three years, the Associated Press names Steve Young, quarterback of the San Francisco 49ers football team, the most valuable player in the National Football League.

1996 The U.S. Postal Service releases a stamp honoring Utah's centennial; it is designed by McRay Magleby, the creative director of BYU's Publications and Graphics Department.

1997 The Mormon Tabernacle Choir performs at Utah governor Michael O. Leavitt's second inauguration, the first time it has performed at such an event since the inauguration of the state's first governor, Heber M. Wells, 101 years earlier.

JANUARY 5

1831 After the third conference of the Church, Joseph Smith receives Doctrine and Covenants 39 on behalf of James Covill, a former Baptist minister, instructing him to be baptized.

1841 Joseph Smith establishes the Nauvoo Lyceum, a theological school to help prepare missionaries for their duties in proclaiming the gospel to the world.

1842 Joseph Smith opens his Red Brick Store in Nauvoo; the building is the site of the organization of the Relief Society and the presentation of the endowment for the first time in this dispensation. It is also the location of Joseph's official office.

1970 Latter-day Saint missionaries enter Indonesia for the first time when six missionaries serving in Singapore are sent to Jakarta.

1986 At the Annandale Virginia Stake conference, President Ezra Taft Benson addresses the Saints for the first time as President of the Church, testifying of the power of the Book of Mormon to change lives and lead people to Christ—a message that would become a recurring theme of his presidency.

1994 The Addis Ababa Branch, the first branch of the Church in Ethiopia, is organized, with Girma Denisa as president.

JANUARY 6

1828 Green Flake, later one of three African-Americans to enter the Salt Lake Valley with the first company of Saints, is born on the Jordan Flake plantation in Anson County, North Carolina. There are no known birth records for Hark Lay and Oscar Crosby, the two other African-Americans in the party.

1831 In Fayette, New York, Joseph Smith receives Doctrine and Covenants 40, a revelation regarding the "fear of persecution and the cares of the world" that cause some to reject the truth.

1834 The general public learns for the first time that Joseph Smith has bodyguards protecting him.

1879 The Supreme Court of the United States upholds the previous conviction of George Reynolds, the First Presidency's secretary, under the 1862 Morrill Anti-Bigamy Act, which the Saints believed violated the First Amendment of the U.S. Constitution. The decision paves the way for more intense prosecution of the Saints in the 1880s and becomes the U.S. Supreme Court's precedent for limiting some religious practices.

1985 The first branch of the Church in the West Indies island of Antigua is organized, with Rex B. Blake as president.

1993 The Church sends two LDS couple missionaries to Hanoi, Vietnam, to teach English; they are the first missionaries to serve in that nation since 1975, when the Church was forced to close the mission as a result of the North Vietnamese victory in the Vietnam War.

▶ *George Reynolds, ca. 1879 (see 1879).*

JANUARY 7

1805 David Whitmer, later one of the Three Witnesses of the Book of Mormon, is born near Harrisburg, Pennsylvania.

David Whitmer, ca. 1880 (see 1805).

1832 Joseph B. Brackenbury, a missionary, is poisoned by anti-Mormons, becoming the first martyr of the dispensation.

1876 Daniel W. Jones leads a small group of missionaries from El Paso, Texas, across the Rio Grande into Ciudad Juárez, Mexico; they become the first missionaries to serve in Mexico.

1880 In Copenhagen, Denmark, Andrew Jenson publishes *Ungdommens Raadgiver,* the first LDS periodical for young people in Scandinavia.

1919 Melvin J. Ballard is ordained an Apostle, filling the vacancy created when Heber J. Grant became President of the Church in November 1918.

1937 N. Eldon Tanner, later a member of the Quorum of the Twelve Apostles and a Counselor in the First Presidency, begins service as Minister of Lands and Mines (equivalent to a U.S. Cabinet position) in Canada.

1976 The Religious Studies Center at Brigham Young University is established to publish scholarly work dealing with topics of interest to Latter-day Saints.

1984 As part of his historic visit to the United States, Premier Zhao Ziyang of the People's Republic of China visits the BYU–Hawaii campus and the Polynesian Cultural Center. This is the first visit of a Chinese premier to the United States since the founding of the People's Republic of China in 1949.

2000 BYUTV, a television station broadcasting twenty-four hours a day seven days a week, begins broadcasting nationally, allowing people across the United States and southern Canada to pick up the station as part of the DISH Network satellite system.

1805 Orson Hyde, later a member of the Quorum of the Twelve Apostles, is born in Oxford, Connecticut.

1808 Louis A. Bertrand, later a missionary and translator of the Book of Mormon into French, is born near Marseilles, France.

1813 Albert Carrington, later a member of the Quorum of the Twelve Apostles and a Counselor in the First Presidency, is born in Royalton, Vermont.

1882 Elder Joseph F. Smith dedicates the Assembly Hall on Temple Square in Salt Lake City.

1900 President Lorenzo Snow issues an official statement reaffirming the Church's position against new plural marriages.

1929 Scott M. Matheson, later governor of Utah (1977–84), is born in Chicago, Illinois.

1955 The Church announces that LDS Boy Scouts can earn the Duty to God Award, similar to other religious groups' awards. This award recognizes faith and activity for young boys in the Church.

1976 David B. Haight is ordained an Apostle, replacing Hugh B. Brown, who had died.

Elder David B. Haight and his wife, Ruby (see 1976).

1982 Polish-speaking missionaries in Chicago help humanitarian groups send aid to people suffering under Poland's marshal law.

Assembly Hall, ca. 1888 (see 1882).

1988 The Argentina Salta, Bolivia La Paz, Mexico Chihuahua, Mexico Tuxtla-Gutierrez, Peru Lima East, and Philippines Cagayan de Oro Missions are organized.

1995 President Howard W. Hunter dedicates the Bountiful Utah Temple.

1999 The Church announces plans to build a temple in Fresno, California.

JANUARY 9

1851 An ordinance is passed by the government of the provisional state of Deseret to incorporate Great Salt Lake City.

1877 The first baptisms for the dead since the Saints had fled Nauvoo thirty years earlier are performed in the St. George Temple (later the St. George Utah Temple).

The St. George Temple, ca. 1877 (see 1877).

1907 Eldred G. Smith, later Patriarch to the Church, is born in Lehi, Utah.

1943 Ariel Bybee, later a mezzo-soprano with the New York Metropolitan Opera, is born.

1950 LDS missionaries arrive in Paraguay for the first time.

1966 Elder Gordon B. Hinckley presents the first copy of the Chinese translation of the Book of Mormon to President David O. McKay.

1979 The first branch of the Church on the Caribbean island of Saint Martin is organized.

1982 The Church introduces a simplified tithing and donation recording system that utilizes the expanding capabilities of computers.

1999 President Gordon B. Hinckley dedicates the Anchorage Alaska Temple.

1999 Ground is broken for two new temples—the Villahermosa México and the Ciudad Juárez Chihuahua México Temples. Elders Richard E. Turley Sr. and Eran A. Call (both of the Second Quorum of the Seventy) preside over the respective ceremonies.

2000 President Gordon B. Hinckley dedicates the St. Paul Minnesota Temple.

JANUARY 10

1832 Joseph Smith and Sidney Rigdon receive Doctrine and Covenants 73, instructing them to go on a short mission and then resume the translation of the Bible.

1847 The Mormon Battalion crosses the Colorado River into what would later become California.

1862 Reed Smoot, later a member of the Quorum of the Twelve Apostles and a U.S. senator from Utah (1903–33), is born in Salt Lake City, Utah.

1870 President Brigham Young drives the last spike for the Utah Central Railroad line, connecting Salt Lake City with Ogden, a distance of thirty-seven miles.

1892 The Church organizes in the Salt Lake City Nineteenth Ward the first Latter-day Saint Sunday School for the deaf.

1907 President Joseph F. Smith announces the payment of the last two $500,000 bonds issued by President Lorenzo Snow; this is a major step in paying off the Church's massive debt incurred during the difficult political and economic period of the 1880s and 1890s.

1939 Ernst Koehler, a German convert who proposed to the Church the microfilming of genealogical records, becomes the Church's first full-time, salaried microfilm photographer.

1986 President Gordon B. Hinckley of the First Presidency dedicates the Lima Peru Temple.

1999 Ground is broken for the Caracas Venezuela Temple (later the Caracas D.F. Venezuela Temple). Elder Francisco J. Vinas, a member of the First Quorum of the Seventy and President of the South America North Area, presides over the ceremony.

The first train to Salt Lake City, 10 January 1870.

JANUARY 11

1827 George Q. Cannon, later a member of the Quorum of the Twelve Apostles, Counselor in the First Presidency, and one of only two men (Joseph F. Smith being the other) to serve in the First Presidencies of four different Church Presidents, is born in Liverpool, England.

1864 William Spry, later governor of Utah (1908–16), is born in Windsor, England.

1877 The first endowments for the dead in this dispensation are performed in the St. George Temple (later the St. George Utah Temple), with President Brigham Young acting as proxy for his father.

1886 Adele M. Cannon (Howells), later the fourth general president of the Primary Association, is born in Salt Lake City, Utah.

1914 Sherman P. Lloyd, later a Utah representative in the U.S. Congress (1962–64, 1966–72), is born in St. Anthony, Idaho.

1927 Bernard (Bernie) F. Fisher, later a Vietnam War Air Force pilot and a recipient of the Congressional Medal of Honor for landing on an enemy airfield long enough to rescue a fellow airman under enemy fire, is born in San Bernardino, California.

U.S. Air Force Major Bernard F. Fisher, ca. 1967 (see 1927).

1931 The Texas Mission is organized.

1971 The Taiwan Mission is organized.

JANUARY 12

1834 Following the Saints' expulsion from Jackson County, Missouri, Parley P. Pratt and Lyman Wight leave Missouri for Ohio to report to the Church leaders in Kirtland concerning the condition of the Missouri Saints and to inform them that Governor Daniel Dunklin is willing to help the Saints return to their lands and property.

1838 Joseph Smith and Sidney Rigdon flee Kirtland to escape mob violence.

1840 Francis M. Lyman, later a member of the Quorum of the Twelve Apostles, is born in Good Hope, Illinois.

1887 Reinhold Stoff, later an early mission president in South America who expanded work into Brazil, is born in Germany.

1936 Merrill C. Oaks, later a member of the Second Quorum of the Seventy, is born in Twin Falls, Idaho.

1975 The Merthyr Tydfil Stake, the first stake in Wales, is organized, with Ralph Pulman as president.

1989 The New York International Film and Video Festival presents three awards to the BYU Motion Picture Studio for the movie *A More Perfect Union,* which chronicles the founding of the United States of America.

JANUARY 13

1870 A large meeting of Latter-day Saint women is held in Salt Lake City to protest the antipolygamy Cullom Bill pending in Congress and to demonstrate the solidarity of Latter-day Saint women with Church leaders.

1901 As part of the Church's efforts to revitalize the priesthood quorums and expand service opportunities for local members, President Joseph F. Smith divides the countywide stake in Utah County into three stakes: the Alpine, Nebo, and Utah Stakes.

1927 Dan W. Anderson, later the fifth president of BYU–Hawaii, is born in Salt Lake City, Utah.

1931 Local Church leaders and students at UCLA, including faculty member Vern O. Knudsen, organize the Deseret Club, the first social organization for LDS college students outside of Utah. Eventually, the club is established Churchwide at schools that do not have fully operating institutes of religion.

1973 Taiwan Mission president Malan R. Jackson baptizes the first Mongolian convert, Wu Rung Fu, in Taipei, Taiwan.

1976 Saints in Arizona host eighty-four Central American members of the Church who had bused more than four thousand miles from Panama to receive their temple blessings.

1994 Emanuel Tov, Hebrew University professor and editor-in-chief of the Dead Sea Scrolls publication projects, invites BYU professor Donald W. Parry to join the international team of editors working on publication of the scrolls. Later BYU professors David R. Seely, Dana M. Pike, and Andrew C. Skinner are added to the team.

1995 The First Presidency announces plans to build temples in Cochabamba, Bolivia, and Recife, Brazil.

JANUARY 14

1833 Joseph Smith sends the revelation known as the "Olive Leaf" (D&C 88) to W. W. Phelps, the editor of the Church's newspaper in Missouri.

1847 While at Winter Quarters, President Brigham Young receives Doctrine and Covenants 136, outlining the "word and will of the Lord" concerning the Saints and their organization for the trek west.

1943 Lex de Azevedo, later a popular LDS composer and playwright, is born in Los Angeles, California.

1959 The Board of Trustees approves the establishment of the College of Religion Instruction (later Religious Education) at BYU, with David H. Yarn as the first dean.

1972 The Church announces the creation of the Church Historical Department, with new archives, history, and library divisions created from the former Church historian's office.

1974 The names of the stakes throughout the Church are changed to identify them uniformly with their geographical area.

1979 The Santa Cruz Bolivia Stake, the first stake in Bolivia, is organized, with Noriharu Ishigaki Haraguichi as president.

JANUARY 15

1867 The Deseret telegraph line opens in St. George, Utah, connecting the Saints in southern Utah with Church headquarters in Salt Lake City.

1877 At the dedication of the St. George Temple (later the St. George Utah Temple) and just eight months before his death, President Brigham Young begins the process of writing down for the first time the endowment ceremony as he received it from Joseph Smith in Nauvoo.

1887 C. Meyer Zulick, governor of Arizona, signs into law a bill repealing the anti-Mormon "test oath" in Arizona, which had barred many Arizona Saints from voting by requiring voters to swear they did not believe in or practice polygamy.

1934 Hugh W. Pinnock, later a member of the Presidency of the Seventy, is born in Salt Lake City, Utah.

1934 Keith Crockett, later a member of the Second Quorum of the Seventy, is born in Pima, Arizona.

1959 *BYU Studies* begins publishing faith-promoting works of LDS scholarship, including articles, essays, and poetry on a variety of subjects.

1988 Lee Roderick assumes duties as president of the (U.S.) National Press Club, a leading forum for world newsmakers, including U.S. presidents and other world leaders.

1998 The First Presidency renews the call for all Church members to be active in volunteer service and political, governmental, and community leadership.

JANUARY 16

1828 Karl G. Maeser, later one of the first Latter-day Saint converts in Saxony, Germany, and the first permanent principal of the Brigham Young Academy, is born in Vorbrucke (a section of the town of Meissen), Saxony, Germany.

1836 In a meeting of the Twelve Apostles in Kirtland, Joseph Smith announces that "the Twelve are not subject to any other than the First Presidency. . . . Where I am not, there is no First Presidency over the Twelve" (*History of the Church,* 2:374).

1908 President Joseph F. Smith dedicates the site for the Maeser Memorial Building, the first building on what would become known as Brigham Young Academy's "upper campus."

1920 The Eighteenth Amendment to the U.S. Constitution goes into effect, prohibiting the manufacture, production, and sale of alcohol. President Heber J. Grant, a fervent supporter of the amendment, believes it is divinely mandated because it outlaws items forbidden by the Word of Wisdom.

1923 Jacob de Jager, later a member of the First Quorum of the Seventy, is born in The Hague, Netherlands.

1981 President Jimmy Carter awards the U.S. Presidential Medal of Freedom to Esther W. Eggertsen Peterson, a national consumer rights advocate and consumer affairs advisor to President Lyndon B. Johnson. She is the first Latter-day Saint to be so honored.

1999 Ground is broken for two new temples—the Mérida México and Memphis Tennessee Temples—with Elders Carl B. Pratt of the First Quorum of the Seventy and Gordon T. Watts of the Second Quorum of the Seventy presiding over the respective ceremonies.

1906 James A. Cullimore, later an Assistant to the Quorum of the Twelve Apostles and a member of the First Quorum of the Seventy, is born in Lindon, Utah.

1971 The Louisville Stake, the first stake in Kentucky, is organized, with Henry H. Griffith as president.

1976 The *Church News* publishes a statement by President Spencer W. Kimball as it begins a campaign against pornography.

1981 The U.S. Republican Party appoints as its national chair Richard N. Richards, the first Latter-day Saint to hold this position.

1986 President Thomas S. Monson of the First Presidency dedicates the Buenos Aires Argentina Temple.

The Buenos Aires Argentina Temple (see 1986).

1798 Christian Whitmer, later one of the Eight Witnesses of the Book of Mormon, is born in Harrisburg, Pennsylvania.

1806 William E. McLellin, later a member of the Quorum of the Twelve Apostles, is born in Smith County, Tennessee.

1827 Joseph Smith and Emma Hale are married by Zachariah Tarbell in South Bainbridge, New York.

1917 Stephen L Richards is ordained an Apostle, filling the vacancy created by the death of Elder Francis M. Lyman.

1925 John Victor Evans, later governor of Idaho (1977–86), is born in Malad City, Idaho.

1929 J. Ballard Washburn, later a member of the Second Quorum of the Seventy, is born in Blanding, Utah.

President David O. McKay (see 1970).

1941 The general Sunday School board announces the first major change in curriculum in more than a decade. The new studies are designed to give a well-rounded knowledge of the gospel to all members of the Church.

1965 The Mormon Tabernacle Choir sings at the inauguration of United States president Lyndon B. Johnson in Washington, D.C.

1970 President David O. McKay dies in Salt Lake City at age ninety-six, after sixty-three years and nine months as an Apostle and Church President, the longest term of service to date.

1972 President Joseph Fielding Smith dedicates the Ogden Temple (later the Ogden Utah Temple). During the service, some of those attending see a brilliant light surrounding the pulpit in the celestial room when members of the First Presidency speak.

1992 Saimoni Tamani, the first Fijian to win a medal in track and field competition at the Commonwealth Games (1970), is inducted into the Fijian Hall of Fame.

1996 The First Presidency and the Quorum of the Twelve Apostles announce the withdrawal of General Authorities from boards of directors of corporations, including Church-owned corporations.

1997 The Public Broadcasting Service (PBS) airs *Ancestors,* a ten-part series on family history produced by KBYU-TV.

JANUARY 19

1841 Joseph Smith receives Doctrine and Covenants 124, which contains instructions for the ordinance of baptism for the dead and calls for the construction of the Nauvoo House and the Nauvoo Temple. The revelation also outlines the reorganization of priesthood quorums decimated by apostasy and death in Missouri and identifies Hyrum Smith as the new Patriarch to the Church and as Assistant President of the Church.

1853 The recently completed Social Hall in Salt Lake City opens with its first theatrical performance. The hall continues to function as a social gathering place until 1922, when it is razed.

1870 Hugh J. Cannon, later a long-time member of the General Sunday School Board, a stake president, and the managing editor of the *Improvement Era* (1928–31), is born in Salt Lake City, Utah.

The Nauvoo Temple, ca. 1846 (see 1841).

1878 James William Robinson, later a Utah representative in the U.S. Congress (1932–46), is born in Coalville, Utah.

1928 RLDS officials begin the process of locating the graves of Joseph and Hyrum Smith, which had been left unmarked since their secret burial in Nauvoo in 1844. After locating and exhuming the bodies, the officials rebury the bodies in nearby, marked graves.

1931 Ronald C. Packard, later a California representative in the U.S. Congress (1983–), is born in Meridian, Idaho.

1947 The Jacksonville Stake, the first stake in Florida, is organized, with Alvin C. Chase as president. During the organizational meeting, Elder Charles A. Callis of the Quorum of the Twelve Apostles prophesies that a temple will be built there in the future. The Orlando Florida Temple, dedicated in 1994, stands within the original geographic boundaries of the Jacksonville Stake.

1953 The First Presidency informs stake presidents of the need for stenographers and other office help in the missions and suggests that a few properly trained women at least twenty-one years old be called as missionaries. The previous minimum age for sister missionaries had been twenty-three.

1961 The French East Mission is organized.

1989 The Mormon Tabernacle Choir performs at events surrounding the inauguration of U.S. president George Bush. Bush calls them the "nation's choir" (*Deseret News 1991–1992 Church Almanac,* 309).

1990 Elder Dallin H. Oaks meets with Chinese leaders and addresses the Chinese Academy of Social Sciences.

1804 Jefferson Hunt, later a colonizer and officer in the Mormon Battalion, is born in Bracken County, Kentucky.

1847 Ellis Reynolds (Shipp), later a pioneer, physician, and women's advocate, is born in Davis County, Iowa.

1860 President Brigham Young affirms the Church's position against suicide but states that the act itself is by no means unforgivable under some circumstances.

1903 The Utah legislature, as was the custom of the time in the United States, elects Reed Smoot of the Quorum of the Twelve Apostles to the U.S. Senate. His election begins a long process of governmental investigation of the Church's doctrines, practices, and history. In 1907 Smoot is allowed to retain his seat in the Senate and eventually becomes one of the most powerful Republican leaders in the nation.

1947 Merrill B. Jenson, later a musician and the composer of the soundtracks for *Legacy* and *The Testaments: Of One Fold and One Shepherd,* is born in Richfield, Utah.

Composer Merrill Jenson, ca. 1999 (see 1947).

1967 In a ceremony at the White House, U.S. president Lyndon B. Johnson presents the Medal of Honor to Major Bernard F. Fisher of the Air Force for rescuing another Air Force pilot under heavy fire during the Vietnam War. Fisher is the first living U.S. Air Force recipient of the honor since World War II.

1969 The Mormon Tabernacle Choir sings at U.S. president Richard M. Nixon's inauguration in Washington, D.C.

1973 Representing Utah, the BYU marching band performs at the inauguration of Richard M. Nixon. Additionally, thirty members of the Mormon Tabernacle Choir sing at a private devotional service at the White House.

1974 Victor Nugent and his family, the first converts to the Church in Jamaica, are baptized.

1977 The San Jose Costa Rica Stake, the first stake in Costa Rica, is organized, with Manuel Najera Guzman as president.

1981 The Mormon Tabernacle Choir participates in the inaugural festivities for U.S. president Ronald Reagan.

1985 The Church of Jesus Christ of Latter-day Saints becomes the fifth largest denomination in the United States.

1991 Local Church leaders participate in services sponsored by the Interreligious Council of Oakland, California, honoring Martin Luther King's dream. The meeting is held at the LDS interstake center next to the Oakland Temple (later the Oakland California Temple).

▶ *United States president Dwight D. Eisenhower looks on as Supreme Court justice Fred M. Vinson administers the oath of office to Secretary Ezra Taft Benson, 21 January 1953.*

JANUARY 21

1804 Eliza R. Snow, later an author, poetess, women's leader, and the second general Relief Society president, is born in Becket, Massachusetts.

1836 Joseph Smith receives Doctrine and Covenants 137, which teaches that "all who have died without a knowledge of this gospel, who would have received it if they had been permitted to tarry, shall be heirs of the celestial kingdom of God" (v. 7) and that "all children who die before they arrive at the years of accountability are saved in the celestial kingdom of heaven" (v. 10).

1953 U.S. Supreme Court justice Fred M. Vinson administers the oath of office for the new secretary of agriculture, Elder Ezra Taft Benson of the Quorum of the Twelve Apostles.

1958 Matthew James Salmon, later an Arizona representative in the U.S. Congress (1995–), is born in Salt Lake City, Utah.

1983 The First Presidency issues a statement reinforcing the policy that members of the Church are expected to pay local, state, and federal taxes.

1990 The Church appoints David Hsiao Hsi Chen, a BYU–Hawaii professor and native of mainland China, as a First Presidency representative to the People's Republic of China.

1995 Church membership reaches nine million.

1836 Joseph Smith meets with members of the Quorum of the Twelve Apostles and the Seventy in the Kirtland Temple and records, "The heavens were opened, and angels ministered unto us. . . . [They] mingled their voices with ours, while their presence was in our midst" (*History of the Church,* 2:383).

1866 President Brigham Young reaches out to the non-Mormon citizens of Utah, allowing the Social Hall to be used as a Masonic Lodge.

1880 Oscar A. Kirkham, later a member of the First Council of the Seventy, is born in Lehi, Utah.

1936 Lowell L. Bennion, director of the University of Utah Institute of Religion, organizes the women's chapter of Lambda Delta Sigma (from the Greek letters for "LDS"), a men's organization recently established at the institute that paralleled the fraternities on campus at the University of Utah.

1939 Elder George Albert Smith ordains and sets apart Moroni Timbimboo, the first Native American Indian to serve as a bishop in the Church, as the presiding officer of the Washakie Ward, in Box Elder County, Utah.

1983 President Gordon B. Hinckley of the First Presidency breaks ground for the Dallas Texas Temple.

1994 Ground is broken for the Hong Kong Temple (later the Hong Kong China Temple). Elder John K. Carmack, a member of the First Quorum of the Seventy and President of the Asia Area, presides over the ceremony.

1994 Elder Boyd K. Packer dedicates a 36,400-square-foot missionary training center in Guatemala.

1998 Governor Pete Wilson of California accepts a copy of a new LDS video depicting the role of the Mormon Battalion in developing the state.

1833 The first session of the School of the Prophets begins in Kirtland with Joseph Smith administering the ordinance of the washing of the feet, as outlined by revelation (D&C 88).

1854 Edward Stevenson, a native of Gibraltar, organizes the first branch of the Church in Gibraltar.

1900 The U.S. House of Representatives refuses to seat duly elected congressman B. H. Roberts, a member of the First Council of the Seventy, because of his religious beliefs.

1918 Elder Hyrum Mack Smith, eldest son of President Joseph F. Smith, dies unexpectedly. His death is one of the events setting the stage for President Smith's vision of the redemption of the dead in October of the same year.

1921 Elder David O. McKay visits members of the Church in Japan during his historic worldwide tour.

Elder David O. McKay, back row third from left, during a visit to Japan, ca. January 1921 (see 1921).

1922 The first annual "Leadership Week," sponsored by BYU, begins. In 1963 the name of the yearly event is changed to Education Week.

1933 Lowell D. Wood, later a member of the Second Quorum of the Seventy, is born in Cardston, Alberta, Canada.

1970 Joseph Fielding Smith is set apart and ordained as the tenth President of the Church, with Harold B. Lee and N. Eldon Tanner as his Counselors.

1976 The *Donny and Marie Show* airs on U.S. national television and runs through January 1979, highlighting two members of the Osmond family performing group.

1977 The Bogotá Colombia Stake, the first stake in Colombia, is organized, with Julio E. Davila P. as president.

1989 Eight large city television stations in the United States begin airing *Together Forever*, a program produced by the Church. Within four months of this event, every commercial station in the United States where mission headquarters are located broadcasts the program.

2000 President Gordon B. Hinckley dedicates the Kona Hawaii Temple.

JANUARY 24

1796 Joseph Smith Sr. and Lucy Mack are married at Tunbridge, Vermont.

1832 Bishop Edward Partridge presents the first report of Church expenditures and revenues.

1839 Joseph Smith petitions the Missouri legislature from Liberty Jail, requesting a change of venue for his trial.

1841 Hyrum Smith is ordained Patriarch to the Church and Assistant President of the Church, and William Law, the first non-U.S. citizen to be called into the First Presidency, is set apart as Second Counselor to Joseph Smith.

1848 Latter-day Saint Henry Bigler records in his journal James W. Marshall's discovery of gold at Sutter's Mill on the South Fork of the American River in California. This discovery sparks the California Gold Rush. Bigler had been a member of the Mormon Battalion and, along with several other Latter-day Saints, had been hired by Sutter to construct a mill following the battalion's discharge the previous summer.

1854 During the time when the Relief Society was not functioning, Matilda Dudley establishes the "Indian Relief Society," a society of women who made clothing for needy Indian women and children.

1894 While visiting the Saints in Cardston, Alberta, Canada, Elder John W. Taylor prophesies that a beautiful temple will be built in this Latter-day Saint community. Dedicated in 1923, the Alberta Temple (later the Cardston Alberta Temple) is the first temple erected outside the United States and its territories.

A choir at the Alberta Temple dedication, ca. 1923 (see 1894).

1895 Clarifying a procedural policy concerning bishops, the First Presidency announces that it will begin ordaining them to their callings as well as setting them apart.

1898 Henry W. Bigler, James S. Brown, Azariah Smith, and William Johnston—four former members of the Mormon Battalion who had participated in the discovery of gold at Sutter's Mill in California—take part in the fiftieth anniversary commemoration of that historic event.

1902 The First Presidency issues an important doctrinal statement regarding the nature of the Holy Ghost, stating that He is a spirit personage while the Spirit of God is an impersonal influence from God.

1927 Paula Hawkins, later a U.S. senator from Florida (1981–87), is born in Salt Lake City, Utah.

1945 D. Todd Christofferson, later a member of the Presidency of the Seventy, is born in American Fork, Utah.

1995 President Thomas S. Monson of the First Presidency welcomes the Most Reverend George H. Niederauer, the new Catholic bishop of Utah, at an evening service in the Cathedral of the Madeleine in Salt Lake City.

~~~ JANUARY 25 ~~~

1832 At a conference held in Amherst, Ohio, Joseph Smith receives Doctrine and Covenants 75, and he is sustained and ordained as "President of the High Priesthood."

1876 Milton Holmes Welling, later a Utah representative in the U.S. Congress (1916–20), is born in Farmington, Utah.

1883 Ab Jenkins, later known for setting numerous land speed records on the Bonneville Salt Flats in his car the *Mormon Meteor III,* is born in Spanish Fork, Utah.

1888 David Whitmer, one of the Three Witnesses of the Book of Mormon and the last surviving of the eleven witnesses of the Book of Mormon plates, dies in Richmond, Missouri.

1936 V. Dallas Merrell, later a member of the Second Quorum of the Seventy, is born in Basalt, Idaho.

◄ *U.S. senator Paula Hawkins, ca. 1981 (see 1927).*

1836 Joshua Seixas begins teaching Biblical Hebrew to Joseph Smith and others in the Kirtland Temple.

1839 The exodus of the Saints from Missouri to Illinois and Iowa begins following Missouri Governor Lilburn W. Boggs's extermination order.

1865 Church agent Francis A. Hammond, under the direction of President Brigham Young, agrees to purchase a six thousand-acre plantation in Laie on the Hawaiian island of Oahu for $14,000. Later the Church establishes the Church College of Hawaii (later known as BYU–Hawaii), the Polynesian Cultural Center, and the Laie Hawaii Temple at the site.

1912 Howard Walter Cannon, later a U.S. senator from Nevada (1959–87), is born in St. George, Utah.

1922 Barbara Bradshaw (Smith), later the tenth general president of the Relief Society, is born in Salt Lake City, Utah.

1964 The Cumorah Mission is organized.

1973 President Marion G. Romney of the First Presidency dedicates the Aloha Center on the Church College of Hawaii campus.

General Relief Society president Barbara B. Smith, ca. 1974 (see 1922).

1800 Jacob Whitmer, later one of the Eight Witnesses of the Book of Mormon, is born in Harrisburg, Pennsylvania.

1822 Thomas L. Kane, later an important non-Mormon advocate of the Church during the second half of the nineteenth century, is born in Philadelphia, Pennsylvania.

1845 The Illinois legislature repeals Nauvoo's city charter, leaving the community without any municipal organizations or police protection.

1847 The Mormon Battalion arrives at the deserted San Luis Rey Mission in California. From a prominence nearby, battalion members catch their first glimpse of the Pacific Ocean.

Title page of the 1855 Hawaiian edition of the Book of Mormon, translated by George Q. Cannon (see 1852).

1849 British sailors George Barber and Benjamin Richey are baptized before sailing to India, where they become the first Latter-day Saints in that land.

1852 As a missionary to Hawaii, George Q. Cannon begins translating the Book of Mormon into Hawaiian.

1878 The Little Colorado Stake, the first stake in Arizona, is organized, with Lot Smith as president.

1884 Fire destroys the first Brigham Young Academy building (known as the Lewis Building).

1910 President Joseph F. Smith dedicates the Bishop's Building on Main Street in Salt Lake City; this is the first time that the Presiding Bishopric of the Church has its own offices.

1985 Members of the Church in Canada and the United States hold a special fast to raise money for victims of famine in Africa and other parts of the world; they raise $6.5 million.

1992 The Argentina Buenos Aires West and the Colombia Bogotá South Missions are organized.

▶ *BYU head football coach R. LaVell Edwards, ca. 1980 (see 1972).*

1836 Joseph Smith meets with various Church leaders in the Kirtland Temple, and they experience great manifestations of the power of God, including the appearance of angels.

1850 Representative Linn Boyd, a member of the U.S. Congress from Kentucky, introduces to the House of Representatives the provisional state of Deseret's application for admission as a state. The petition ultimately fails, and Utah is granted territorial status instead.

1940 California state senator Edward Fletcher acts as master of ceremonies at the unveiling and dedication of the Mormon Battalion Monument in San Diego, California.

1964 The U.S. federal government identifies Temple Square and the Lion House as National Historic Landmarks.

1967 *The History of the Relief Society,* compiled under the direction of Marianne C. Sharp, a counselor in the Relief Society general presidency, is released.

1967 The Philippine Mission is organized.

1972 BYU names R. LaVell Edwards as its new head football coach. His twenty-nine year distinguished career includes a national championship in 1984.

1981 The first missionaries to the island of Saint Croix (in the Virgin Islands) arrive and begin their missionary labors.

1982 The Pro Football Hall of Fame, in Canton, Ohio, inducts Latter-day Saint Merlin Olsen, a former all-pro tackle for the Los Angeles Rams.

1989 Elders Russell M. Nelson and Dallin H. Oaks of the Quorum of the Twelve complete an eight-day visit to China, during which they visited government leaders.

1990 The Tallinn Branch, the first branch in Estonia and in the Soviet Union, is organzied.

JANUARY 29

1839 While Joseph Smith and other Church leaders remain incarcerated in Liberty Jail, President Brigham Young meets with the Saints at Far West to appoint a committee to help remove the Saints from the state of Missouri. President Young puts them and himself under covenant to "stand by and assist each other to the utmost of our abilities in removing from this state" and to "never desert the poor who are worthy, till they shall be out of the reach of the exterminating order" (*History of the Church,* 3:250).

1844 At a meeting in Nauvoo, Joseph Smith is nominated as an independent candidate for president of the United States.

1847 The Mormon Battalion arrives at the San Diego Mission, the oldest Spanish mission in California. This marks the end of its 103-day march from Ft. Leavenworth, during which they had traveled approximately two thousand miles.

1888 The Saints dedicate the first meetinghouse of the Church in Canada at Lee's Creek (later Cardston), Alberta.

1972 The Adult Aaronic Priesthood program is renamed the Prospective Elders program.

1980 The first branch of the Church in the Canary Islands is organized in Las Palmas.

1982 During U.S. vice president George Bush's visit to Utah, President N. Eldon Tanner of the First Presidency presents him with a replica of the Monument to Women statue.

JANUARY 30

1831 Sidney Rigdon returns home to Ohio after his first visit with Joseph Smith in New York and bears strong witness of the Prophet's call and of the truthfulness of the Book of Mormon.

1841 Joseph Smith assumes the position of trustee-in-trust for the Church, an office that would administer Church finances until 1923.

1847 U.S. military officer Philip St. George Cooke issues "Order Number 1," stating: "The lieutenant-colonel commanding congratulates the [Mormon] battalion on their safe arrival on the shore of the Pacific ocean, and the conclusion of the march of over two thousand miles. History may be searched in vain for an equal march of infantry" (*Exploring Southwestern Trails 1846–1854,* 4:238).

1899 Joseph Fielding Smith, the son of Hyrum M. and Ida Elizabeth Smith and later Patriarch to the Church, is born in Salt Lake City, Utah.

1909 During a two-day meeting, local Church leaders in Auckland, New Zealand, dedicate new mission headquarters and an assembly hall.

1951 Church leaders decide that no young man of draft age in the United States will be recommended for missionary service during the Korean War.

1982 General Primary president Dwan J. Young announces major changes in curriculum for the Primary, including the introduction of a Valiant A and B course, a combined Sunday School class of eleven-year-olds, and a new Gospel in Action award.

1821 Zina Diantha Huntington (Young), later the third general president of the Relief Society, is born in Watertown, New York.

1846 President Brigham Young receives a revelation dealing with succession in the Church Presidency. Although never canonized, the revelation is one of a number of inspired written documents Brigham Young receives as the senior Apostle of the Church during the period between Joseph Smith's death and the beginning of his own tenure as President of the Church.

1852 The first Latter-day Saint emigrants from Scandinavia set sail from Copenhagen, Denmark, for the United States.

1872 John Andreas Widtsoe, later a member of the Quorum of the Twelve Apostles, is born in Daloe, Island of Froyen, Trondhjem, Norway.

1886 The Saints living at what would later be known as Colonia Juárez, Chihuahua, Mexico, hold the first meeting in their newly erected chapel, the first built in Mexico.

1907 The New Zealand Mission publishes the first number of the *Elders' Messenger,* a semimonthly periodical in English and Maori.

1920 Stewart Udall, later an Arizona representative in the U.S. Congress (1955–61) and secretary of the interior under U.S. presidents Kennedy and Johnson (1961–69), is born in St. Johns, Arizona.

1926 Merlin R. Lybbert, later a member of the Second Quorum of the Seventy, is born in Cardston, Alberta, Canada.

1960 The Baseball Writers Association of America names Vernon Law the best pitcher in professional baseball and winner of the Cy Young Award.

Elder John A. Widtsoe and family, ca. 1912 (see 1872).

1964 During a meeting with President David O. McKay, U.S. president Lyndon B. Johnson asks the Church President for advice and indicates that he has felt inspired during previous visits with President McKay.

FEBRUARY 1

1831 Joseph and Emma Smith arrive in Kirtland, Ohio, from New York and take up temporary residence with Newel K. Whitney.

1847 The Mormon Battalion leaves the San Diego Mission and marches to San Luis Rey, where the soldiers are instructed to defend the mission as a military post.

1885 President John Taylor delivers his last public sermon in the Tabernacle in Salt Lake City and goes "underground" to avoid arrest for practicing plural marriage.

1895 Cavendish W. Cannon, later a U.S. ambassador (Yugoslavia, 1947; Syria, 1950; Portugal, 1952; Greece, 1953; and Morocco, 1956), is born in Salt Lake City, Utah.

1926 Helio da Rocha Camargo, later a member of the First Quorum of the Seventy, is born in Resende, Rio de Janeiro, Brazil.

1951 Hugh Hodgkiss, the first convert to the Church in Zimbabwe, is baptized.

1962 The Southwest British Mission is organized.

1980 The Honduras Tegucigalpa Mission is organized.

1993 The Brazil Ribeiro Preto and the Brazil Rio de Janeiro North Missions are organized.

FEBRUARY 2

1833 Joseph Smith completes his translation of the New Testament.

1842 Moses Thatcher, later a member of the Quorum of the Twelve Apostles, is born in Springfield, Illinois.

1848 With the signing of the treaty of Guadalupe Hidalgo, the Mexican War officially ends and the region now divided among Utah, California, Arizona, and New Mexico becomes part of the United States. Mexico had previously claimed this region.

1874 Levi E. Young, later one of the First Seven Presidents of the Seventy, is born in Salt Lake City, Utah.

1944 E. Gordon Gee, later president of West Virginia University (1981), University of Colorado System (1985), Ohio State University (1990), Brown University (1998), and Vanderbilt (2000), is born in Vernal, Utah.

1968 Six missionaries arrive in Thailand, having been transferred from the Taiwan and Hong Kong zones of the Southern Far East Mission. They are the first LDS missionaries in Thailand since 1854.

1986 Brazil becomes the third country outside the United States to have 50 stakes.

1996 In a special telecast from Salt Lake City, the Mormon Tabernacle Choir is featured on *CBS This Morning,* a national news program.

❧ ❧ ❧ FEBRUARY 3 ❧ ❧ ❧

1851 President Brigham Young takes the oath of office as governor of the territory of Utah.

1885 William M. Bunn, governor of Idaho, signs a law prohibiting Mormons from voting in Idaho through the device of a "test oath." This law requires all voters to swear that they are not members of "any sect or organization which teaches, advises, or encourages the practice of polygamy or bigamy" (Roberts, *Comprehensive History of the Church,* 6:213).

1902 Merlo John Pusey, later the first Latter-day Saint to receive the Pulitzer Prize (1952), is born in Woodruff, Utah.

1913 Owen J. Cook, later the third president of the Church College of Hawaii (later known as BYU–Hawaii), is born in Tremonton, Utah.

1925 President Heber J. Grant dedicates the first Mission Home in Salt Lake City. LeRoi Snow is its first director.

1926 During two important meetings (on 3 and 8 February), the Church Board of Education decides to continue expanding seminary programs throughout the Church and to turn its junior colleges over to state governments. Schools later converted to state colleges include Snow College (Ephraim), Weber College (Ogden), Dixie College (St. George), and Gila College (Thatcher, Arizona). When the state of Idaho chooses not to take Ricks College in Rexburg, the Church decides to keep it open.

1937 Patricia Peterson (Pinegar), later the ninth general president of the Primary, is born in Cedar City, Utah.

1963 The Milwaukee Stake, the first stake in Wisconsin, is organized, with DeWitt C. Smith as president.

1977 LDS missionaries enter the Marshall Islands for the first time.

1979 The Church Genealogical Department announces a new "family entry system," which makes it possible for families to submit for temple work the names of deceased ancestors whose birthplaces and birth dates are unknown.

1982 The first district of the Church in Czechoslovakia is organized.

1992 The Russia St. Petersburg Mission is organized.

1998 In Washington, D.C., Elder Neal A. Maxwell of the Twelve and Elder Merrill J. Bateman (BYU president and member of the Seventy), along with several LDS members of the U.S. Congress, host a gathering of diplomats from ten predominantly Muslim countries to celebrate BYU's publication of the first English translation of the Islamic text *The Incoherence of the Philosophers* by Al-Ghazali, a twelfth-century Muslim philosopher.

Elder Neal A. Maxwell (center), BYU President Merrill J. Bateman and his wife, Marilyn (second and third from right), BYU professor Daniel C. Peterson (second from left), and LDS members of Congress host Muslim diplomats in Washington, D.C., 3 February 1998.

❧❧❧ FEBRUARY *4* ❧❧❧

1795 Patty Bartlett (Sessions), later a pioneer midwife and diarist, is born in Bethel, Maine.

1831 Joseph Smith receives Doctrine and Covenants 41, which designates Edward Partridge as the first bishop in this dispensation and indicates that the "law" of the Church would shortly be given.

1832 Charles W. Penrose, later a member of the Quorum of the Twelve Apostles and a Counselor in the First Presidency, is born in London, Surrey County, England.

1841 Under the provisions of the Nauvoo charter granted by the Illinois state legislature, the Nauvoo Legion is organized.

1846 Charles Shumway and his family cross the Mississippi River, thus beginning the Saints' exodus from Nauvoo. On the same day, the ship *Brooklyn* sets sail from New York for California with 238 Saints aboard.

1851 The government of the provisional state of Deseret passes an ordinance that incorporates The Church of Jesus Christ of Latter-day Saints.

1864 Brigham Young Jr. and Joseph Angell Young are ordained Apostles but are not placed in the Quorum of the Twelve Apostles. On 9 October 1868, four and a half years later, Brigham Young Jr. is sustained a member the Quorum of the Twelve Apostles.

1881 The Zion's Cooperative Mercantile Institution store (ZCMI) in Ogden is dedicated.

1902 The First Presidency announces the policy that full-time missionaries need not pay tithing.

1911 G. Homer Durham, later a member of the Presidency of the Seventy, is born in Parowan, Utah.

1996 The Honaira Branch, the first branch of the Church in the Solomon Islands, is organized, with Eddie Misi as president.

1996 Church members commemorate the sesquicentennial of the Saints' 1846 exodus from Nauvoo.

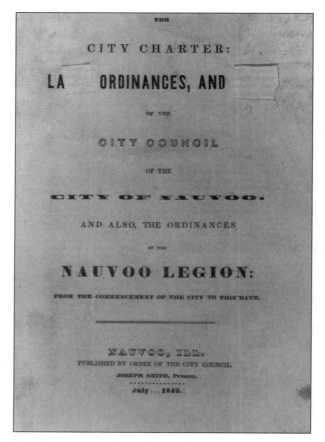

The Nauvoo Legion Charter (see 1841).

FEBRUARY 5

1795 Newel K. Whitney, later the second Presiding Bishop of the Church, is born in Marlborough, Vermont.

1840 While preaching to a congregation in Philadelphia, Joseph Smith teaches that "all children dying at an early age (say eight years) not knowing good from evil, were incapable of sinning; and that all such assuredly go to heaven" (*History of the Church,* 4:78).

1844 Joseph Smith instructs William Weeks, architect of the Nauvoo Temple, concerning several features he wants included in the building, stating, "I wish you to carry out *my* designs. I have seen in vision the splendid appearance of that building illuminated, and will have it built according to the pattern shown me" (*History of the Church,* 6:197).

A Nauvoo Temple sunstone (see 1844).

1846 John Christopher Cutler, later the second governor of the state of Utah, is born in Sheffield, England.

1849 Charles W. Nibley, later the fifth Presiding Bishop of the Church and a Counselor in the First Presidency, is born in Hunterfield, Midlothian Region, Scotland.

1928 Waldo P. Call, later a member of the First Quorum of the Seventy, is born in Colonia Juárez, Chihuahua, Mexico.

1936 Joseph C. Muren, later a member of the Second Quorum of the Seventy, is born in Richmond, California.

1942 Jay E. Jensen, later a member of the First Quorum of the Seventy, is born in Payson, Utah.

1977 The First Presidency announces that the Quorum of the Twelve Apostles will direct ecclesiastical matters and that the Presiding Bishopric will oversee temporal programs of the Church.

1994 The Church announces the launching of a television series that will make LDS programs available in 85 percent of the English-speaking homes across Canada during 1994 over the VISION/TV network.

FEBRUARY 6

1816 Horace S. Eldredge, later one of the First Seven Presidents of the Seventy, is born in Brutus, New York.

1840 Joseph Smith preaches a sermon in Washington, D.C.

1851 Ordinances passed by the government of the provisional state of Deseret incorporate Ogden City, Provo City, Parowan City, and Manti City.

1855 A festival honoring the Mormon Battalion commences in Salt Lake City.

1886 LeGrand Richards, later the seventh Presiding Bishop of the Church and a member of the Quorum of the Twelve Apostles, is born in Farmington, Utah.

1928 The First Presidency authorizes the purchase of the Hill Cumorah, adding to the growing number of historical sites owned by the Church.

1951 Ronald A. Rasband, later a member of the First Quorum of the Seventy, is born in Salt Lake City.

1993 Lamjav Purevsuren and Tsendkhuu Bat-Ulzii, the first converts of the Church in Mongolia, are baptized.

1999 Ground is broken for the Raleigh North Carolina Temple. Elder Loren C. Dunn, a member of the First Quorum of the Seventy and First Counselor in the North America East Area Presidency, presides over the ceremony.

FEBRUARY 7

1794 Oliver Granger, later appointed by revelation to settle the Church's debts in Kirtland following the Prophet Joseph Smith's removal to Missouri in 1838 (see D&C 117:12–13), is born in Phelps, New York.

1839 In company with a small group of Saints, Emma Smith leaves Far West, Missouri, to join the main body of Saints gathering in Quincy, Illinois.

1844 Having been aided by W. W. Phelps, Joseph Smith finishes a manuscript outlining his political ideas. It was later published under the title *Views of the Powers and Policy of the Government of the United States.*

1846 Brigham Young, President of the Quorum of the Twelve Apostles, finishes administering temple blessings in the Nauvoo Temple as the Saints prepare to move west. Over 5,600 Saints were endowed in the temple before the exodus.

1849 Elder Orson Hyde issues the first number of *The Frontier Guardian,* a semimonthly newspaper, at Kanesville, Iowa.

1872 Amy Brown (Lyman), later a pioneer in the field of social services and the eighth general Relief Society president, is born in Pleasant Grove, Utah.

1901 President Lorenzo Snow dedicates LDS Business College in Salt Lake City.

1957 The St. John's Branch, the first branch of the Church in Newfoundland, Canada, is organized.

1960 Tauna Kay Vandeweghe-Mullackey, later a silver medalist in swimming in the 1976 Montreal Olympic games, is born in Green Valley, California.

From left: Lorenzo D., Brigham, Phineas, Joseph, and John Young, 13 September 1866 (see 1835).

1835 Joseph Smith tells Brigham and Joseph Young of a vision in which he saw those who had died in Zion's Camp: "If I get a mansion as bright as theirs, I ask no more." Additionally, he tells them that Brigham Young will be called as a member of the Quorum of the Twelve Apostles and that Joseph Young will be called as a member and President of the Seventy (*History of the Church,* 2:180–81).

1846 Brigham Young, President of the Quorum of the Twelve Apostles, dedicates the Nauvoo Temple, as thus far completed, in a private ceremony.

1886 Approximately twenty U.S. deputy marshals search the Gardo House (the official residence of President John Taylor), the Tithing Yards, and various Church offices in an unsuccessful attempt to arrest Presidents John Taylor and George Q. Cannon.

1990 Elder Russell M. Nelson dedicates Romania for the preaching of the gospel.

1800 Hyrum Smith, later one of the Eight Witnesses of the Book of Mormon, Church Patriarch, and Assistant President of the Church, is born in Tunbridge, Vermont.

1831 Joseph Smith receives portions of Doctrine and Covenants 42, with additional portions revealed on 23 February. Called by Joseph "the law of the Church," this revelation includes instructions concerning the implementation of the law of consecration.

Nauvoo House Association stock certificate (see 1841).

1841 Obedient to instructions given on 19 January (see D&C 124), Church leaders incorporate the Nauvoo House Association in an effort to raise money to build the Nauvoo House, which is to be "a delightful habitation for man, and a resting-place for the weary traveler, that he may contemplate the glory of Zion, and, the glory of this, the corner-stone thereof" (D&C 124:60).

1843 Joseph Smith explains the "three grand keys" for the detection of angels and false spirits. His instructions later make up Doctrine and Covenants 129.

1873 Melvin J. Ballard, later a member of the Quorum of the Twelve Apostles, is born in Logan, Utah.

1919 The U.S. Congress awards Private Thomas C. Neibur the Medal of Honor, making him the first Latter-day Saint and the first private in the U.S. Army to receive the award.

1923 J. Elliot Cameron, later the sixth president of BYU–Hawaii, is born in Panguitch, Utah.

1972 President Joseph Fielding Smith dedicates the Provo Temple (later the Provo Utah Temple).

1999 The First Presidency announces plans to build a temple in Palmyra, New York.

1999 Deseret Management Corporation, the Church's holding company for commercial entities, announces plans to purchase Bookcraft, Inc., a Salt Lake City publisher of LDS books and products.

FEBRUARY 10

1846 Joseph Young, brother of Brigham Young, is appointed to preside temporarily over the Church in Nauvoo.

1846 Patty Sessions begins recording in her diary the story of the Saints' exodus from Nauvoo. Her writings for the next several years reveal the daily life of a Mormon midwife and Utah pioneer.

1870 The Utah territorial legislature, composed of an LDS majority, passes an act allowing women to vote in Utah; it is only the second territory to pass woman suffrage laws.

1919 In a letter to stake presidents, the First Presidency urges local congregations to increase the number of missionaries because of the conclusion of World War I.

◀ *The Provo Temple (see 1972).*

1798 Alvin Smith, an older brother of the Prophet Joseph Smith, is born in Tunbridge, Vermont.

1800 John Snyder, later one of the first missionaries to England, is born in New Brunswick, Nova Scotia, Canada.

1900 The Church holds services in the Salt Lake Tabernacle to honor Utah soldiers killed in Manila during the Spanish-American War.

1917 Ruth Hardy (Funk), later the seventh general president of the Young Women, is born in Chicago, Illinois.

1921 While touring the Kilauea Volcano in Hawaii, Elder David O. McKay is impressed by the Spirit to move those with him away from a ledge overlooking the volcano just before the ledge collapses into the volcano.

1950 Ernest James Istook Jr., later an Oklahoma representative in the U.S. Congress (1993–), is born in Fort Worth, Texas.

1951 Michael O. Leavitt, later the governor of Utah (1992–), is born in Cedar City, Utah.

1972 Dr. Stephen L. Brower is inaugurated as the fourth president of the Church College of Hawaii, later known as BYU–Hawaii.

1973 The Southampton England Stake, the six hundredth stake of the Church, is organized, with Reginald V. Littlecott as president.

1849 President Brigham Young calls and ordains to the Quorum of the Twelve Apostles Charles C. Rich, Lorenzo Snow, Erastus Snow, and Franklin D. Richards (replacing himself, Heber C. Kimball, and Willard Richards, who had been called to the First Presidency, and Lyman Wight, who had apostatized).

1851 The provisional state of Deseret authorizes and requests President Brigham Young, as governor of the territory, to procure a block of marble to be used in building the Washington Monument, which is under construction at the nation's capital.

1870 Acting Governor S. A. Mann signs an act of the territorial legislature granting Utah women the right to vote.

1955 President David O. McKay dedicates grounds for the Church College of Hawaii before hundreds of Latter-day Saints gathered in an open field on the north shore of the island of Oahu, Hawaii.

1955 Construction begins on the first chapel in Niue, a small island in the South Pacific.

1989 The Church announces that worthy unendowed members whose spouses are not members of the Church or are not worthy to enter the temple may receive their individual endowments.

FEBRUARY 13

1841 Elder Orson Hyde sets sail from New York City for Liverpool, England, on his mission to the Holy Land.

The Papeete Tahiti Temple, ca. 1983 (see 1981).

1981 President Spencer W. Kimball breaks ground for the Papeete Tahiti Temple.

1990 Elder Russell M. Nelson dedicates Bulgaria for the preaching of the gospel.

1992 The Papua New Guinea Port Moresby Mission is organized.

1994 The First Presidency announces plans to convert the Uintah Tabernacle into the Vernal Utah Temple.

FEBRUARY 14

1835 The Three Witnesses of the Book of Mormon—Oliver Cowdery, David Whitmer, and Martin Harris—select the first members of the Quorum of the Twelve Apostles. Lyman E. Johnson, Brigham Young, and Heber C. Kimball are ordained that day by the Three Witnesses and the First Presidency.

1835 Lyman Eugene Johnson is ordained an Apostle.

1839 As a result of Governor Lilburn Boggs's 1838 extermination order, several families, including those of Brigham Young and Heber C. Kimball, begin their exodus from Far West, Missouri, to relocate in Quincy, Illinois.

1853 President Brigham Young breaks ground for the Salt Lake Temple.

1870 Seraph C. Young, a grand-niece of Brigham Young, becomes the first woman to vote legally in the United States (at a municipal election in Salt Lake City).

Elder Robert C. Oaks at the time he received BYU Air Force ROTC's Patriots Award, 1996 (see 1936).

1901 President Lorenzo Snow announces plans to open Japan to missionary work, an important first step in expanding the foreign missions of the Church.

1936 Robert C. Oaks, later a four-star brigadier general in the U.S. Air Force and member of the Second Quorum of the Seventy, is born in Los Angeles, California.

1998 President Gordon B. Hinckley begins an eight-day tour of African nations, including Nigeria, Ghana, Kenya, Zimbabwe, and South Africa, becoming the first Church President to tour West Africa.

1835 Orson Hyde, David W. Patten, Luke S. Johnson, William E. McLellin, John F. Boynton, and William Smith are ordained members of the Quorum of the Twelve Apostles.

1839 Emma Smith and her children arrive safely in Quincy, Illinois, after fleeing Missouri.

1846 Brigham Young, President of the Quorum of the Twelve Apostles, leaves Nauvoo for the West, crossing the Mississippi River and traveling nine miles to the camp on Sugar Creek.

1926 Albert Choules Jr., later a member of the First Quorum of the Seventy, is born in Driggs, Idaho.

1964 Ernest L. Wilkinson begins his term as the sixth president of Brigham Young University.

1970 The Jakarta Branch, the first branch of the Church in Indonesia, is organized.

1976 The Canada Winnipeg Mission is organized.

1987 The Mormon Tabernacle Choir performs its three thousandth radio broadcast in a series that had become the longest-running network program in America.

1989 The mayor of Quincy, Illinois, officially declares this "Latter-day Saints Day" and presents Elder Loren C. Dunn with a key to the city in commemoration of the refuge the residents of Quincy provided the Saints as they fled Missouri 150 years earlier.

1991 Former U.S. president Ronald Reagan speaks at Brigham Young University and pays a courtesy call to Church headquarters.

1832 While translating the Gospel of John, Joseph Smith and Sidney Rigdon receive a vision that comprises Doctrine and Covenants 76. In the vision they see the Savior on the right hand of God, events in the premortal life, and the three degrees of glory.

1846 Brigham Young, President of the Quorum of the Twelve Apostles, organizes the Camp of Israel at Sugar Creek, Iowa, preparatory to the Saints' trek across the plains. The organization includes captains of tens, fifties, and hundreds.

Sugar Creek, *by C.C.A. Christensen, ca. 1885 (see 1846).*

1951 Lee Groberg, later an award-winning film producer and director, is born in Ogden, Utah.

1961 The Texas Mission is organized.

1983 Relief Society general president Barbara B. Smith receives the BYU Exemplary Womanhood Award.

1998 During his tour of the continent, President Gordon B. Hinckley announces plans to build a temple in Accra, Ghana.

▶ *W. W. Phelps, ca. 1853 (see 1792).*

FEBRUARY 17

1792 W. W. Phelps, later a poet and a Church printer, is born in Hanover, New Jersey.

1796 Peter Haws, later a prominent property holder in Nauvoo and a member of the Nauvoo House building committee (see D&C 124:62, 70), is born in Young Township, Leeds County, Ontario, Canada.

1815 Abraham O. Smoot, later an early civic, Church, and business leader in Utah County, is born in Owentown County, Kentucky.

1834 The Kirtland Stake, the first stake in the Church, is established with Joseph Smith, Sidney Rigdon, and Frederick G. Williams as the stake presidency and Joseph Smith Sr., John Smith, Joseph Coe, John Johnson, Martin Harris, John S. Carter, Jared Carter, Oliver Cowdery, Samuel H. Smith, Orson Hyde, Sylvester Smith, and Luke S. Johnson as members of the high council (see D&C 102).

1844 Anti-Mormon activists hold a convention at Carthage, Illinois, to devise ways to expel the Saints from the state.

1847 Brigham Young, President of the Quorum of the Twelve Apostles, has a vision at Council Bluffs, Iowa, in which the martyred prophet Joseph Smith asks him to tell the Saints to "keep the Spirit of the Lord and it will lead them right. Be careful and not turn away the small still voice; it will teach them what to do and where to go; it will yield the fruits of the kingdom" (Andrus, *Doctrinal Commentary on the Pearl of Great Price*, 122).

1855 In New York City Elder John Taylor publishes the first issue of a newspaper entitled the *Mormon*.

1939 Douglas L. Callister, later a member of the Second Quorum of the Seventy, is born in Glendale, California.

1998 Members of the Church from Somalia travel to Kenya to see President Hinckley during his visit to that country. The Church had sent relief supplies to Somalia but had no organized missionary effort in that country. During the years of civil unrest and drought, many Somalians had accepted the gospel while living as refugees in nearby Kenya.

▶ *Patriarch John Smith (seated) and his half-brother President Joseph F. Smith, ca. May 1895 (see 1855).*

❧ ❧ ❧ FEBRUARY ❧ ❧ ❧

1855 John Smith, son of Hyrum Smith, is ordained Patriarch to the Church.

1857 Joseph Howell, later a Utah representative in the U.S. Congress (1902–16), is born in Brigham City, Utah.

1887 As part of the continuing antipolygamy crusade, the Edmunds-Tucker Act becomes law without the signature of United States president Grover Cleveland. This law unincorporates the Church, dissolves the Perpetual Emigrating Fund Company and escheats its property to the government, abolishes female suffrage in Utah Territory, and allows the government to confiscate practically all the property of the Church.

1979 Ezra Taft Benson, President of the Quorum of the Twelve Apostles, organizes the Nauvoo Illinois Stake, the Church's one thousandth stake, with Gene Lee Roy Mann as president.

1981 President Spencer W. Kimball and King Taufa'ahau Tupou IV break ground for the Nuku'alofa Tonga Temple. Nearly seven thousand attend the ceremony.

1996 Members of the Church from Botswana and Namibia attend the Johannesburg South Africa Regional Conference, showing Church growth in that country.

FEBRUARY 19

1793 Sidney Rigdon, later a spokesman for the Prophet and member of the First Presidency, is born in St. Clair, Pennsylvania.

1937 Wilford C. Wood purchases the first of ten lots eventually acquired by the Church of the original Nauvoo Temple site.

Wilford C. Wood presents the deed for the Nauvoo Temple lot to President Heber J. Grant, as Counselor David O. McKay looks on, ca. 1937 (see 1937).

1981 President Spencer W. Kimball, assisted by Malieotoa Tanumafil II, the Samoan head of state, breaks ground for the Apia Samoa Temple. Nearly four thousand attend.

1994 The First Presidency issues a statement opposing efforts to legalize same-sex marriages in the United States.

1995 Elder Neil L. Andersen of the Seventy organizes the Cadiz Spain Stake, which encompasses the island of Gibraltar.

FEBRUARY 20

1829 Christian D. Fjeldsted, later one of the First Seven Presidents of the Seventy, is born in Amagar, Denmark.

1840 Joseph Smith leaves Washington, D.C., to return to Nauvoo, having gone there to petition U.S. president Martin Van Buren and the U.S. Congress to redress the Saints for their losses in Missouri.

1874 George Q. Morris, later an Assistant to the Twelve and a member of the Quorum of the Twelve Apostles, is born in Salt Lake City, Utah.

1890 Alma Richards, later the first Latter-day Saint gold medalist (winner of the high jump in the 1912 Olympics in Stockholm, Sweden), is born in Parowan, Utah.

1901 Henry Eyring, later an internationally recognized research scientist in chemistry; member of the National Academy of Sciences (1945); and winner of the National Medal of Science (1967), the Priestley Medal (1975), the Swedish Berzelius Gold Medal (1979), and the Wolf Prize (1980), is born in Colonia Juárez, Mexico.

1907 Ending a five-year battle, the U.S. Senate votes to allow Elder Reed Smoot, a member of the Quorum of the Twelve Apostles and a republican senator from Utah, to retain his seat in the Senate. Some senators had accused him of practicing plural marriage, and when this was easily disproved, they accused him of believing in the practice and upholding it.

1910 Arthur Henry King, later a British convert to the Church and renowned English-language scholar, is born in Gosport, England.

1977 The Brussels Belgium Stake, the first stake in Belgium, is organized, with Joseph Scheen as president.

Arthur Henry King at BYU commencement exercises, 18 April 1986 (see 1910).

1981 J. Elliot Cameron is inaugurated as the sixth president of BYU–Hawaii.

1987 Alton L. Wade is inaugurated as the seventh president of BYU–Hawaii.

1802 Addison Pratt, later a diarist and missionary to Society Island (French Polynesia) (1843 and 1852), is born in Winchester, New Hampshire.

1816 Jedediah M. Grant, later one of the Presidents of the Seventy and a member of the First Presidency, is born in Windsor, New York.

1835 Parley P. Pratt is ordained an Apostle by Joseph Smith, Oliver Cowdery, and David Whitmer.

1977 President Spencer W. Kimball begins a nineteen-day tour of Latin America, attending area conferences and meeting with heads of state in Mexico, Guatemala, Chile, and Bolivia.

1990 The Czechoslovakian government renews recognition of the Church; it had originally been granted in 1928.

1990 Elder Neal A. Maxwell of the Twelve dedicates Swaziland for the preaching of the gospel.

Elder Parley P. Pratt, ca. 1853 (see 1835).

❦ ❦ ❦ FEBRUARY 22 ❦ ❦ ❦

1811 Ezra T. Benson, later a member of the Quorum of the Twelve Apostles and great-grandfather of Church President Ezra Taft Benson, is born in Mendon, Massachusetts.

1834 Parley P. Pratt and Lyman Wight arrive in Kirtland after a five-week journey from Missouri and inform Church leaders in Kirtland that Missouri governor Daniel Dunklin is willing to help restore the Saints to their lands and property in Jackson County, from which they had been driven in November 1833.

1849 The original nineteen wards in the Salt Lake Valley are organized, giving a model for future establishment of Church units throughout the world.

1875 Elder Wilford Woodruff performs the marriage sealing of Sagwhitch and Mogogah and of Ohetocump (James Laman) and Minnie, two Shoshone Indian couples in the Endowment House on the Temple Block in Salt Lake City; these are the first sealings of American Indian couples.

1958 Kurt Roland Bestor, later an Emmy Award–winning composer (1988), an arranger, and a performer, is born in Waukesha, Wisconsin.

1970 Elder Gordon B. Hinckley organizes the Lima Stake, the first stake in Peru, with Roberto Vidal as president.

Kurt Bestor, December 1995 (see 1958).

1987 President Ezra Taft Benson addresses the mothers of the Church in a fireside for parents broadcast over the Church satellite network, urging them to fulfill the Lord's commandments regarding their families.

1990 Elder Neal A. Maxwell dedicates the African country of Lesotho for the preaching of the gospel; Elder M. Russell Ballard dedicates the Caribbean islands of Trinidad and Tobago for the preaching of the gospel.

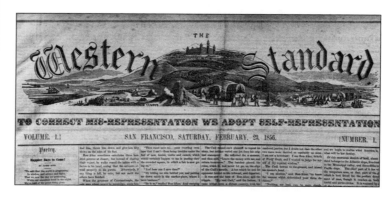

▶ *Masthead for the* Western Standard, *a newspaper published by George Q. Cannon in San Francisco (see 1856).*

1856 George Q. Cannon publishes the first issue of the *Western Standard,* a Church newspaper published in San Francisco, California.

1861 George F. Richards, later a member of the Quorum of the Twelve Apostles, is born in Farmington, Utah.

1888 J. Spencer Cornwall, later the Mormon Tabernacle Choir director (1935–57), is born in Millcreek, Utah.

1925 Gunn McKay, later a Utah representative in the U.S. Congress (1971–81), is born in Ogden, Utah.

1935 Gordon T. Watts, later a member of the Second Quorum of the Seventy, is born in South Weber, Utah.

1990 Elder M. Russell Ballard dedicates the South American country of Guyana for the preaching of the gospel.

1999 The First Presidency announces plans to build a temple in Oaxaca, Mexico.

1834 Joseph Smith receives Doctrine and Covenants 103, which calls for the organization of Zion's Camp, a company of men who would travel to Jackson County to assist the Saints there in reclaiming their lands and property.

1846 En route from New York to California aboard the ship *Brooklyn,* Mormon emigrant Sarah Burr gives birth to a baby boy, whom she names John Atlantic Burr. He is the first of two children to be born onboard the ship.

1858 Colonel Thomas L. Kane, a nonmember friend of the Church, arrives in Salt Lake City to negotiate peace between the Church and the U.S. Army. Under the command of Albert Sidney Johnston, the army had attempted to seize control of the territory of Utah.

1937 Hilton A. and Hazel Robertson arrive in Hawaii to reopen the Japanese Mission (the mission in Japan had been closed in 1924). From this beginning, many Japanese converts in the Hawaiian Islands are prepared to reopen the island of Japan following World War II.

1990 Elder M. Russell Ballard dedicates the South American country of Suriname for the preaching of the gospel.

▶ The Lord's Army Marching to the Deliverance of Zion's Camp, *1873 (see 1834).*

FEBRUARY 25

1799 John E. Page, later a member of the Quorum of the Twelve Apostles, is born in Trenton, New York.

1844 Joseph Smith prophesies that within five years the Saints will be beyond the power of their old enemies.

1871 Anthony Lund, later the Mormon Tabernacle Choir director (1916–35), is born in Ephraim, Utah.

1883 The Wautu New Zealand Branch, the first branch organized among the Maoris in New Zealand, is organized, with Hare Te Katere as president.

1950 Elders H. Grant Heaton and William K. Paalani arrive in Hong Kong; they are the first missionaries to labor in Hong Kong in nearly one hundred years.

1979 The Asuncion Paraguay Stake, the first stake in Paraguay, is organized, with Carlos Ramon Espinola as president.

1982 The first branch of the Church on the Indian Ocean island of Mauritius is established.

1990 The Church receives official recognition in Kenya.

1999 The First Presidency announces plans to build a temple in Tuxtla Gutiérrez, Chiapas, Mexico.

FEBRUARY 26

1834 Joseph Smith and several elders leave Kirtland on short-term missions to northeastern Ohio, Pennsylvania, and western New York to recruit members for Zion's Camp.

1852 The Malta Mission is organized.

1989 President Gordon B. Hinckley, First Counselor in the First Presidency, speaks at the Church's first fireside broadcast by satellite for single-adult members.

1995 The Singapore Singapore Stake, the first stake in Singapore, is organized, with Woo Hoi Seng Leonard as president.

1996 The Church announces that Latter-day Saints living outside the United States outnumber members living in the United States. The only other time this had happened was in the 1850s when the membership in the British Isles exceeded that in the United States.

2000 President Gordon B. Hinckley dedicates the Ciudad Juárez México Temple.

~ ~ ~ FEBRUARY 27 ~ ~ ~

1833 Joseph Smith receives Doctrine and Covenants 89, which comes to be known as the Word of Wisdom.

BYU president Rex E. Lee with Ronald Reagan, 15 February 1991 (see 1935).

1835 Joseph Smith assembles nine of the Twelve who are present in Kirtland for instruction and laments that the Church has been slothful in record keeping. He admonishes the Twelve to record every decision and discussion of the quorum.

1839 The members of the Democratic Association and the citizens of Quincy, Illinois, pass resolutions recommending that the refugee Mormons be allowed to live and find employment in Quincy.

1846 Severe cold causes the Mississippi River to freeze over, allowing many Saints to drive their wagons over the river in their exodus from Nauvoo.

1932 David B. Bleak, later a Korean War army medical aid and U.S. Congressional Medal of Honor recipient (1953) for saving a wounded soldier while also wounded and under enemy attack, is born in Idaho Falls, Idaho.

1935 Rex Edwin Lee, later the founding dean of the J. Reuben Clark Law School at BYU, tenth president of BYU, and solicitor general of the United States, is born in Los Angeles, California.

1941 Leigh A. Harline, the first Latter-day Saint to receive an award from the Academy of Motion Pictures Arts and Sciences, wins two Oscars—one for the musical score of *Pinocchio* and another for best song for "When You Wish Upon a Star."

1972 J. Spencer Kinard becomes the voice for *Music and the Spoken Word.*

1983 The sesquicentennial anniversary of the Word of Wisdom is observed throughout the Church and at the Newel K. Whitney store in Kirtland, Ohio, the location of the 1833 revelation.

1988 President Ezra Taft Benson breaks ground for the San Diego California Temple.

1990 Elder M. Russell Ballard dedicates the South American country of French Guiana for the preaching of the gospel.

1999 Ground is broken for the Edmonton Alberta Temple. Elder Yoshihiko Kikuchi of the Seventy presides over the ceremony.

2000 President Gordon B. Hinckley dedicates the Hermosilla Sonora México Temple.

The San Diego California Temple, 1 May 1993 (see 1988).

❧❧❧ FEBRUARY 28 ❧❧❧

1835 Joseph Smith organizes the First Quorum of the Seventy and ordains Joseph Young, Hazen Aldrich, Levi W. Hancock, Leonard Rich, Zebedee Coltrin, Sylvester Smith, and Lyman Sherman as the First Seven Presidents.

1839 Members of the Democratic Association of Quincy pass a resolution condemning Missouri governor Lilburn W. Boggs's extermination order and expulsion of the Mormons from Missouri.

1850 The government of the provisional state of Deseret passes an ordinance that incorporates the University of the State of Deseret (later renamed the University of Utah).

1934 Honam Rhee, later a pioneer of the Church in Korea and a BYU professor, is born in Shimonoseki, Japan.

1960 The Morristown New Jersey Stake, the first stake in New Jersey, is organized, with George H. Mortimer as president.

1961 The Scottish-Irish Mission is organized.

1993 Eugene and Ruth Hilton arrive in Ethiopia as the first official missionaries of the Church to that country.

▶ *Emmeline B. Wells, 14 January 1879 (see 1828).*

❧❧❧ FEBRUARY 29 ❧❧❧
(Leap Day)

1784 Alpheus Cutler, later a prominent member of the early Church, is born in Plainfield, New Hampshire.

1828 Emmeline Blanche Woodward (Wells), later a publisher of the *Woman's Exponent,* a woman's advocate, and the fifth general president of the Relief Society, is born in Petersham, Massachusetts.

1860 The *Deseret News* publishes a guide for the Deseret Alphabet, an experimental phonetic alphabet developed under the direction of President Brigham Young. The effort, headed by Church member George D. Watt, was intended to help foreign converts immigrating to Utah learn English.

2000 The one hundred millionth copy of the Book of Mormon published by the Church since 1830 is released (making the scripture the third most published book in the world).

1830 Palmyra N.Y.

Kirtland Ohio 1837

1840 Nauvoo Ill.

Liverpool England 1852

1869 Deseret Alphabet N.Y.

Compact, S.L.C., Utah 1907

1920 S.L.C., Utah, in columns

S.L.C. Utah 1961

1965 London England

Worlds Fair edition 1974

1977 S.L.C., Utah

S.L.C., Utah 1990

Book of Mormon editions (see 2000).

❧❧❧ MARCH *1* ❧❧❧

1807 Wilford Woodruff, later a member of the Quorum of the Twelve Apostles and the fourth President of the Church, is born in Avon (Farmington), Connecticut.

1832 The Prophet Joseph Smith receives Doctrine and Covenants 78 on this day (according to the Kirtland Revelation Book). The revelation contains instructions to members of the united order concerning their consecrated properties.

1841 The Nauvoo City Council divides the city into four political areas called wards. This political division into wards (often called districts or precincts in other areas of the United States) becomes the basis for the modern ecclesiastical use of the term *ward*.

1842 Joseph Smith publishes extracts from the Book of Abraham (including facsimiles) in the *Times and Seasons* in Nauvoo, Illinois. Later, the Book of Abraham is published by Franklin D. Richards in England as part of the Pearl of Great Price and is canonized as part of the standard works in 1880.

"Facsimile No. 1" from the Book of Abraham (see 1842).

On this day, Joseph Smith also publishes the Wentworth Letter in the *Times and Seasons,* giving a brief history of the Church and including what are now called the Articles of Faith. In the Wentworth Letter, Joseph Smith prophesies concerning the future destiny of the Church: "The standard of truth has been erected; no unhallowed hand can stop the work from progressing; persecutions may rage, mobs may combine, armies may assemble, calumny may defame, but the truth of God will go forth boldly, nobly, and independent, till it has penetrated every continent, visited every clime, swept every country, and sounded in every ear, till the purposes of God shall be accomplished, and the Great Jehovah shall say the work is done" (*History of the Church,* 4:540).

1846 Under the direction of Brigham Young, President of the Quorum of the Twelve Apostles, the first wagons leave the encampment at Sugar Creek in Iowa, headed for the Great Salt Lake Valley.

1917 Mark Austin, president of the Church Board of Education, announces that Ricks Academy in Rexburg, Idaho, will be known as Ricks Normal College.

1988 The Liberia Monrovia Mission is organized.

1861 The U.S. Congress creates the territory of Nevada out of the western half of Utah Territory.

1904 President Joseph F. Smith appears before the U.S. Senate during the Reed Smoot hearing.

1919 A. Theodore Tuttle, later an Assistant to the Twelve and a member of the Presidency of the Seventy, is born in Manti, Utah.

1951 Ana Villasenor, the first convert in El Salvador, is baptized.

Primary Children's Hospital (see 1952).

1952 President David O. McKay dedicates the new Primary Children's Hospital in Salt Lake City. Half the cost of the construction had been raised by children of the Church through a penny drive that commenced during the administration of President Heber J. Grant.

1964 Ilka Josephina Frau, the first native Puerto Rican to join the Church on the island, is baptized.

1980 Church members in the United States and Canada begin a Sunday meeting schedule that consolidates priesthood meetings, sacrament meeting, and most auxiliary meetings into a three-hour time block.

1850 Oliver Cowdery, one of the Three Witnesses of the Book of Mormon and former Assistant President of the Church, dies in Richmond, Missouri.

1852 Martha James Cragun (Cox), later a pioneer schoolteacher and author of a handwritten autobiography over three hundred pages long, is born at Mill Creek, Utah.

1968 The Huntsville Stake, the first stake in Alabama, is organized, with Raymond D. McCurdy as president.

1991 Latter-day Saint missionaries enter Madagascar for the first time.

Oliver Cowdery, ca. 1846 (see 1850).

1995 President Howard W. Hunter dies in Salt Lake City, Utah, at age eighty-seven, after more than thirty-five years of service as a General Authority.

1840 Joseph Smith arrives in Nauvoo after spending over four months in the East (primarily in Washington, D.C., and Philadelphia), unsuccessfully petitioning the nation's leaders to redress the losses the Saints had suffered in Missouri.

1844 Joseph Smith recommends that work on the Nauvoo House be suspended until the temple is completed.

1865 The Saints in Salt Lake City join the nation in celebrating the reinauguration of United States president Abraham Lincoln.

1895 Church Apostle John Henry Smith is elected by the Utah Constitutional Convention to preside over the delegates as they begin to prepare a constitution for the new state.

1902 On the Mount of Olives in Jerusalem, Elder Francis M. Lyman, president of the European Mission, rededicates the Holy Land for the gathering of the Jews.

1925 The Church Missionary Home and Preparatory Training School opens in Salt Lake City for the training of new missionaries.

1930 Feith Foote Nyborg, later the U.S. ambassador to Finland (1981), is born in Ashton, Idaho.

1962 The Bavarian Mission is organized.

1994 The Church receives legal recognition from the government of Cambodia.

1849 A constitutional convention meets in Salt Lake City, where a constitution for the proposed state of Deseret is adopted. However, the U.S. Congress, in the famous Compromise of 1850, makes Utah a territory instead of a state, denying the Saints local home rule and leading to a nearly fifty-year struggle for statehood.

1884 Alma Sonne, later an assistant to the Quorum of the Twelve Apostles and a member of the First Quorum of the Seventy, is born in Logan, Utah.

1902 The name of the Smith Academy in Rexburg, Idaho, is changed to Ricks Academy in honor of Thomas E. Ricks, founder of Rexburg.

1994 Elder Joseph B. Wirthlin dedicates a new missionary training center near the Buenos Aires Argentina Temple.

2000 President Gordon B. Hinckley dedicates the Albuquerque New Mexico Temple.

1862 President Brigham Young dedicates the Salt Lake Theater.

1906 Joseph T. Bentley, later the superintendent of the Young Men's Mutual Improvement Association (1958–62), is born in Colonia Juárez, Mexico.

1935 Horacio A. Tenorio, later a member of the Second Quorum of the Seventy, is born in Mexico City, Mexico.

1948 President Edward "Vaun" Clissold and his wife, Irene, arrive in Japan, the first official missionaries in Japan since the closure of the Japanese mission in 1924.

1961 The Central British Mission is organized.

1986 Stanley Howard Watts, a BYU men's basketball coach (1949–72) whose teams won eight conference titles and two National Invitational Tournaments (NIT), is inducted into the Basketball Hall of Fame.

1988 Native priesthood leaders representing the Amman, Irbid, and Husn branches in the Jordan District of the Church gather in the first priesthood leadership training meeting held for Arab branches.

1999 President Gordon B. Hinckley dedicates the Colonia Juárez Chihuahua México Temple.

Priesthood leadership training meeting in the Jordan District in Amman, 6 March 1988.

1821 Rachel Ridgway Ivins (Grant), later the mother of Heber J. Grant, is born in Hornerstown, New Jersey.

1831 Joseph Smith receives Doctrine and Covenants 45, which sheds greater light on events associated with the Second Coming.

1832 Joseph Smith receives Doctrine and Covenants 80 on this day (according to the Kirtland Revelation Book). The revelation calls Stephen Burnett and Eden Smith on short-term missions.

Rachel Ridgway Ivins Grant and her son, Heber J. Grant, ca. 1868 (see 1821).

1840 Elders Brigham Young and Heber C. Kimball board the *Patrick Henry* in the New York Harbor, leaving the United States for their famous mission to England.

1853 The Gibraltar Mission is organized.

1943 The Navajo-Zuni Mission is organized, the first mission in the twentieth century directed to Native Americans.

1981 President Spencer W. Kimball breaks ground for the Atlanta Georgia Temple.

1992 The United States Internal Revenue Service announces that contributions to the missionary program of The Church of Jesus Christ of Latter-day Saints qualify as deductible charitable donations.

1998 Ground is broken for the Colonia Juárez Chihuahua México Temple. Elder Eran A. Call, a member of the Second Quorum of the Seventy and President of the Mexico North Area, presides over the ceremony.

1821 Christopher Layton, later a Mormon Battalion member and colonizer, is born in Thorncutt, England.

1831 Joseph Smith and Sidney Rigdon begin work on the Joseph Smith Translation of the New Testament. The Prophet receives Doctrine and Covenants 46, which gives instructions on conducting Church meetings and on the proper use of the gifts of the Spirit. He also receives Doctrine and Covenants 47, in which John Whitmer is called to keep a history of the Church.

1832 Joseph Smith ordains Sidney Rigdon and Jesse Gause as Counselors in the First Presidency, organizing the First Presidency for the first time in this dispensation.

1833 Joseph Smith receives Doctrine and Covenants 90, which brings a deepened understanding of the purpose and importance of the First Presidency.

1849 A constitutional convention opens in Salt Lake City, and a constitution for the proposed state of Deseret is adopted.

1869 The Union Pacific Railway reaches Ogden, Utah.

1958 The West-Spanish American Mission is organized.

1973 The Seoul Stake, the first stake organized on mainland Asia, is organized in Korea, with Ho Nam Rhee as president.

2000 *God's Army,* an independent film directed by LDS filmmaker Richard Dutcher about missionary life in southern California, premieres in Sandy, Utah.

2000 President Gordon B. Hinckley is the featured speaker at a sold-out National Press Club Newsmakers Luncheon, becoming the first President of the Church to address such an audience.

1811 Jacob Gates, later one of the First Seven Presidents of the Seventy, is born in Saint Johnsbury, Vermont.

1833 Joseph Smith receives Doctrine and Covenants 91, which informs him "that it is not needful that the Apocrypha should be translated."

1920 George I. Cannon, later a member of the First Quorum of the Seventy, is born in Salt Lake City, Utah.

1982 President Marion G. Romney of the First Presidency dedicates the Spencer W. Kimball Tower, the tallest building on the Brigham Young University campus, with President Kimball attending in his first public appearance after having been sick for six months.

1997 The Church creates the Puerto Varas Chile Stake, with Gerardo J. Wilhelm Kretschmar as president, making Chile the fourth nation in the world to have one hundred or more stakes.

The Spencer W. Kimball Tower on BYU campus (see 1982).

1838 At a meeting of the Seventies in Kirtland, discussion focuses on the possibility of the quorum as a whole moving to Far West following the Kirtland apostasy and Joseph Smith's flight to Missouri earlier in the year. The Spirit touches each man in attendance until all present are satisfied that they should move immediately.

1841 Illinois Governor Thomas Carlin commissions Joseph Smith as lieutenant general of the Nauvoo Legion.

1843 Meliton G. Trejo, later the translator of the Book of Mormon into Spanish, is born in Garganto-la-Olla, Spain.

1844 Joseph Smith addresses the Saints at the Nauvoo Temple site about the work and calling of Elias, Elijah, and the Messiah.

1946 Elder Ezra Taft Benson, a member of the Twelve and the European Mission president, arrives in Germany with Frederick Babbel, European Mission secretary, to begin their assessment of the status of the Saints in Europe after the conclusion of World War II.

1970 The first meetinghouse in Guam is dedicated, and the Guam Branch becomes a ward.

1985 A Churchwide fireside is held to teach members how to use the new LDS edition of the scriptures.

1996 Mike Wallace of CBS's *60 Minutes* interviews President Gordon B. Hinckley for a story on the Church to be aired in April 1996.

1998 President Thomas S. Monson rededicates Brigham Young University's Eyring Science Center, which is named in honor of LDS scientist Carl F. Eyring.

1786 Isaac Morley, later one of the first converts to the Church in Kirtland, a counselor to Bishop Edward Partridge, a stake president in Illinois, and a pioneer in Manti, Utah, is born in Montague, Massachusetts.

1882 A town site in the Snake River Valley in Idaho is selected and named Rexburg after Thomas E. Ricks.

1893 Herbert Brown Maw, later governor of Utah (1940–48), is born in Ogden, Utah.

1956 President David O. McKay dedicates the Los Angeles Temple (later the Los Angeles California Temple), which was one of only four temples erected during the 1950s.

1982 The restored Sarah Granger Kimball home, the site of the preliminary meetings of what would become the Relief Society, is dedicated in Nauvoo, Illinois.

1992 President Gordon B. Hinckley of the First Presidency presents the Vatican Library in Vatican City, Italy, with a copy of the five-volume *Encyclopedia of Mormonism*.

2000 President James E. Faust, Second Counselor in the First Presidency, dedicates the Oaxaca México Temple.

1832 Joseph Smith receives Doctrine and Covenants 79 on this day (according to the Kirtland Revelation Book). The revelation appoints Jared Carter to serve a short-term mission for the Church.

1835 Joseph Smith proposes that the newly called Quorum of the Twelve Apostles embark on a mission to the eastern states and the Atlantic seaboard.

1849 The officers of the first provisional government of the state of Deseret are elected as follows: Brigham Young (governor), Willard Richards (secretary of state), Newel K. Whitney (treasurer), Heber C. Kimball (chief justice), John Taylor and Newel K. Whitney (associate justices), Daniel H. Wells (attorney general), Horace S. Eldredge (marshal), Albert Carrington (assessor and collector of taxes), and Joseph L. Heywood (surveyor of highways).

1857 Rudger Clawson, later President of the Quorum of the Twelve Apostles and Second Counselor in the First Presidency, is born in Salt Lake City, Utah.

President Heber J. Grant presents a copy of the Book of Mormon in Braille to Helen Keller, an activist for the deaf and blind, 12 March 1941.

1859 Abraham H. Cannon, later one of the First Seven Presidents of the Seventy and a member of the Quorum of the Twelve Apostles, is born in Salt Lake City, Utah.

1930 Vernon Law, later a professional baseball star and Cy Young Award winner in 1960, is born in Meridian, Idaho.

1941 President Heber J. Grant presents a copy of the Book of Mormon in braille to Helen Keller, a well-known advocate for the deaf and the blind.

1947 Willard Mitt Romney, later founder and partner of Bain Capital, Inc., and director of the Salt Lake City 2002 Olympics Organizing Committee, is born in Detroit, Michigan.

1956 Dale Murphy, later a professional baseball all-star, National League MVP (1982, 1983), 1987 *Sports Illustrated* Sportsman of the Year, and Church mission president, is born in Portland, Oregon.

1961 The Holland Stake, the first stake in the Netherlands and the first non-English-speaking stake in the Church, is organized at The Hague, with Johan Paul Jongkees as president.

1987 The Church announces that the seventy-six-year-old Hotel Utah, in downtown Salt Lake City, will be renovated and will function as a meetinghouse, family history library, and Church office building.

1995 Gordon B. Hinckley is ordained and set apart as the fifteenth President of the Church, with Thomas S. Monson and James E. Faust as Counselors; Elder Boyd K. Packer of the Twelve is set apart as Acting President of the Twelve.

1995 The Dublin Ireland Stake, the first stake in the Republic of Ireland, is organized, with Liam Gallagher as president.

2000 President James E. Faust, Second Counselor in the First Presidency, dedicates the Tuxtla Gutiérrez México Temple.

1795 Josiah Butterfield, later one of the First Seven Presidents of the Seventy, is born in Saco, Maine.

1808 Samuel H. Smith, brother of Joseph Smith and later one of the Eight Witnesses of the Book of Mormon, is born in Tunbridge, Vermont.

1811 William B. Smith, brother of Joseph Smith and later a member of the Quorum of the Twelve Apostles and an ordained Patriarch to the Church (although he was never sustained as such), is born in Royalton, Vermont.

1838 Under the supervision of Hyrum Smith, the seventies draft the constitution for the organization and government of Kirtland Camp (sometimes called the "poor camp"). The camp was composed of impoverished Latter-day Saints who were fleeing Kirtland, Ohio, for Far West, Missouri, following the apostasy in Kirtland.

1850 Isaac Morley, leader of the Saints settling San Pete County, Utah, baptizes Ute Indian Chief Wakara ("Walker").

1857 Brigham Henry Roberts, later a prominent historian and theologian and one of the First Seven Presidents of the Seventy, is born in Warrington, England.

1963 Peter R. Huntsman, later president and CEO of Huntsman Chemical (founded by his father, Jon M. Huntsman Sr.), is born in Los Angeles, California.

1970 President Hugh B. Brown of the First Presidency and Elders Ezra Taft Benson and Gordon B. Hinckley conduct the dedication of the Mormon Pavilion at the World's Fair in Osaka, Japan. Some 6.65 million people attend the pavilion in the first six months of the fair.

President Gordon B. Hinckley's first press conference, 13 March 1995.

1979 President Spencer W. Kimball rededicates the Logan Temple (later the Logan Utah Temple), which had undergone extensive remodeling.

1981 United States president Ronald Reagan hosts President Spencer W. Kimball and Elder Gordon B. Hinckley.

1992 Elder Joseph Anderson, who had served as secretary to the First Presidency, Assistant to the Quorum of the Twelve Apostles, and member of the First Quorum of the Seventy, dies at age 102 in Salt Lake City, Utah.

1995 President Gordon B. Hinckley holds his first press conference as President of the Church in the lobby of the Joseph Smith Memorial Building in Salt Lake City.

1999 Ground is broken for three new temples—the Oaxaca México Temple, the Kona Hawaii Temple, and the Nashville Tennessee Temple. Elders Carl B. Pratt, John B. Dickson, and John K. Carmack (all of the First Quorum of the Seventy) preside over the respective ceremonies.

1802 Orson Spencer, later a missionary, educator, and author, is born in West Stockbridge, Massachusetts.

1804 Vinson Knight, later an early bishop and defender of Joseph Smith, is born in Norwhich, Massachusetts.

1811 Robert D. Foster, who later rose to prominence in Nauvoo before apostatizing and supporting William Law in his quest to destroy Joseph Smith, is born in Braunston, England.

1838 Joseph Smith arrives in Far West, Missouri, after escaping from apostates in Kirtland, Ohio.

1982 The Madrid Spain Stake, the first stake in Spain, is organized, with Jose Maria Oliveira Aldamiz as president.

1992 The women of the Church celebrate the sesquicentennial of the founding of the Relief Society through an international satellite broadcast.

1832 Joseph Smith receives a revelation on this day (according to the Kirtland Revelation Book) calling Jesse Gause to the "Presidency of the High Priesthood." When Gause later proves unfaithful, the calling is extended to Frederick G. Williams, whose name is now found in the revelation as recorded in Doctrine and Covenants 81.

1833 Joseph Smith receives Doctrine and Covenants 92, which appoints Frederick G. Williams as a member of the united order.

1877 Romania Pratt (Penrose) graduates from the Women's Medical College in New York. She is one of the first LDS women to earn a medical degree.

1931 Richard B. Wirthlin, later a member of the Second Quorum of the Seventy, is born in Salt Lake City, Utah.

1961 The Central German Mission is organized.

1970 The Tokyo Stake, the first stake in Asia, is organized in Japan, with Kenji Tanaka as president.

1970 The Japan East Mission is organized.

1989 The first LDS branch in Kenya is organized in Nairobi.

1842 Joseph Smith completes his translation of the Book of Abraham.

1844 The last meeting of the Female Relief Society of Nauvoo is held.

1892 Dr. Charles William Elliott, president of Harvard University, gives an address in the Salt Lake Tabernacle, honoring Latter-day Saint pioneer women.

1964 Sharlene C. Wells (Hawkes), later the second Latter-day Saint to be crowned Miss America (1985), is born in Asuncion, Paraguay.

▶ *Danny Ainge during his basketball career at BYU, ca. 1980 (see 1959).*

1842 Joseph Smith organizes the Female Relief Society of Nauvoo, with Emma Smith as president, Elizabeth Ann Whitney and Sarah M. Cleveland as counselors, and Eliza R. Snow as secretary.

1892 The Saints celebrate the fiftieth anniversary of the organization of the Relief Society.

1896 Archibald F. Bennett, later a hymn composer, pioneer genealogist for the Church, and diligent worker in the Genealogical Society of Utah, is born in Dingle, Idaho.

1921 John A. Widtsoe is ordained a member of the Quorum of the Twelve Apostles, replacing Anthony W. Ivins, who had been called to be the Second Counselor in the First Presidency.

1959 Daniel "Danny" Ainge, later a BYU basketball star, a major league baseball player, and an NBA player and coach, is born in Eugene, Oregon.

1984 Elder Thomas S. Monson of the Quorum of the Twelve breaks ground for the Stockholm Sweden Temple.

1993 Elder James E. Faust dedicates the Baltic republic of Latvia for the preaching of the gospel.

1999 The First Presidency announces plans to build new temples in Louisville, Kentucky; Medford, Oregon; Oklahoma City, Oklahoma; Adelaide, Australia; Copenhagen, Denmark; and San José, Costa Rica.

MARCH 18

1856 Susa Young (Gates), daughter of Brigham Young and later an accomplished writer and speaker, is born in Salt Lake City, Utah.

Susa Young Gates, ca. 1874 (see 1856).

1926 Richard P. Lindsay, later a member of the Second Quorum of the Seventy, is born in Salt Lake City, Utah.

1934 H. Bryan Richards, later a member of the Second Quorum of the Seventy, is born in Salt Lake City, Utah.

1962 The Apia Samoa Stake, the first stake in Western Samoa, is organized, with Percy John Rivers as president.

1970 The Japan West Mission is organized.

1982 Three Church executive committees are created—the Missionary Executive Council, the Priesthood Executive Council, and the Temple and Genealogy Executive Council (later known as the Temple and Family History Executive Council).

1995 President Boyd K. Packer, Acting President of the Quorum of the Twelve Apostles, addresses ambassadors and members of the diplomatic community from twenty-six nations at a BYU Management Society dinner held in Washington, D.C.

1999 Presidents Gordon B. Hinckley and Thomas S. Monson and Elder Jeffrey R. Holland visit Spain's King Juan Carlos and Queen Sofia at the royal palace in Madrid.

MARCH 19

1830 An advertisement in the *Wayne Sentinel*, a Palmyra newspaper, notes that the first copies of the Book of Mormon will be ready for sale in a week.

1851 President Brigham Young organizes the Provo Stake, the first stake in Utah south of Salt Lake City, with Isaac Higbee as president.

1903 Reuben D. Law, later the first president of the Church College of Hawaii, later known as BYU–Hawaii, is born in Avon, Utah.

1925 Brent Scowcroft, later the U.S. national security advisor (1975–77 and 1989–93), is born in Ogden, Utah.

1931 Ardeth Greene (Kapp), later the ninth general president of the Young Women, is born in Cardston, Alberta, Canada.

1968 LDS missionaries arrive in Singapore for the first time.

1999 President Gordon B. Hinckley dedicates the Madrid Spain Temple.

2000 President Thomas S. Monson, First Counselor in the First Presidency, dedicates the Louisville Kentucky Temple.

MARCH 20

1826 Joseph Smith stands trial in South Bainbridge, New York, on the charge of being a "disorderly person." Although he is exonerated, this is the first of many such trials he is forced to endure.

1839 While confined in Liberty Jail, Joseph Smith begins a letter to Church leaders, extracts from which would become the basis for Doctrine and Covenants 121–23.

1875 Some two hundred Shivwit Indians are baptized at St. George, Utah. This is one of the largest groups of North American Indians to be baptized in a single day.

1949 Kim Clark, later dean of faculty at the Harvard Business School, is born in Salt Lake City, Utah.

1976 Elder James E. Faust, an Assistant to the Twelve, breaks ground for the São Paulo Temple (later the São Paulo Brazil Temple).

1977 The Providence Stake, the first stake in Rhode Island, is organized, with Morgan W. Lewis Jr. as president.

1995 The U.S. Postal Service issues a new stamp designed by fourteen-year-old Brian Hailes of Millville, Utah.

1999 Ground is broken for three new temples—the Tuxtla Gutiérrez México, Fresno California, and Melbourne Australia Temples—with Elders Richard E. Turley Sr. (of the Second Quorum of the Seventy), John B. Dickson (of the First Quorum of the Seventy), and P. Bruce Mitchell (an Area Authority) presiding over the respective ceremonies.

2000 Daniel Oswald of the Foundation for Ancient Research and Mormon Studies (FARMS) at Brigham Young University meets with Vatican officials and signs a publishing agreement between the Vatican Apostolic Library and BYU's Center for the Preservation of Ancient Religious Texts (CPART).

MARCH 21

1858 President Brigham Young supervises the evacuation of the northern Utah settlements as the United States Army, led by Albert Sidney Johnston, prepares to enter the territory during the "Utah War."

1867 President Brigham Young is named president of the Deseret Telegraph Company.

1872 Hyrum Mack Smith, later a member of the Quorum of the Twelve Apostles, is born in Salt Lake City, Utah.

1886 The Saints living on the Peadres Verdes River in Chihuahua, Mexico, hold a celebration and name their community Juárez.

1912 In an effort to prevent the transmission of germs, Church leaders encourage local congregations to use individual sacrament cups instead of the "common cup."

1940 Glenn L. Pace, later a member of the First Quorum of the Seventy, is born in Provo, Utah.

1953 The first converts in Honduras are baptized.

1994 Jerry Molen receives an Oscar from the Academy of Motion Picture Arts and Sciences as co-producer of the 1993 film *Schindler's List*.

1996 The First Presidency appoints Rodney H. Brady as president and chief executive officer of Deseret Management Corporation, the holding company that oversees businesses owned by the Church.

MARCH 22

1821 Elijah F. Sheets, later the bishop of the Salt Lake City Eighth Ward for forty-eight years (the longest tenure of any bishop in Church history), is born in Charlestown, Pennsylvania.

1856 John G. Hafen, later a Utah landscape artist and Salt Lake Temple muralist, is born in Thurgin Canton, Switzerland.

John Hafen, ca. 1900 (see 1856).

1882 United States president Chester A. Arthur signs the antipolygamy Edmunds Bill into law. The law defines polygamous living as "unlawful cohabitation," makes contracting plural marriages a punishable offense, and disenfranchises polygamists.

1885 The United States Supreme Court annuls the Utah Commission's "test oath," which had been designed to prevent polygamists in Utah from voting. This restores the right to vote to a number of Saints in the territory.

1922 Robert L. Backman, later a member of the Presidency of the Seventy, is born in Salt Lake City, Utah.

1928 Elaine Low (Jack), later twelfth general president of the Relief Society, is born in Cardston, Alberta, Canada.

1934 Orrin G. Hatch, later an influential member of the U.S. Senate (1976–) and candidate in the 2000 U.S. presidential election, is born in Homestead Park, Pennsylvania.

1937 Jerald L. Taylor, later a member of the Second Quorum of the Seventy, is born in Colonia Dublan, Mexico.

1970 The Transvaal South Africa Stake, the first stake in Africa, is organized, with Louis P. Hefer as president.

1970 The Merrimack New Hampshire Stake, the first stake in New Hampshire, is organized, with William A. Fresh as president.

1970 The Mandenville Branch, the first branch of the Church in Jamaica, is organized.

1972 Shawn Paul Bradley, later a professional basketball player, is born in Landstuhl, West Germany.

1981 The Managua Nicaragua Stake, the first stake in Nicaragua, is organized, with Jose R. Armando Garcia A. as president.

1833 The Prophet Joseph Smith appoints Joseph Coe, Moses Dailey, and Ezra Thayer to purchase the Peter French farm as the site for the Kirtland Temple.

1844 Joseph Smith is informed that William Law, Wilson Law, Robert D. Foster, Chauncey L. Higbee, and Joseph Jackson are conspiring to kill the Smith family.

1847 Companies A, C, D, and E of the Mormon Battalion arrive at Pueblo de Los Angeles after a four-day journey from the San Luis Rey Mission.

1876 Advance companies of Saints called to settle in Arizona arrive from Utah at the Little Colorado River.

1906 Richard L. Evans, later a member of the First Council of the Seventy and of the Quorum of the Twelve Apostles, as well as the narrator of *Music and the Spoken Word* for nearly forty years, is born in Salt Lake City, Utah.

1935 Stephen A. West, later a member of the Second Quorum of the Seventy, is born in Salt Lake City, Utah.

1943 George P. Lee, later a member of the First Quorum of the Seventy, is born in Towaoc, Ute Mountain Indian Reservation, Colorado.

1974 The Church gives the state of Utah the Brigham Young Forest Farm home in Salt Lake City for use in the state's Pioneer State Park. In exchange the Church receives Brigham Young's winter home in St. George, Utah, and the Jacob Hamblin home in Santa Clara, Utah, to be used as visitors' and information centers.

1986 The Santo Domingo Dominican Republic Stake, the first stake in the Dominican Republic, is organized, with Jose Delio Ceveno as president.

1832 Fifty men led by former Church member Symonds Ryder tar and feather Joseph Smith in Hiram, Ohio. The same mob drags Sidney Rigdon by his heels along the frozen ground, severely injuring his head. Joseph and Emma's eleven-month-old adopted son, Joseph, dies a few days later as a result of exposure during the mobbing.

1851 Five hundred settlers leave Payson, Utah, for California, where they would found a Church-sponsored settlement at San Bernardino that was intended to be the first permanent settlement in California.

1927 Dean L. Larsen, later a member of the Presidency of the Seventy, is born in Hyrum, Utah.

1933 F. Burton Howard, later a member of the First Quorum of the Seventy, is born in Logan, Utah.

1958 Bruce Hurst, later a professional baseball pitcher, is born in St. George, Utah.

1988 At a dinner commemorating the 350th anniversary of the first Swedish settlement in the United States, the king and queen of Sweden entertain a group of guests that includes President Thomas S. Monson, Second Counselor in the First Presidency, and his wife, Frances.

◄ *Richard L. Evans delivering the "Spoken Word" (see 1906).*

2000 *The Testaments: Of One Fold and One Shepherd*, a film portraying the mission of the Savior in the Holy Land and on the American continent, opens to the public in the Legacy Theater of the Joseph Smith Memorial Building.

1793 Titus Billings, later a Counselor in the Presiding Bishopric, an early settler in Jackson County, and a pioneer to Manti, Utah, is born in Greenfield, Massachusetts.

1815 William H. Folsom, later the architect of many buildings in Utah, including the Manti Temple (later the Manti Utah Temple), is born in Portsmouth, New Hampshire.

1816 Don Carlos Smith, brother and lifelong supporter of Joseph Smith, is born in Norwich, Vermont.

1832 After spending the night having tar and feathers removed from his skin, Joseph Smith preaches on the Sabbath to a congregation that includes members of the mob that had attacked him the night before. Joseph baptizes three people later in the day.

1949 Claudio R. M. Costa, later a member of the Second Quorum of the Seventy, is born in Santos, Brazil.

1953 The First Presidency announces that returning missionaries will now report to their local stake presidency and high council rather than to General Authorities.

1982 The Mormon Tabernacle Choir leaves for a concert tour of Europe.

1984 With the announcement of the four-phase genealogical facilities program, wards and branches are authorized to establish genealogical facilities in their meetinghouses.

1995 President Gordon B. Hinckley speaks at the annual Young Women meeting in his first address from the Salt Lake Tabernacle pulpit after becoming President of the Church.

1797 Joseph Fielding, later a missionary companion to Heber C. Kimball to England in 1837 and the subsequent president over that mission, is born in Honeydon, England.

The first edition of the Book of Mormon (see 1830).

1830 The Book of Mormon goes on sale at the E. B. Grandin bookstore in Palmyra, New York.

1844 Joseph Smith meets with the Quorum of the Twelve Apostles in what is his last opportunity to address the group before his martyrdom. This is probably when he gives his "last charge" and bestows on them the keys, rights, and responsibility to lead the kingdom.

1847 Jacob Spori, later a distinguished educator and missionary to the Middle East, is born in Oberwyl, Switzerland.

1850 Colonel Thomas L. Kane, a nonmember friend of the Latter-day Saints, gives a lecture on the "Mormons" to the Historical Society of Pennsylvania. Kane's address is one of the few non-Mormon descriptions of the Church during this period that portrays the Saints in a favorable light.

1904 President John R. Winder of the First Presidency dedicates the Bureau of Information, the first visitors' center on Temple Square. The building is an octagonal frame structure about twenty feet across, costing $500; it serves as the base for the seventy-five guides called to answer tourists' questions about Salt Lake City and the Church.

Servicemen on the island of Sardina meet outside of the brick chapel they built for the Latter-day Saints stationed at their base (see 1944).

1906 Morris Blaine Peterson, later a Utah representative in the U.S. Congress (1960–62), is born in Ogden, Utah.

1931 Vaughn J. Featherstone, later a member of the First Quorum of the Seventy, is born in Stockton, Utah.

1944 American servicemen stationed on the Mediterranean island of Sardina at a B-26 Marauder station meet for the first time in a small brick chapel. With the help of local Italian bricklayers, twelve servicemen had used their own funds and efforts to construct a chapel large enough to accommodate the thirty Latter-day Saints on the base.

1960 Michael S. Evans, later a silver medalist in water polo at the 1988 Seoul Olympic games, is born in Fontana, California.

1960 Jon M. Huntsman Jr., later U.S. ambassador to Singapore (1992–93) and vice chairman of Huntsman Chemical Corporation, is born in Palo Alto, California.

1989 The first convert in Suriname is baptized.

1998 President Gordon B. Hinckley dedicates a replica of the Palmyra, New York, log home where the Joseph Smith Sr. family resided at the time of the First Vision and the appearances of the angel Moroni.

1836 Reading a prayer given by revelation (D&C 109), Joseph Smith dedicates the Kirtland Temple, the first temple completed in this dispensation.

1893 Utah Saints gather in their meetinghouses for a special fast in anticipation of the 6 April dedication of the Salt Lake Temple.

1898 President Brigham Young Jr. of the Quorum of the Twelve Apostles sets apart Harriet Maria Horsepool Nye as a missionary; she is generally identified as the first full-time sister missionary of the Church, although sources indicate that other missionaries' wives were also blessed prior to leaving for their missions.

1907 Theodore M. Burton, later an Assistant to the Twelve and a member of the First Quorum of the Seventy, is born in Salt Lake City, Utah.

1910 Hugh W. Nibley, later a renowned educator, linguist, author, scriptorian, and social critic, is born in Portland, Oregon.

Hugh W. Nibley, ca. 1980 (see 1910).

1960 The Sydney and Manchester Stakes, the first stakes in Australia and England, are organized, with Dell C. Hunt and Robert G. Larson, respectively, as presidents.

1960 The North British Mission is organized.

1963 The Southeast Mexican Mission is organized.

1980 An essay on Joseph Smith written by Elder Gordon B. Hinckley of the Quorum of the Twelve Apostles, is placed in the United States *Congressional Record*.

1998 President Gordon B. Hinckley dedicates the newly restored Egbert B. Grandin Building in Palmyra, New York.

1784 William Huntington Sr., later a stalwart friend of Joseph Smith, Nauvoo Temple stonemason, and prominent leader during the Saints' trek across Iowa, is born in New Grantham, New Hampshire.

1834 Joseph Smith returns to Kirtland after traveling to western New York to recruit men and secure means for the establishment of Zion's Camp.

1835 Joseph Smith receives Doctrine and Covenants 107 at a special meeting of the Quorum of the Twelve Apostles, although portions were received as early as 1831. The revelation clarifies the duties of many Church offices and explains the distinction between the Aaronic and Melchizedek Priesthoods.

1850 Joseph L. Rawlins, later the Utah Territory delegate to the U.S. Congress (1892–94) and a U.S. Senator (1897–1903), is born in Salt Lake City, Utah.

1851 The general assembly of the provisional state of Deseret meets and recognizes the act of the U.S. Congress that created the territory of Utah.

1895 Spencer W. Kimball, later a member of the Quorum of the Twelve Apostles and twelfth President of the Church, is born in Salt Lake City, Utah.

1896 United States president Grover Cleveland signs an act to return to the Church real estate properties confiscated by the federal government during the polygamy prosecutions of the 1880s.

1899 Harold B. Lee, later a member of the Quorum of the Twelve Apostles, a Counselor in the First Presidency, and the eleventh President of the Church, is born in Clifton, Idaho.

President Harold B. Lee (see 1899).

1903 Spencer W. Kimball is baptized in the family bathtub at eight years of age. He is baptized again in October 1907 because of concern about the appropriateness of his previous baptism.

1929 Ruth May Fox is called as the third general president of the Young Ladies' Mutual Improvement Association (the predecessor of the Young Women program), with Lucy Grant Cannon and Clarissa A. Beesley as counselors.

1998 Ground is broken for the Billings Montana Temple. Elder Hugh W. Pinnock of the First Quorum of the Seventy presides over the ceremony.

1830 The local Palmyra Presbyterian Church suspends Lucy Mack, Hyrum, Samuel, and Sophronia Smith for nonattendance.

1832 Joseph Murdock, one of the twins taken in by Joseph and Emma Smith, dies as a result of exposure to the cold during the 24 March mob attack on Joseph Smith and Sidney Rigdon.

1836 A number of Church leaders and elders assemble in the Kirtland Temple, where they participate in the sacred ordinance of the washing of the feet and afterward remain all night, prophesying and praising God.

Richard Erastus Egan, ca. 1860 (see 1842).

1842 Richard Erastus Egan, later one of the original Pony Express riders (1860), is born in Salem, Massachusetts.

1934 Alton L. Wade, later the seventh president of BYU–Hawaii, is born in Leamington, Utah.

1970 The first Indonesian converts are baptized.

1995 In a testimony at a U.S. Senate Finance Committee hearing regarding welfare reform, Presiding Bishop Merrill J. Bateman highlights Church welfare programs and shares the history, principles, and lessons learned by the Church while establishing these programs.

1813 Amasa M. Lyman, later a member of the Quorum of the Twelve Apostles, is born in Lyman, New Hampshire.

1836 After a full day of instruction in the Kirtland Temple, the congregation experiences spiritual manifestations similar to those on the day of Pentacost, and several witness the appearance of angels.

1909 Elizabeth Fetzer (Bates), later the composer of several hymns and children's songs, including "Pioneer Children Sang as They Walked" and "Book of Mormon Stories," is born in Salt Lake City, Utah.

1925 Teddy E. Brewerton, later a member of the First Quorum of the Seventy, is born in Raymond, Alberta, Canada.

1927 Graham W. Doxey, later a member of the Second Quorum of the Seventy, is born in Salt Lake City, Utah.

❧❧❧ MARCH ❧❧❧

1836 Joseph Smith repeats the dedicatory service of the Kirtland Temple for the benefit of those members who were unable to participate in the 27 March meeting.

1864 While trying to land at Lahaina, Maui, in the Hawaiian Islands, Elder Lorenzo Snow drowns when a boat he and Elder Ezra T. Benson are in capsizes. After an hour of prayer and artificial resuscitation, Elder Snow revives.

The general Relief Society presidency, ca. 1990. From left: Chieko Okazaki, President Elaine Jack, and Aileen Clyde (see 1990).

1875 George Reynolds's trial for breaking the antipolygamy Morrill Act of 1862 commences in the Third District Court. Reynolds was asked by the First Presidency to submit to this trial in an effort to test the constitutionality of the Morrill Act. The next day he is found guilty, which sets the stage for a series of appeals that eventually leads to a hearing before the United States Supreme Court. The Court upholds the constitutionality of the Morrill Act, paving the way for several more antipolygamy bills in the 1880s.

1903 Sterling W. Sill, later an Assistant to the Quorum of the Twelve Apostles and a member of the First Quorum of the Seventy, is born in Layton, Utah.

1978 President Spencer W. Kimball announces that stake conferences will be held semiannually instead of quarterly beginning in 1979.

1982 The First Presidency announces plans to build a temple in Guayaquil, Ecuador.

1990 Elaine L. Jack is called as the twelfth general president of the Relief Society, with Chieko Nishimura Okazaki and Aileen Hales Clyde as counselors.

1990 David M. Kennedy is released as the First Presidency's international representative.

APRIL 1

1775 James Foster, later one of the First Seven Presidents of the Seventy, is born in Morgan County, New Hampshire.

1832 In obedience to the Lord's command given in Doctrine and Covenants 78, Joseph Smith, Newel K. Whitney, Peter Whitmer Jr., and Jesse Gause leave for Jackson County, Missouri, to establish the united order. This is Joseph's second trip to Jackson County.

1873 Alice Louise Reynolds, later an important writer, librarian, and early female professor at Brigham Young University for more than forty years, is born in Salt Lake City, Utah.

1898 Lucy Jane Brimhall and Amanda Inez Knight, the first single sister missionaries, receive calls to serve as full-time missionaries to England.

1917 Mark Evan Austad, later a U.S. ambassador (Finland, 1975; Norway, 1981), is born in Ogden, Utah.

1920 The Danish and Norwegian Missions are organized.

1931 Gordon Jump, later a TV and movie star and a Maytag representative, is born in Dayton, Ohio.

1980 The Micronesia Guam Mission is organized.

1981 President Spencer W. Kimball announces plans to build temples in nine cities in Africa, Asia, Central America, Europe, and the United States: Chicago, Illinois; Dallas, Texas; Frankfurt, Germany; Guatemala City, Guatemala; Johannesburg, South Africa; Lima, Peru; Manila, Philippines; Seoul, South Korea; and Stockholm, Sweden.

1982 The Church announces that membership has reached five million.

1989 The creation of the Second Quorum of the Seventy is announced at general conference.

1995 President Gordon B. Hinckley is sustained as President of the Church during a solemn assembly at general conference. He announces that the position of regional representative in the Church will be replaced by that of Area Authority. Unlike the General Authorities, Area Authorities continue their current employment and reside in their homes.

1999 Deseret Management Corporation finalizes the purchase of Bookcraft, Inc., bringing the book publisher and the electronic media group InfoBases under the Church's ownership.

1999 Mayor Hal Daub of Omaha, Nebraska, deeds the Winter Quarters Cemetery to the Church.

2000 General conference is held for the first time in the nearly completed Conference Center.

The interior of the Conference Center, April 2000 (see 2000).

APRIL 2

1821 Franklin D. Richards, later a member of the Quorum of the Twelve Apostles, is born in Richmond, Massachusetts.

1843 While visiting the Saints in Ramus, Illinois, Joseph Smith gives instruction on such topics as the nature of the Godhead, intelligence, and obedience, found today in Doctrine and Covenants 130.

1921 Clarissa Smith Williams is called as the sixth general president of the Relief Society, with Jennie Brimhall Knight and Louise Yates Robison as counselors.

1936 Dale E. Miller, later a member of the Second Quorum of the Seventy, is born in Los Angeles, California.

1974 Kieth Merrill receives an Oscar for best documentary from the Academy of Motion Picture Arts and Sciences for *The Great American Cowboy.*

1982 The Church announces changes in the financing of Church meetinghouses. Construction costs are to be paid by general Church funds, whereas utility costs are to be borne by local units.

1988 Michaelene Packer Grassli is called as the eighth general president of the Primary, with Betty Jo Nelson Jepsen and Ruth Broadbent Wright as counselors.

1990 The Church releases FamilySearch®, a new software package, in an effort to simplify the task of family history research.

1994 Elder Merrill J. Bateman of the Second Quorum of the Seventy is sustained as Presiding Bishop of the Church.

2000 Following the closing session of the first general conference in the new Conference Center, the First Presidency opens the building to the public in an open house that lasts until 10:00 P.M.

The Conference Center, April 2000 (see 2000).

❦❦❦ APRIL 3 ❦❦❦

1814 Lorenzo Snow, later a member of the Quorum of the Twelve and fifth President of the Church, is born in Mantua, Ohio.

1836 Joseph Smith and Oliver Cowdery pray in the recently dedicated Kirtland Temple and witness the appearance of Jesus Christ, Moses, Elias, and Elijah (D&C 110).

1852 The German Mission is organized.

1976 In General Conference, the First Presidency and the Quorum of the Twelve Apostles propose to the Church to include Joseph Smith's vision of the celestial kingdom and Joseph F. Smith's vision of the redemption of the dead in the standard works of the Church. The vote is unanimous in the affirmative.

Melchizedek Priesthood pulpits in the Kirtland Temple (see 1836).

1983 President Gordon B. Hinckley of the First Presidency rededicates the newly renovated Assembly Hall on Temple Square.

1993 *The Mountain of the Lord,* a motion picture produced by the Church about the building of the Salt Lake Temple, premieres between sessions of general conference as part of a year-long commemoration of the centennial of the Salt Lake Temple.

1997 The First Presidency announces plans to build temples in Albuquerque, New Mexico; and Campinas, Brazil.

❦❦❦ APRIL 4 ❦❦❦

1838 Sidney Rigdon arrives and takes up permanent residence with his family at Far West after leaving Kirtland.

1839 Joseph Smith writes a letter to his wife from Liberty Jail: "It is I believe now about five months and six days since I have been under the grimace of a guard night and day, and within the walls, grates, and screeching iron doors of a lonesome, dark, dirty prison. With emotions known only to God, do I write this letter. . . . This night we expect is the last night we shall try our weary joints and bones on our dirty straw couches in these walls, let our case hereafter be as it may . . . we cannot get into a worse hole than this. . . . We shall never cast a lingering wish after Liberty in Clay County Missouri. We have enough of it to last forever" (Dean C. Jessee, comp. and ed. *The Personal Writings of Joseph Smith,* 425–26; spelling and punctuation have been standardized).

1870 George Albert Smith, later a member of the Quorum of the Twelve Apostles and eighth President of the Church, is born in Salt Lake City.

1880 The first public meetings are held in the Salt Lake Assembly Hall.

George Albert Smith, ca. 1950 (see 1870).

1919 Walter Spat, later the first president of the São Paulo Brazil Stake, the first stake in South America, is born in Stimptach, Germany.

1920 Howard W. Hunter is baptized in a swimming pool in Boise, Idaho. (He is twelve years and five months old.)

1927 John R. Clarke, later a member of the Presidency of the Seventy, is born in Rexburg, Idaho.

1932 Ben B. Banks, later a member of the First Quorum of the Seventy, is born in Murray, Utah.

1951 President George Albert Smith dies in Salt Lake City on his eighty-first birthday, after more than forty-seven years of ministry as an Apostle and Church President.

1981 President Spencer W. Kimball announces that the three-fold mission of the Church is to proclaim the gospel, perfect the Saints, and redeem the dead.

1984 President Gordon B. Hinckley of the First Presidency dedicates the Museum of Church History and Art, located on the block east of Temple Square in Salt Lake City.

The Museum of Church History and Art, ca. 1984 (see 1984).

1992 Janette Hales Beckham is called as the tenth general president of the Young Women, with Virginia Hinckley Pearce and Patricia Peterson Pinegar as counselors.

1999 President Gordon B. Hinckley closes conference with electrifying news: "I feel impressed to announce that among all of the temples we are constructing, we plan to rebuild the Nauvoo Temple" (in Conference Report, April 1999, 117).

⚜ **APRIL** ⚜

5

1829 Oliver Cowdery arrives in Harmony, Pennsylvania, and meets Joseph Smith for the first time.

1847 Elder Heber C. Kimball, the first pioneer to leave Winter Quarters for the overland journey to Utah, leaves the settlement with six wagons.

1850 The first Latter-day Saint branch in France is organized in Boulogne-sur-Mer.

1900 The First Presidency decides that seniority in the Quorum of the Twelve is based on when one becomes a member of the Quorum, not when one is ordained to the office of Apostle; thus Joseph F. Smith is placed ahead of Brigham Young Jr.

1905 Martha Horne Tingey is called as the second general president of the Young Ladies' Mutual Improvement Association (the predecessor to the Young Women program), with Ruth May Fox and Mae Taylor Nystrom as counselors.

1930 F. Enzio Busche, later a member of the First Quorum of the Seventy, is born in Dortmund, Germany.

1942 The First Presidency closes the Salt Lake Tabernacle for the duration of World War II. Meetings are to be held in the Assembly Hall and in the solemn assembly room in the Salt Lake Temple.

1943 Gordon B. Hinckley accepts the position of assistant superintendent of the Salt Lake City Union Depot and Railroad Company.

1952 The Church begins transmitting the priesthood session of general conference by direct wire to buildings outside of Temple Square.

1980 Dwan Jacobsen Young is called as the seventh general president of the Primary, with Virginia Beesley Cannon and Michaelene Packer Grassli as counselors.

1995 The Utah Salt Lake City Temple Square Mission is organized.

1996 A group of Church members purchases Southern Virginia College and announces that it will establish a four-year program with standards similar to LDS Church schools.

1997 President Gordon B. Hinckley announces the formation of the Third, Fourth, and Fifth Quorums of the Seventy, which are to be composed of Area Authority Seventies.

1997 Mary Ellen W. Smoot is called as the thirteenth general president of the Relief Society, with Virginia U. Jensen and Sheri L. Dew as counselors.

The general Relief Society presidency, ca. 1997. From left: Virginia U. Jensen, President Mary Ellen W. Smoot, and Sheri L. Dew (see 1997).

APRIL

1819 Jacob Hamblin, later a famous missionary to Native Americans and colonizer of southern Utah, Arizona, and New Mexico, is born in Salem, Ohio.

1830 Joseph Smith organizes The Church of Jesus Christ in Fayette, New York, and receives Doctrine and Covenants 21 during the course of the meetings. According to the Book of Commandments, the material found in Doctrine and Covenants 23 is also received on this date.

1839 Joseph and Hyrum Smith, Alexander McRae, Caleb Baldwin, and Lyman Wight are taken under guard from Liberty Jail to Gallatin, Missouri, to stand trial.

1841 President Joseph Smith presides at the cornerstone laying ceremony for the Nauvoo Temple.

1847 Newell K. Whitney is sustained as Presiding Bishop of the Church.

1852 The Old Tabernacle, built on the site later occupied by the Assembly Hall on Temple Square, is dedicated. It is torn down in 1870, following completion of the modern, dome-shaped Tabernacle.

1853 President Brigham Young presides at the laying and dedication of the cornerstones for the Salt Lake Temple.

1854 The Siam Mission is organized.

1877 President Daniel H. Wells of the First Presidency dedicates the St. George Temple (later the St. George Utah Temple), the first temple in Utah.

1880 Celebrating its jubilee year, the Church forgives $802,000 of indebtedness to those who still owe money to the Perpetual Emigrating Fund and distributes one thousand cows and five thousand sheep to the worthy poor.

1884 William Bowker Preston is sustained as Presiding Bishop of the Church.

1892 At a ceremony attended by about forty thousand people, President Wilford Woodruff presses an electric button to lower into place the capstone for the Salt Lake Temple.

1893 President Wilford Woodruff dedicates the Salt Lake Temple.

1904 President Joseph F. Smith issues the "Second Manifesto," reemphasizing the Church's stand against new plural marriages performed in or outside the United States.

1930 Elder B. H. Roberts presents his monumental six-volume work, *A Comprehensive History of The Church of Jesus Christ of Latter-day Saints,* to the membership of the Church as part of the centennial celebration of the organization of the Church.

1936 Latter-day Saints in Europe hear a message from the First Presidency via shortwave radio for the first time.

1941 President Heber J. Grant institutes the office of Assistant to the Quorum of the Twelve Apostles, which exists until April 1976.

1941 The first general conference broadcasts beyond Utah commence when the Saints in Idaho and southern California receive the proceedings by radio.

1945 Belle Smith Spafford is called as the ninth general president of the Relief Society, with Marianne Clark Sharp and Gertrude Ryberg Garff as counselors.

1948 Bertha Stone Reeder is called as the fifth general president of the Young Women's Mutual Improvement Association (the predecessor to the Young Women program), with Emily Higgs Bennett and LaRue Carr Longden called later as counselors.

1952 Joseph L. Wirthlin is sustained as Presiding Bishop of the Church.

1972 Victor Lee Brown is sustained as Presiding Bishop of the Church.

1973 Immediately following the end of the Vietnam War, the first missionaries to Vietnam arrive from Hong Kong.

1980 On the Church's sesquicentennial, President Spencer W. Kimball conducts part of general conference via satellite broadcast from the newly restored Peter Whitmer farmhouse in Fayette, New York, the site where the Church was organized in 1830.

1985 Robert D. Hales is sustained as Presiding Bishop of the Church.

1993 The Church celebrates the centennial of the Salt Lake Temple.

1995 Henry B. Eyring is ordained as a member of the Quorum of the Twelve Apostles.

1996 President Gordon B. Hinckley announces in the opening session of general conference that a new meeting hall that will hold three to four times more people than the Salt Lake Tabernacle is being designed.

The Palmyra New York Temple (see 2000).

1996 H. David Burton is sustained as Presiding Bishop of the Church.

2000 President Gordon B. Hinckley dedicates the Palmyra New York Temple. The dedication is broadcast by satellite to stake centers and institute buildings throughout North America and Canada.

APRIL 7

1797 Joseph Young, brother of Brigham Young and later one of the First Seven Presidents of the Seventy, is born in Hopkinton, Massachusetts.

1803 Levi W. Hancock, later one of the First Seven Presidents of the Seventy, is born in Springfield, Massachusetts.

1829 Joseph Smith recommences his translation of the Book of Mormon with Oliver Cowdery as his newly appointed scribe. Martin Harris had lost virtually everything that Joseph had previously translated.

1831 Martin Harris sells part of his farm and pays E. B. Grandin for the cost of printing the Book of Mormon.

1844 During what would be his last general conference, Joseph Smith delivers the King Follett discourse, declaring that man has an immortal soul and can become like God and that the greatest responsibility resting on the Saints is to seek after their dead.

1851 Edward Hunter is sustained as the Presiding Bishop of the Church.

1851 The First Presidency issues the "Fifth General Epistle" to the Church, regarding the need to establish home manufacturing in Utah.

1854 Jedediah M. Grant is ordained an Apostle but is not placed in the Quorum of the Twelve Apostles.

1860 After a four-day trip from California, the first pony express carrier arrives in Salt Lake City.

Angel Moroni statue installation, ca. April 1892 (see 1892).

1879 Moses Thatcher is ordained a member of the Quorum of the Twelve Apostles.

1889 Wilford Woodruff is sustained as the fourth President of the Church, with George Q. Cannon and Joseph F. Smith as Counselors.

1892 The statue of the angel Moroni atop the Salt Lake Temple is illuminated with electric lights for the first time.

1907 Members of the Church attending general conference sustain the First Presidency's plans to send flour to those suffering from a famine in China.

1910 Joseph Fielding Smith is ordained a member of the Quorum of the Twelve Apostles, replacing John Henry Smith, who had been called to the First Presidency, and fulfilling a prophecy in his 1896 patriarchal blessing.

1913 Florence Smith (Jacobsen), later the sixth general president of the Young Women's Mutual Improvement Association (the predecessor to the Young Women organization), is born.

1918 Richard R. Lyman is ordained a member of the Twelve, replacing Hyrum M. Smith, who had died. Richard Lyman is the son of Francis M. Lyman and the grandson of Amasa M. Lyman, who had both served as members of the Quorum of the Twelve Apostles.

1951 President George Albert Smith's funeral is held in the Tabernacle in Salt Lake City.

1961 Thurl Bailey, later a professional basketball player in the NBA and a recording artist (*Faith in Your Heart*), is born in Washington, D.C.

1973 The First Presidency announces the creation of the Welfare Services Department, which brings the existing Church welfare units into full correlation.

1980 NBC news anchor Tom Brokaw interviews Elder Gordon B. Hinckley and J. Willard Marriott Jr. on the *Today* show.

1984 Russell M. Nelson is ordained a member of the Quorum of the Twelve Apostles.

1984 Barbara Woodhead Winder is sustained as the eleventh general president of the Relief Society, with Joy Frewin Evans and Joanne Bushman Doxey as counselors.

1984 Ardeth Greene Kapp is sustained as the ninth general president of the Young Women, with Patricia Terry Holland and Maurine Johnson Turley later called as counselors.

1994 Robert D. Hales is ordained a member of the Quorum of the Twelve Apostles.

1994 The First Presidency announces plans to build a temple in Bogotá, Colombia.

1996 President Gordon B. Hinckley is featured in an interview with Mike Wallace on *60 Minutes* on U.S. national television.

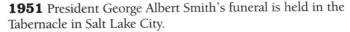

APRIL 8

1839 Joseph and Hyrum Smith, Alexander McRae, Caleb Baldwin, and Lyman Wight arrive in Gallatin, Missouri, to stand trial.

1841 Lyman Wight is ordained a member of the Quorum of the Twelve Apostles, replacing Elder David W. Patten, who was killed in a skirmish with non-Mormons in Missouri.

1844 In his last general conference address, the Prophet Joseph Smith explains that Zion includes all of North and South America.

1848 At a conference held in the log tabernacle at Miller's Hollow on the east side of the Missouri River, the settlement is renamed Kanesville in honor of Colonel Thomas L. Kane, a friend to the Mormons. The name is later changed to Council Bluffs, Iowa.

1876 In Chihuahua about five hundred people attend the first Latter-day Saint meeting ever held in Mexico. The missionaries had received permission to hold the meeting from Governor Luis Terrazas.

1888 Zina Diantha Huntington Young is called as the third president of the Relief Society, with Jane Snyder Richards and Bathsheba Wilson Smith later called as counselors.

1898 Elders Brigham F. Duffin and Thomas H. Chambers, two missionaries from Utah, hold the first Latter-day Saint meeting in Caldwell County, Missouri, since the Saints were expelled from the state in 1838.

1900 Reed Smoot is ordained a member of the Quorum of the Twelve Apostles, replacing Franklin D. Richards, who had died.

1937 Albert Ernest Bowen is ordained a member of the Quorum of the Twelve Apostles, replacing Alonzo Hinckley, who had died.

1954 George Q. Morris is ordained a member of the Quorum of the Twelve Apostles at eighty years of age (making him the oldest man ordained an Apostle in this dispensation), replacing Matthew Cowley, who had died.

1964 The Northern Indian Mission is organized.

1990 The Umtata Branch, the first branch of the Church in the South African country of Transkei, is organized, with Emmanuel Danso as president.

Reed Smoot, ca. 1900 (see 1900).

APRIL

1818 Mary Elizabeth Rollins (Lightner), later a folk heroine for saving pages of the Book of Commandments (the predecessor of the Doctrine and Covenants) in 1833 after a mob had destroyed the printing press in Independence, Missouri, is born in Lima, New York.

1831 Joseph Smith ordains John Whitmer as the first Church historian, pursuant to an earlier revelation given on 8 March (see D&C 47).

1849 The First Presidency issues the "First General Epistle" from the Salt Lake Valley. The epistle brings Church members up to date by recounting all that had transpired in Winter Quarters, in the Salt Lake Valley, and with the Mormon Battalion and gives directions for Saints preparing to immigrate to Utah.

1852 A number of Saints on their way to Utah are killed when the *Saluda,* the steamboat they are riding, explodes at Lexington, Missouri.

1884 John W. Taylor is ordained a member of the Quorum of the Twelve Apostles, replacing Charles C. Rich, who had died.

1906 George F. Richards and Orson Ferguson Whitney are ordained members of the Quorum of the Twelve Apostles, replacing John W. Taylor and Matthias Cowley, who had both resigned from the Twelve.

1906 David O. McKay is ordained a member of the Quorum of the Twelve Apostles, replacing Marriner W. Merrill, who had died.

1906 Charles H. Hart is ordained a member of the Seventy and becomes the first General Authority with a law degree.

1922 Elaine Anderson Cannon, later the eighth general president of the Young Women, is born in Salt Lake City, Utah.

President David O. McKay, ca. 1960 (see 1951).

1951 Following the death of President George Albert Smith, David O. McKay is sustained as the ninth President of the Church, with Stephen L Richards and J. Reuben Clark as Counselors. President Clark, who had been serving as President George Albert Smith's First Counselor, took this opportunity to teach that "in the service of the Lord, it is not where you serve but how" (in Conference Report, April 1951, 154).

1953 Adam S. Bennion is ordained a member of the Quorum of the Twelve Apostles, replacing John A. Widtsoe, who had died.

1970 Boyd K. Packer is ordained a member of the Quorum of the Twelve Apostles, replacing Joseph Fielding Smith, who was called to the First Presidency.

1999 Ground is broken for the Montreal Quebec Temple. Elder Gary J. Coleman of the Seventy and Second Counselor in the North America Northeast Area Presidency, presides over the ceremony.

1854 The First Presidency issues the "Eleventh General Epistle" to the Saints. This epistle reviews the status of missionary work throughout the world, discusses current events in Utah (including the Walker Indian War and the creation of the Deseret Alphabet), and offers counsel on a variety of topics to Latter-day Saints throughout the world.

1884 George R. Hill, later general superintendent of the Sunday School (1949–66), is born in Ogden, Utah.

1921 Francis M. Gibbons, later a member of the First Quorum of the Seventy, is born in St. Johns, Arizona.

1941 Harold B. Lee is ordained a member of the Twelve, replacing Reed Smoot, who had died.

Pavilion at HemisFair, ca. 1968 (see 1968).

1947 Eldred Gee Smith is ordained Patriarch to the Church by George Albert Smith.

1947 Henry D. Moyle is ordained a member of the Quorum of the Twelve Apostles, replacing Charles A. Callis, who had died.

1952 LeGrand Richards is ordained a member of the Quorum of the Twelve Apostles, replacing Joseph F. Merrill, who had died.

1958 Hugh B. Brown is ordained a member of the Quorum of the Twelve Apostles, replacing Adam S. Bennion, who had died.

1968 President Hugh B. Brown dedicates the LDS pavilion at the HemisFair '68. Fair directors had set this day apart to recognize the Church's founding on 6 April.

1977 The San Pedro Sula Honduras Stake, the first stake in Honduras, is organized, with Samuel Ben-Zion Ventura as president.

1991 The *New York Times* announces that Laurel Thatcher Ulrich has won the Pulitzer Prize in history for *A Midwife's Tale: The Life of Martha Ballard, Based on Her Diary, 1785–1812* (1990).

APRIL 11

1779 John Johnson, later a prominent Church member and owner of the home in Hiram, Ohio, where Joseph received several revelations, is born in Chesterfield, New Hampshire.

1813 William Weeks, later architect of the Nauvoo Temple, is born in Martha's Vineyard, Massachusetts.

1830 Oliver Cowdery preaches at the first public meeting of the Church and baptizes six people: Hiram and Katherine Page, and Christian, Anne, Jacob, and Elizabeth Whitmer.

1901 Annie Taylor Hyde organizes the Daughters of Utah Pioneers in Salt Lake City.

1922 John Sonnenberg, later a member of the First Quorum of the Seventy, is born in Schneidemuhle, Germany.

1954 José D. Guzman, the first convert in Nicaragua, is baptized.

Elder L. Tom Perry, ca. 1975 (see 1974).

1974 L. Tom Perry is ordained a member of the Quorum of the Twelve Apostles, replacing Spencer W. Kimball, who had been called to the First Presidency.

1976 The Montpelier Stake, the first stake in Vermont, is organized, with C. Lynn Fife as president.

1992 Marlize Gomez Lima, the first convert of the Church in Andorra, is baptized.

APRIL 12

1807 Parley P. Pratt, later a member of the Quorum of the Twelve Apostles and one of the early Church's most influential writers and missionaries, is born in Burlington, New York.

1828 Joseph Smith commences translating the Book of Mormon with Martin Harris acting as scribe. Translation continues until 14 June.

1850 The First Presidency issues the "Third General Epistle" to the Saints. This epistle reviews the conditions of the Saints in the Salt Lake Valley following their third winter since arriving, discusses exploration and new settlements in the territory, counsels the Saints against going to California for gold, and offers advice for those preparing to immigrate to Zion.

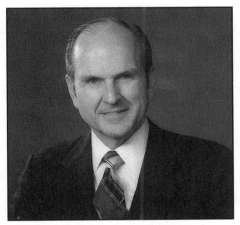

Elder Russell M. Nelson, ca. 1984 (see 1984).

1858 Alfred Cumming, the newly appointed Utah territorial governor, arrives in Salt Lake City and is kindly received by President Brigham Young.

1930 Neil D. Schaerrer, later the first Young Men general president (1977–79), is born in Payson, Utah.

1943 Robert J. Whetten, later a member of the Second Quorum of the Seventy, is born in Chuichupa, Mexico.

1973 The first Sperry Symposium is held at BYU in honor of Sydney B. Sperry, former professor and dean of Religious Education. The annual symposium focuses on one of the standard works or LDS Church history and doctrine.

1984 Russell M. Nelson is ordained a member of the Quorum of the Twelve Apostles, replacing LeGrand Richards, who had died.

1985 U.S. Senator Jake Garn (Utah) blasts off in the space shuttle *Discovery,* becoming the first Latter-day Saint to enter space. A few weeks later aboard the *Challenger,* astronaut Don Lind becomes the second member of the Church to travel in space.

1999 The First Presidency announces a temple to be built in Reno, Nevada.

1784 George Lane, later a Methodist minister and apparently the one who referred Joseph Smith to passages in the New Testament book of James about seeking out God, is born in Kingston, New York.

1833 Joseph Smith writes a letter to Jared Carter wherein he teaches that "it is contrary . . . for any member of the Church to receive instruction for those in authority, higher than themselves" (*History of the Church,* 1:338).

1889 In an effort to find support for the Church's quest to convince Congress to allow the practice of plural marriage, Presidents Wilford Woodruff and George Q. Cannon leave Salt Lake City to meet with political and business leaders in California.

1953 Elder Ezra Taft Benson, the U.S. secretary of agriculture, appears on the cover of *Time* magazine, which highlights his national and international influence as a member of Dwight D. Eisenhower's cabinet.

1999 Tal Bachman, a returned missionary, Juno Award winner, and son of rock star Randy Bachman, releases a self-titled album featuring the hit "She's So High."

1999 The Salt Lake City Council approves a plan to build a pedestrian plaza connecting the Church offices grounds to Temple Square.

Apostle and U.S. secretary of agriculture Ezra Taft Benson on the cover of Time *magazine, 13 April 1953.*

1773 Peter Whitmer Sr., in whose home Joseph Smith later translated much of the Book of Mormon and organized the Church, is born in Pennsylvania.

1832 Brigham Young and his wife, Miriam, are baptized in a millpond near Mendon, New York.

1840 Willard Richards is ordained a member of the Quorum of the Twelve Apostles following the apostasy of four of the original Twelve Apostles during the Kirtland era.

1847 Brigham Young leaves Winter Quarters to begin the overland trek to the Rocky Mountains. His party consists of 143 men, 3 women, 2 children, 72 wagons, 93 horses, 52 mules, 66 oxen, 19 cows, and 17 dogs.

1929 Bertha Sell and her children, the first converts to the Church in Brazil, are baptized.

1938 Sylvester Quayle Cannon is ordained an Apostle by Heber J. Grant. On 6 October 1939 he is sustained as a member of the Quorum of the Twelve Apostles, replacing Melvin J. Ballard, who had died.

1999 The First Presidency announces a temple to be built in Veracruz, Mexico.

1839 After securing a change of venue, Joseph and Hyrum Smith, Alexander McRae, Caleb Baldwin, and Lyman Wight leave Gallatin, Missouri, to stand trial in Columbia, Missouri. In the evening they are allowed to "escape," and they begin their journey to Illinois.

1840 Orson Hyde leaves Commerce (Nauvoo), Illinois, for his mission to Jerusalem.

1846 While encamped with the main pioneer company near Locust Creek (Middle Fork), Iowa, William Clayton receives word that his wife, Diantha, gave birth to a baby boy in Nauvoo on 30 March and that both are in good health. This experience inspires him to write the lyrics to the hymn "All Is Well," later known as "Come, Come, Ye Saints."

1865 Upon receiving news of Abraham Lincoln's assassination the previous day, all Salt Lake City businesses close, and the entire city is declared to be in a state of mourning.

1912 Irene C. Corbett, a member of the Church from Utah who had been studying in London, is among the fifteen hundred casualties when the luxury liner *Titanic* sinks in the Atlantic Ocean after colliding with an iceberg.

1928 Anthony Ozodimma Obinna, later the first West African baptized by missionaries following the 1978 revelation on priesthood and the first to preside over a branch composed entirely of black members, is born in Aboh Mbaise, Nigeria.

1975 President Spencer W. Kimball rededicates the renovated Arizona Temple (later the Mesa Arizona Temple).

1993 Elder Neal A. Maxwell of the Quorum of the Twelve Apostles dedicates the Asian country of Mongolia for the preaching of the gospel.

1774 Polly Peck (Knight), later a faithful follower of Joseph Smith and the first Saint to die in Jackson County, is born in Guilford, Vermont.

1840 During a two-day conference, Church leaders and members in the British Isles vote to publish the *Latter-day Saints' Millennial Star,* a monthly periodical in pamphlet form that would continue to be published until 1970.

1842 William Smith publishes the first issue of the *Wasp,* a Nauvoo community newspaper.

1873 Brigham Young, depicted as the "Mormon Moses," appears on the cover the *Daily Graphic,* a national newspaper.

1904 George H. Brimhall begins his term as the third president of Brigham Young University.

1905 Kim Ho Jik, credited with being the first Korean convert, is born in Bok Dong, Korea.

1918 Richard W. Young, a nephew of Brigham Young, becomes the first Latter-day Saint to obtain the rank of general in the U.S. Army.

Brigham Young caricature published in the Daily Graphic, *16 April 1873.*

1993 The first convert in the African nation of Ethiopia is baptized.

1994 The city of Palo Alto, California, honors Elder David B. Haight of the Quorum of the Twelve, who served as mayor of Palo Alto from 1961 to 1963.

1803 Levi Hancock, later one of the original First Seven Presidents of the Seventy, is born in Springfield, Massachusetts.

1836 Mary Duty Smith, the ninety-three-year-old maternal grandmother of Joseph Smith, arrives in Kirtland as one of the oldest people to make the move from New York.

1838 Joseph Smith receives Doctrine and Covenants 114, directing Apostle David W. Patten to prepare to serve a mission to Great Britain the following year.

1839 Brigham Young, President of the Quorum of the Twelve Apostles, decides that the Twelve would return to Far West, Missouri, to fulfill the Lord's commandment for the Twelve to leave on their mission to Great Britain from the temple site at Far West (see D&C 118:4–5).

1969 The Church announces the construction of the new twenty-eight-story Church Office Building in Salt Lake City.

1998 Ground is broken for the Anchorage Alaska Temple. Elder F. Melvin Hammond, a member of the First Quorum of the Seventy and President of the North America Northwest Area, presides over the ceremony.

The Church Office Building, located at 50 E. North Temple, ca. 1975 (see 1969).

1839 Brigham Young, in company with Orson Pratt, John Taylor, Wilford Woodruff, George A. Smith, and Alpheus Cutler, leaves Quincy, Illinois, for Far West, Missouri. From there, the elders will officially leave on their mission to Great Britain. This fulfills the injuction in Doctrine and Covenants 118.

1852 The First Presidency issues the "Seventh General Epistle" to the Saints. This epistle recounts missionary work and events of the previous winter, including the April conference and the construction of the Old Tabernacle. The epistle concludes by counseling Saints throughout the world to sustain their governments and keep the commandments of the Lord.

1894 After receiving a revelation, President Wilford Woodruff discontinues the law of adoption, a practice from the early days of the Church, when members were often sealed directly to prominent priesthood leaders.

1906 A devastating earthquake strikes San Francisco, and in the ensuing fire the mission home is destroyed. This results in the California Mission headquarters being moved to Los Angeles in southern California.

1928 Jack H. Goaslind Jr., later a member of the Presidency of the Seventy, is born in Salt Lake City, Utah.

1947 Minerva K. Teichert, the first woman to receive a commission to create a temple mural, commences to paint *The Pageant of History* for the world room of the Manti Temple (later the Manti Utah Temple).

1965 The Memphis Stake, the first stake in Tennessee, is organized, with Richard Stoddard as president.

1853 The South African Mission is organized.

1915 Elder James E. Talmage finishes writing the book *Jesus the Christ,* a classic in Church literature.

1932 Robert B. Harbertson, later a member of the First Quorum of the Seventy, is born in Ogden, Utah.

1938 A group of LDS missionaries, including future Apostle Marvin J. Ashton, wins the Great Britain national basketball championship.

1948 The Church Board of Education announces that, beginning in the 1949–50 school year, Ricks College will begin granting four-year degrees. Ricks later reverts to a junior college.

James E. Talmage, ca. 1911 (see 1915).

1991 At a special meeting of Church members in Abidjan, Elder Richard P. Lindsay, a member of the Second Quorum of the Seventy and President of the Africa Area, announces that the country of Ivory Coast has officially recognized the Church.

1997 One company of the Mormon Trail Wagon Train departs from Council Bluffs, Iowa, in reenactment of the epic journey of the 1847 pioneers led by Brigham Young to the Great Basin. The second company departs from Omaha, Nebraska, two days later.

1785 Henry G. Sherwood, later Nauvoo's first marshal and an early prominent member of the Church, is born in Kingsbury, New York.

1838 Elders Heber C. Kimball and Orson Hyde set sail from Liverpool, England, for New York City, ending their first mission to England.

1839 The last group of the Saints in Far West, Missouri, leaves under the expulsion order.

1873 Elder Franklin D. Richards and others organize a society in Ogden for the mutual improvement of young men in the Church, the forerunner of the Young Men's Mutual Improvement Association.

A tree-planting project on the New Zealand Temple grounds, ca. 1958 (see 1958).

1887 Latter-day Saint settlers arrive in Chihuahua, Mexico, where several LDS colonies are eventually established.

1907 George Edward Anderson leaves Springville, Utah, on a train heading east, beginning his famous photographic mission to LDS Church history sites.

1927 Douglas J. Martin, later a member of the First Quorum of the Seventy, is born in Hastings, New Zealand.

1944 Mark Edward Petersen is ordained a member of the Quorum of the Twelve Apostles, replacing Richard R. Lyman, who had been excommunicated.

1958 President David O. McKay dedicates the New Zealand Temple (later the Hamilton New Zealand Temple).

1975 The Stockholm Sweden Stake, the first stake in Sweden, is organized, with Evert W. Perciwall as president.

1980 The Vienna Austria Stake, the first stake in Austria, is organized, with Johann Anton Wondra as president.

1983 Ground is broken for the Buenos Aires Argentina Temple. Elder Bruce R. McConkie of the Quorum of the Twelve Apostles presides over the ceremony.

APRIL 21

1834 During a conference of the Church held in Norton, Ohio, the Prophet Joseph Smith declares, "Take away the Book of Mormon and the revelations, and where is our religion? We have none" (*History of the Church,* 2:52).

1841 Elders Brigham Young, Heber C. Kimball, Orson Pratt, George A. Smith, Wilford Woodruff, John Taylor, and Willard Richards, along with 120 converts, board the ship *Rochester* to return to the United States, thus ending the mission of the Twelve Apostles to Great Britain.

1859 Clarissa West Smith (Williams), later the sixth general president of the Relief Society, is born in Salt Lake City, Utah.

1898 Lucy Jane Brimhall and Inez Knight arrive in Liverpool, England, as the first single sister missionaries.

1940 Captain William Losey, military advisor to the U.S. ambassador to Norway, dies during the German invasion of Norway, becoming the first Latter-day Saint killed during World War II.

Clarissa West Smith Williams, ca. 1921 (see 1859).

1990 Devin Knight, later the 1995 March of Dimes national ambassador, is born in Springville, Utah.

1991 The Accra Ghana Stake, the first stake in Ghana, is organized, with Emmanuel Ohene Opare as president.

1994 The Church announces to priesthood leaders in the United States and Canada that a uniform curriculum will be implemented over a two-year period. The new curriculum focuses on the scriptures and combines various age-groups in the auxiliaries.

APRIL 22

1839 Joseph and Hyrum Smith, Alexander McRae, Caleb Baldwin, and Lyman Wight arrive in Quincy, Illinois, after their escape from Missouri.

1889 Henry D. Moyle, later a member of the Quorum of the Twelve Apostles and First Presidency, is born in Salt Lake City, Utah.

1938 Duane B. Gerrard, later a member of the Second Quorum of the Seventy, is born in Murray, Utah.

1966 The *Church News* announces publication of the Book of Mormon in Korean, translated by Han In San and seven assistants, and notes that the more than three thousand members in that country have been anxious to have it completed. The first copies are presented to President David O. McKay and Elder Gordon B. Hinckley.

1976 The Taipei Taiwan Stake, the first stake in Taiwan, is organized, with I-Ching Chang as president.

1978 The Church announces the name extraction program, through which Church members research the names and vital information of deceased individuals and families for temple work.

1995 Elder M. Russell Ballard, chair of the Church pioneer sesquicentennial committee, announces plans for the commemoration of the pioneer trek to Utah with the theme "Faith in Every Footstep, 1847–1997."

APRIL 23

1834 Joseph Smith receives Doctrine and Covenants 104, which calls for the separation of the United Order of Kirtland and the United Order of Zion in Missouri.

1861 The first of several Church wagon trains leaves the Salt Lake Valley with provisions for incoming Saints, whom they later meet at the Missouri River. This program to help immigrating Saints lasts until the railroad comes in 1869.

1870 Alonzo Arza Hinckley, later a member of the Quorum of the Twelve Apostles, is born at Cove Fort, Utah.

1912 Joseph F. Merrill, a member of the stake presidency and board of education of the Granite Stake, announces that the first seminary program will be established during the coming academic year at Granite High School in Salt Lake City.

1983 President Thomas S. Monson of the First Presidency breaks ground for the Freiberg Germany Temple, the first temple to be built in an Eastern European country.

1993 Elder Dallin H. Oaks of the Twelve dedicates Albania for missionary work.

Mormon wagon train, ca. 1866 (see 1861).

APRIL 24

1832 Joseph Smith and his companions arrive in Independence, Missouri, on their visit to organize the United Order.

1834 Non-Mormon citizens of Jackson County begin burning the homes of the Saints who had been driven from the county the previous fall. Over the next six days, they burn around 150 homes.

1839 Parley P. Pratt, Morris Phelps, Luman Gibbs, King Follett, Darwin Chase, and Norman Shearer are brought before the grand jury of Ray County, Missouri, at Richmond. The six had been charged with murder during the "Mormon War" in Missouri. Darwin Chase and Norman Shearer are dismissed after having been imprisoned for six months.

1846 The Saints establish Garden Grove, a way station on the trail through Iowa.

1857 Brigham Young travels to the Salmon River Indian Mission in Idaho in the aftermath of an Indian attack there that left two missionaries dead.

1876 Karl G. Maeser begins his term as the first principal of Brigham Young Academy.

1924 Paul H. Dunn, later a member of the Presidency of the Seventy, is born in Provo, Utah.

1936 The Church announces that stake missions will be established Churchwide.

1939 John M. Madsen, later a member of the First Quorum of the Seventy, is born in Washington, D.C.

1999 President Gordon B. Hinckley dedicates the Bogotá Colombia Temple (later the Bogotá D.C. Colombia Temple).

1999 Ground is broken for the San José Costa Rica Temple. Elder Julio E. Alvarado of the Seventy presides over the ceremony.

1999 Elder Spencer J. Condie, a member of the First Quorum of the Seventy and President of the Europe North Area, presides at the site dedication of a Denmark chapel that is to become the Copenhagen Denmark Temple. This marks the second time in this dispensation that an existing building is renovated to become a temple.

APRIL

1827 Joseph Ridges, later the builder of the original Tabernacle organ, is born in Eling, England.

1835 Thomas B. Marsh is ordained a member of the Quorum of the Twelve Apostles.

1877 President Brigham Young dedicates the site for the Manti Temple (later the Manti Utah Temple).

1922 President Heber J. Grant breaks ground for the Arizona Temple (later the Mesa Arizona Temple).

1947 Reed Smoot, later the cinematographer of such movies as *Where the Red Fern Grows* and *Legacy,* is born in Provo, Utah.

1967 Jane Clayson, later a KSL television anchor and reporter and cohost with Bryant Gumbel on CBS television's *Early Show,* is born in Salt Lake City, Utah.

1976 The Hong Kong Stake, the first stake in Hong Kong, is organized, with Shiu-Tat Sheldon Poon as president.

1987 The First Presidency announces the creation of four new areas as part of the Church's realignment of worldwide administrative areas.

1990 Elder Russell M. Nelson dedicates Estonia for the preaching of the gospel. Estonia is the first country of the former Soviet Union to be opened for missionary work.

1991 Elder Russell M. Nelson of the Quorum of the Twelve Apostles meets Ivan S. Silaev, the prime minister of Russia, in Los Angeles as part of the Church's efforts to receive official recognition in that country.

1993 President Gordon B. Hinckley of the First Presidency dedicates the San Diego California Temple.

From left to right: LDS businessman Stephen H. Smoot, Elder Russell M. Nelson, and Russian prime minister Ivan S. Silaev in Los Angeles, 25 April 1991.

1996 Elder Merrill J. Bateman of the Seventy is inaugurated as the eleventh president of Brigham Young University; he is the first General Authority to serve as president.

1998 President Gordon B. Hinckley announces plans to build a temple in Columbus, Ohio.

1999 President Gordon B. Hinckley addresses a gathering of 57,500 members at a soccer stadium in Santiago Chile. This is one of the largest gatherings of Latter-day Saints in Church history.

1832 Joseph Smith receives Doctrine and Covenants 82, containing instructions to the leaders of the Church in Missouri concerning the united order.

1835 Orson Pratt is ordained a member of the Quorum of the Twelve Apostles.

1838 Joseph Smith receives Doctrine and Covenants 115, indicating that the Church is to be known as The Church of Jesus Christ of Latter-day Saints. The revelation also instructs the Saints concerning the building of the temple at Far West, Missouri.

1839 During the early hours of the morning, Elders Brigham Young, Heber C. Kimball, Orson Pratt, John Taylor, and John E. Page assemble at the temple site in Far West, Missouri, in fulfillment of the revelation appointing them to leave for their missions to Great Britain from Far West (see D&C 118). While there they ordain Wilford Woodruff and George A. Smith as members of the Quorum of the Twelve Apostles (replacing members who had been excommunicated during the Kirtland apostasy).

1938 H. David Burton, later the Presiding Bishop of the Church, is born in Salt Lake City, Utah.

1944 Lawrence "Larry" H. Miller, later a successful businessman and owner of the Utah Jazz NBA basketball team, is born in Salt Lake City, Utah.

1958 President David O. McKay dedicates the Church College of New Zealand just six days after the dedication of the New Zealand Temple (later the Hamilton New Zealand Temple).

1964 Elder Gordon B. Hinckley dedicates a meetinghouse for the Tokyo North Branch; it is the first LDS meetinghouse in Asia.

1853 Elders Hosea Stout, Chapman Duncan, and James Lewis arrive in Hong Kong and open China for the preaching of the gospel.

1887 Charles Ora Card and his companions select a site for a Latter-day Saint settlement on Lee's Creek, Alberta, Canada; it is later named Cardston.

1913 W. Jay Eldredge, later the general superintendent (1969–72) and president (1972) of the Young Men's Mutual Improvement Association, is born.

1915 The First Presidency inaugurates the home evening program, inviting all families to participate.

1955 The First Presidency and Church Board of Education send out a letter stating that Ricks would return to its status as a junior college after having been a four-year school since the 1949–50 school year.

◀ *The Church College of New Zealand* (see 1958).

1971 James C. Fletcher, a former president of the University of Utah, is appointed as the chief administrator of the National Aeronautics and Space Administration (NASA) until 1977. The space shuttle program is developed under his leadership. (He holds the position again from 1986 to 1989, in the aftermath of the space shuttle *Challenger* disaster).

1990 Yuri V. Dubinin, the Soviet Union's ambassador to the United States, makes a historic visit to Utah. During the visit, he announces that Church missionaries are welcome in Russia.

1991 The Church begins computerizing membership records worldwide, fifty years after it began keeping individual membership records.

1994 President Thomas S. Monson of the First Presidency represents the Church at the funeral of former U.S. president Richard M. Nixon in Yorba Linda, California.

1999 Elder Richard G. Scott of the Quorum of the Twelve Apostles breaks ground for the Montevideo Uruguay Temple.

APRIL 28

1862 Adjutant-General L. Thomas calls upon Brigham Young to provide cavalry to protect the mail route between Fort Bridger and North Platte during the Civil War.

1883 President John Taylor receives a revelation calling for the reestablishment of the School of the Prophets.

1898 A First Presidency statement encourages Latter-day Saint youth to support the American War effort in the Spanish-American War.

1919 Gordon B. Hinckley is baptized at eight years of age, location unknown. Of the site he states: "It's the only secret I have left! It was done by proper authority in a proper place" (quoted by Clarke Hinckley in a letter to Michael Taylor, as reported in *LDS Gems*).

1934 The Church announces that the official representative of the king of England has been allowed to visit the interior of the Alberta Temple (later the Cardston Alberta Temple), even though it had been dedicated.

1961 During a sunrise service at the American Battle Memorial Cemetery in Manila, Elder Gordon B. Hinckley dedicates the Philippines, opening the country for missionary work.

1982 Brigham Young University's Lamanite Generation embarks on a ground-breaking tour of the People's Republic of China.

1996 American Mothers, Inc., names Carolyn M. Shumway, wife of BYU–Hawaii president Eric Shumway, the National Mother of the Year.

1999 Some five thousand Latter-day Saint women gather at BYU in what is called the largest humanitarian event held by the Church in a single setting. Participants donate approximately 6,955 service hours making hygiene kits and other items for needy families.

1853 The Church holds its first conference in India two years after missionary work was begun there by Elder Joseph Richards.

1943 President J. Reuben Clark introduces a new financial reorganization plan for the Church, emphasizing the point that every financial operation must help the purpose and mission of the Church.

1947 John "Johnny" Lawrence Miller, later a professional golfer and winner of numerous PGA titles, is born in San Francisco, California.

Elder Gordon B. Hinckley on his way to visit Asia, ca. May 1960 (see 1960).

1960 Elder Gordon B. Hinckley makes his first trip to Asia (visiting Japan, Korea, Okinawa, Taiwan, the Philippines, and Hong Kong) after being asked by President Henry D. Moyle to supervise the Southern Far East and Northern Far East Missions.

1972 The Church releases the translation of the Book of Mormon into Afrikaans.

1985 Don Lind, a professional astronaut, participates in a journey aboard the space shuttle *Challenger.*

1989 Steven D. Bennion is appointed thirteenth president of Ricks College.

1994 Salt Lake City hosts the fifty-ninth annual American Mothers National Convention under the leadership of Barbara B. Smith, a former general president of the Relief Society.

1790 Reynolds Cahoon, later an early Church leader and friend of Joseph Smith, is born in Cambridge, New York.

1831 Emma Smith gives birth to twins, a boy and girl, whom she and Joseph name Thaddeus and Louisa. The infants live only about three hours.

1832 Joseph Smith receives Doctrine and Covenants 83, containing additional instructions concerning principles governing the support of women and children under the law of consecration.

1844 The Society Islands Mission is organized.

1846 Joseph Young, brother of Brigham Young and one of the First Seven Presidents of the Seventy, privately dedicates the completed Nauvoo Temple.

1879 Emma Hale Smith, wife of the Prophet Joseph Smith and first president of the Nauvoo Female Relief Society, dies in Nauvoo, Illinois.

1961 The West European Mission is organized. Serving more of an administrative than a proselyting function, it is discontinued in 1965.

1984 BYU president Jeffrey R. Holland announces the Church Board of Education's endorsement of a university-sponsored women's conference, an annual event to be held at BYU and cosponsored by the general Relief Society presidency.

1986 Church membership is estimated to have arrived at six million members.

1993 Elder Thales Haskell Smith (a pediatrician) and Sister Charone Smith (a nurse), two of the first four missionaries to serve in a humanitarian capacity in Albania, visit with Mother Teresa, a native Albanian, at the Tirana Dystrophy Hospital.

1994 Tahiti issues a new postage stamp to honor the 150th anniversary of the LDS missionaries' arrival to that Pacific island nation.

Sister Charone Smith with Mother Teresa in Albania, 30 April 1993.

MAY 1

1820 Edward Stevenson, later one of the First Seven Presidents of the Seventy, is born in Gibraltar, Spain.

1832 Presided over by the Prophet Joseph Smith, a Church council in Independence, Missouri, decides to print three thousand instead of ten thousand copies of the Book of Commandments. W. W. Phelps, Oliver Cowdery, and John Whitmer are appointed to review and prepare it for printing; W. W. Phelps is also appointed to correct and print the hymns Emma Smith had selected for the first LDS hymnbook.

1834 The first members of Zion's Camp leave Kirtland and travel to New Portage, Ohio.

1846 Elders Orson Hyde and Wilford Woodruff preside at the public dedicatory services of the Nauvoo Temple.

1869 President Brigham Young dedicates the first Zion's Co-operative Mercantile Institution (ZCMI) store in Salt Lake City. More than 150 retail cooperatives are later established in LDS settlements throughout the Intermountain West.

1881 May Green (Hinckley), later the third general president of the Primary, is born in Brampton, England.

1927 Elder Richard R. Lyman dedicates a Mormon pioneer monument in San Bernardino, California, commemorating the settlement of five hundred Latter-day Saints in the area in 1851.

1931 Dwan Jacobsen (Young), later the seventh general president of the Primary, is born in Salt Lake City, Utah.

1957 Richard Swett, later a New Hampshire representative in the U.S. Congress (1991–95) and U.S. ambassador to Denmark (1998), is born in Bryn Mawr, Pennsylvania.

1960 The Tulsa Stake, the first stake in Oklahoma, is organized, with Robert N. Sears as president.

J. Reuben Clark Law School groundbreaking (from left: Robert J. Smith, Rex E. Lee, Dallin H. Oaks, unknown, Elder Ezra Taft Benson, Ben E. Lewis), 1 May 1973.

1966 The São Paulo Brazil Stake, the first stake in both Brazil and South America, is organized, with Walter Spat as president.

1973 Elder Ezra Taft Benson, Brigham Young University president Dallin H. Oaks, and newly appointed dean of the J. Reuben Clark Law School Rex E. Lee participate in the groundbreaking ceremonies for the law school.

1991 The Church calls the five hundred thousandth full-time missionary in this dispensation.

1997 The Church closes the Deseret Gymnasium to make room for a new assembly building (later named the Conference Center) announced by President Gordon B. Hinckley during April 1996 conference.

1998 President James E. Faust of the First Presidency breaks ground for the Campinas Brazil Temple.

1835 At a council of the officers of the Church held in Kirtland, Joseph Smith organizes the Quorum of the Twelve Apostles by order of age. Seniority is as follows: Thomas B. Marsh, David W. Patten, Brigham Young, Heber C. Kimball, Orson Hyde, William E. McLellin, Parley P. Pratt, Luke S. Johnson, William Smith, Orson Pratt, John F. Boynton, and Lyman E. Johnson.

1867 Maud May Babcock, later a first lady of theater, a physical education teacher, and the first woman to serve as chaplain in the Utah State Senate, is born in East Worcester, New York.

1901 President Lorenzo Snow instructs members of the Quorum of the Twelve Apostles to preach tithing until all non-tithe payers are converted.

1937 Wayne Owens, later a Utah representative in the U.S. Congress (1972–74 and 1986–92), is born in Panguitch, Utah.

1965 The Jackson Stake, the first stake in Mississippi, is organized, with Neil J. Ferrill as president.

1992 In Los Angeles, California, local Church members join with other volunteers in clean-up and relief efforts in the aftermath of rioting ignited by the acquittal of four white policemen charged with abusing a black motorist.

1992 President Ezra Taft Benson breaks ground for the Bountiful Utah Temple.

1993 The Mormon Tabernacle Choir performs in the newly renovated Catholic Cathedral of the Madeleine in Salt Lake City.

The Bountiful Utah Temple (see 1992).

1998 President James E. Faust of the First Presidency breaks ground for the Porto Alegre Brazil Temple.

MAY 3

1822 Bathsheba Wilson (Smith), later the fourth general president of the Relief Society, is born near Shinnston, West Virginia.

Bathsheba Wilson Smith, ca. 1895 (see 1822).

1831 Members of the Church living in Fayette and Waterloo, New York, embark on their journey to relocate to Ohio. They are led by the Prophet's mother, Lucy Mack Smith, and Thomas B. Marsh.

1839 Near Quincy, Illinois, six members of the Quorum of the Twelve Apostles meet with Joseph Smith in the first such meeting since the Prophet's escape from Liberty Jail in Missouri.

1843 The first number of the *Nauvoo Neighbor,* a Nauvoo-based newspaper edited by John Taylor, is released.

1900 The last Church-sponsored pioneer settlement company leaves Kemmerer, Wyoming, for the Big Horn Basin under the direction of Elder Abraham O. Woodruff.

1937 Eduardo Ayala, later a member of the Second Quorum of the Seventy, is born in Coronel, Chile.

1966 The Church receives permission to proselyte in Bermuda.

1975 The First Presidency assigns six Assistants to the Twelve to reside outside the United States and Canada and oversee Church activities there. This action sets up an area supervisory program.

1984 Dallin H. Oaks is ordained an Apostle, replacing Mark E. Petersen, who had died.

MAY 4

1835 Members of the newly organized Quorum of the Twelve Apostles leave on their first mission to the eastern United States.

1842 Joseph Smith administers the endowment for the first time in this dispensation in the upstairs room of the Red Brick Store on Water Street in Nauvoo.

1846 After three months of sailing, the ship *Brooklyn,* transporting over two hundred Latter-day Saints to California, drops anchor off the Island of Juan Fernandez, near the coast of Chile, the island made famous by Alexander Selkirk (Robinson Crusoe).

1856 The ship *Thornton* leaves Liverpool, England, carrying a company of 764 Saints led by James G. Willie. Most in the company are those who later make up the ill-fated Martin and Willie handcart companies, which become stranded on their way to Utah later that year.

1865 Charles Albert Callis, later a member of the Quorum of the Twelve Apostles, is born in Dublin, Ireland.

1875 Hyrum W. Mikesell baptizes Shoshone chief Pocatello in Salt Lake City. The chief is ordained an elder and prophesies that many of his people will soon join the Church. By the end of the year, nearly all his people join, as had hundreds of other Native Americans from other western tribes.

1899 Ernest L. Wilkinson, later president of BYU and a renowned leader in Church education, is born in Ogden, Utah.

1934 Augusto A. Lim, a member of the Second Quorum of the Seventy, is born in Santa Cruz, Philippines.

Presidents of the San Diego and Los Angeles Temples, Floyd L. and H. Von Packard, ca. 1993 (see 1992).

1946 President George Albert Smith autographs five specially bound leather copies of the recently completed Tongan translation of the Book of Mormon for Tonga's Queen Salote, Tupou III; Prince Tupou To'a; Premier Ata; and two Tongan governors.

1964 Richard Dutcher, later the producer, writer, and director of *God's Army,* an independent film portraying missionary life in southern California, is born in Oak Park, Illinois.

1984 For the first time, missionaries arrive in the group of the Carribean islands of Martinique and Guadeloupe.

1992 Elder H. Von Packard, a regional representative, receives a call to serve as president of the Los Angeles Temple (later the Los Angeles California Temple). At the time of his call, his brother Floyd L. Packard is serving as the first president of the San Diego California Temple, making them the first brothers to serve simultaneously as temple presidents.

MAY

1832 Hubert Howe Bancroft, later a historian and author of one of the first histories of the Church written by a sympathetic non-Mormon, is born in Granville, Ohio.

1834 Joseph Smith, in company with approximately eighty-five men recruited as members of Zion's Camp, leaves Kirtland and travels to Streetsborough, Ohio, on his way to Missouri.

1850 Sarah Louise Bouton (Felt), later the first general president of the Primary, is born in Norwalk, Connecticut.

1855 President Heber C. Kimball dedicates the Endowment House on the Temple Block in Salt Lake City. The building functions as a temporary temple and is used by the Saints until 1889.

1873 George Washington Hill baptizes Sagwitch, the leader of a group of Shoshone Indians, and 101 of his tribe in the Bear River in Box Elder County, Utah. This is the beginning of an important relationship between the Church and the Shoshone. From this group come one of the first Native Americans to be called as a full-time missionary (Sagwitch's son) and the first Native American called as a bishop (Sagwitch's grandson). Sagwitch's family's

Sarah Louise Bouton Felt, ca. 1880 (see 1850).

service continues today with numerous descendents serving missions in the beginning of the twenty-first century.

1887 Mervyn S. Bennion, later a World War II Navy captain and U.S. Congressional Medal of Honor recipient (1942, awarded posthumously) for working to preserve his crew and ship, the *USS West Virginia,* after being mortally wounded during the Japanese attack on Pearl Harbor, is born in Vernon, Utah.

1936 The Mormon Tabernacle Choir sings with the Philadelphia Orchestra in Salt Lake City. Conductor Leopold Stokowski voices his high praise for the choir, and at the conclusion of the climax of Handel's "Hallelujah Chorus," he turns to the audience and says, "That was thrilling, wasn't it? A wonderful choir!" (*Improvement Era,* June 1936, 372).

1949 Bishop Joseph L. Wirthlin of the Presiding Bishopric dedicates Sanpete LDS Hospital at Mount Pleasant, Utah.

1957 The Atlanta Stake, the first stake in Georgia, is organized, with William L. Nicholls as president.

1980 Latter-day Saint missionaries arrive for the first time in the Central American country of Belize.

1981 The First Presidency releases a strongly worded statement decrying the proposed building of large arsenals of nuclear weaponry and basing of the MX missile system in the Utah-Nevada desert.

1994 In Papeete, Tahiti, Elder Russell M. Nelson speaks at the opening ceremonies of festivities marking the sesquicentennial of the arrival of Latter-day Saint missionaries in Tahiti.

MAY 6

1833 Joseph Smith receives Doctrine and Covenants 93, which instructs on the concepts of intelligence and eternal progression and commands the brethren to set their families in order. Joseph also receives section 94, calling for the construction of a print shop and a building for the use of the First Presidency and appointing Hyrum Smith, Reynolds Cahoon, and Jared Carter as the Church's building committee.

1839 The Eastern States Mission is organized.

1878 The Northwestern States Mission is organized.

1915 Marvin J. Ashton, later a member of the Quorum of the Twelve Apostles, is born in Salt Lake City, Utah.

1922 President Heber J. Grant dedicates KZN (later known as KSL), the Deseret News radio station, and speaks on the station's first broadcast.

President Heber J. Grant at the dedication and first broadcast of KZN, 6 May 1922.

1928 James M. Paramore, later a member of the Presidency of the Seventy, is born in Salt Lake City, Utah.

1931 Hyrum Manwaring is appointed seventh president of Ricks College.

1946 Merrill Cook, later a Utah representative in the U.S. Congress (1997–), is born in Philadelphia, Pennsylvania.

1987 The University of Alberta sponsors a three-day conference entitled "The Mormon Presence in Canada," highlighting the contributions of the LDS pioneers to Canada one hundred years earlier.

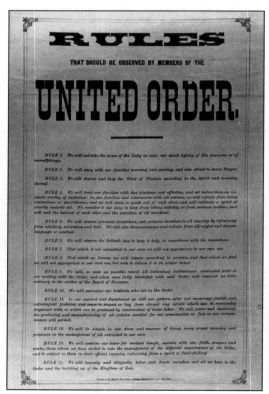

▶ *Rules for the united order (see 1874).*

1811 Peter Maughan, later a pioneer, colonizer, bishop, and the first stake president in Cache Valley, Utah, is born in Milton, England.

1850 Louisa Barnes Pratt, wife of missionary Addison Pratt, is called and set apart to go to the islands of the sea with her husband to help proclaim the gospel. Louisa's calling represents an important step toward the calling of single sisters in the Church as full-time missionaries, which did not take place until 1898.

1874 During general conference President Brigham Young organizes the united order in the Salt Lake City wards. Over the course of the following months, the order is organized in dozens of towns throughout the territory.

1942 Alan Ashton, later a philanthropist, businessman, co-founder of WordPerfect Corporation, and one of the four hundred richest people in America (according to *Forbes Magazine*), is born in Salt Lake City, Utah.

1998 The Church announces plans to build temples in Halifax, Nova Scotia; Fukuoka, Japan; Suva, Fiji; Ciudad Juárez, Chihuahua, Mexico; and Kona, Hawaii.

~ ~ ~ MAY 8 ~ ~ ~

1831 Following the birth and death of their own set of twins on 30 April, Joseph and Emma Smith adopt the twins of John and Julia Murdock. Julia Murdock had died as a result of childbirth.

1834 Zion's Camp leaves New Portage, Ohio, where the camp's two companies had rendezvoused after leaving Kirtland, on its way to Jackson County, Missouri.

1889 Charles "Charlie" Redd, later a well-known rancher, civic leader, philanthropist, and recipient of the Order of the British Empire by Queen Elizabeth II for his service to and friendship with Great Britain, is born in Bluff, Utah.

The BYU men's volleyball team, 8 May 1999.

1895 After sixty-six days of deliberation, delegates to Utah's constitutional convention sign the new Utah State Constitution, paving the way for statehood after more than forty years of waiting.

1899 At a conference in St. George, Utah, President Lorenzo Snow announces a renewed emphasis on the payment of tithing, which members have been neglecting for some time, stating, "The time has now come for every Latter-day Saint . . . to do the will of the Lord and pay his tithing in full" (in James R. Clark, *Messages of the First Presidency,* 3:312).

1938 Sheldon F. Child, later a member of the First Quorum of the Seventy, is born in Ogden, Utah.

1976 The Spain Barcelona Mission is organized.

1988 On Nassau's New Providence Island, the first meetinghouse in the Bahamas is dedicated. It serves an English-speaking branch and a French Creole-speaking branch.

1999 Ground is broken for the Baton Rouge Louisiana and Fiji Suva Temples. Elders Monte J. Brough and Earl M. Monson, members of the First Quorum of the Seventy, preside over the respective ceremonies.

1999 The BYU men's volleyball team wins the (NCAA) national title at UCLA's Pauley Pavilion.

1796 Lyman Wight, later a member of the Quorum of the Twelve Apostles, is born in Fairfield, New York.

1830 William Fowler, later the author of the hymn "We Thank Thee, O God, for a Prophet," is born in Auburn, Australia.

1831 Joseph Smith receives Doctrine and Covenants 50 on this date (according to the *Evening and Morning Star*). The revelation describes the procedure for discerning false and evil spirits.

1836 John Taylor is baptized in a stream near Toronto, Canada. (He is twenty-seven years old.)

1891 U.S. president Benjamin Harrison arrives in Utah Territory on a visit. The Saints cordially receive him despite the long years of persecution by the federal government over the issue of plural marriage.

1898 Nathan Eldon Tanner, later a member of the Quorum of the Twelve Apostles and a Counselor in the First Presidency, is born in Salt Lake City, Utah.

1903 The Church publishes the Book of Mormon in Samoan.

1912 Joseph F. Smith ordains Hyrum Gibbs Smith, son of Hyrum Fisher and Annie Maria Gibbs Smith, as Patriarch to the Church.

1931 Barbara Woodhead (Winder), later the eleventh general president of the Relief Society, is born in Midvale, Utah.

1983 Elder Marvin J. Ashton breaks ground for the Seoul Korea Temple (later the Seoul South Korea Temple).

1992 President Gordon B. Hinckley dedicates historic Cove Fort, near Kanosh, Utah. Under the direction of Brigham Young, his grandfather Ira N. Hinckley had built the fort in central Utah in 1867.

1809 Sutcliffe Maudsley, later a portrait artist in Nauvoo who painted some of the earliest known paintings of Joseph Smith, is born in Whitehouse, England.

1837 The panic of 1837 begins when U.S. banks in New York cease making specie payments. The panic causes widespread bank closures throughout the United States and contributes to the failure of the Kirtland Anti-Banking Safety Society, leading to major apostasy among the Saints in Kirtland.

◄ *Broadside announcing U.S. president Benjamin Harrison's visit to Springville, Utah (see 1891).*

1839 Joseph Smith and his family move into a house in Commerce (later Nauvoo), Illinois. The house, which had been owned by Hugh White, becomes known as the Homestead.

1869 The first transcontinental railroad is completed when the Union Pacific Railroad line meets the Central Pacific Railroad line at Promontory Summit in Utah Territory. The new railroad allows Church leaders, missionaries, and converts to travel quickly to their destinations.

1905 The Beneficial Life Insurance Company, owned by the Church, is incorporated.

1928 Ronald E. Poelman, later a member of the First Quorum of the Seventy, is born in Salt Lake City, Utah.

1931 John K. Carmack, later a member of the First Quorum of the Seventy, is born in Winslow, Arizona.

1937 Robert K. Dellenbach, later a member of the Second Quorum of the Seventy and First Quorum of the Seventy, is born in Salt Lake City, Utah.

The meeting of the rails, 10 May 1869.

1966 In Bogotá, Elder Spencer W. Kimball dedicates the South American country of Colombia for the preaching of the gospel.

1994 Presidents Gordon B. Hinckley and Thomas S. Monson speak at a ceremony at Promontory Summit, marking 125 years since the completion of the transcontinental railway.

1995 The First Presidency announces the release of the Book of Mormon on videotape in American Sign Language.

MAY 11

1808 John Gould, later one of the First Seven Presidents of the Seventy, is born in Ontario, Canada.

1850 The Scandinavian Mission is organized.

1881 Antoine R. Ivins, later one of the First Seven Presidents of the Seventy, is born in St. George, Utah.

1921 Douglas H. Smith, later a member of the First Quorum of the Seventy, is born in Salt Lake City, Utah.

1978 The Laura Branch, the first branch in the Marshall Islands, is organized, with Misao Lokeijak as president.

1980 The first LDS Sunday services in Belize are held.

1993 Elder Russell M. Nelson dedicates the eastern European republic of Belarus for the preaching of the gospel.

1847 Appleton Harmon completes the construction of a wooden "roadometer," an instrument designed by Orson Pratt to measure the distances traveled each day by the first pioneer company. The roadometer is not installed on a wagon until 16 May.

1849 David Eccles, later one of Utah's richest industrialists, is born in Paisley, Scotland.

Granite Seminary Building, ca. 1915 (see 1912).

1912 The Church Board of Education approves the establishment of the first seminary, which is to be built near Granite High School in Salt Lake City, Utah.

1918 Richard T. Wootton, later the second president of the Church College of Hawaii (later known as BYU–Hawaii), is born in Salt Lake City, Utah.

1924 Evan Mecham, later the governor of Arizona (1987–88), is born in Duchesne, Utah.

1985 The Dartmouth Nova Scotia Stake, the first stake in Nova Scotia, Canada, is organized, with Terry Lee Livingstone as president.

1993 The government of Italy formally grants legal status to the Church, even though there has been missionary activity in the country since 1963.

1993 Pope John Paul II greets industrialist and Regional Representative Jon M. Huntsman at the Vatican in Rome.

1810 Anson Call, later a pioneer and colonizer, is born in Fletcher, Vermont.

1854 Ferdinand Hintze, later one of the first missionaries to the Near East and the first mission president in Turkey, is born in Roskilde, Denmark.

1857 While on a trip to visit Saints in the eastern and southern states, Elder Parley P. Pratt is murdered in Arkansas and buried near the town of Alma. Before dying, he states: "I die a firm believer in the Gospel of Jesus Christ as revealed through the Prophet Joseph Smith. . . . I am dying a martyr to the faith" (*Autobiography of Parley P. Pratt*, xxvii).

Susan B. Anthony surrounded by LDS women during visit to Utah, ca. 13 May 1895.

1885 A delegation appointed by a mass meeting held in the Tabernacle in Salt Lake City on 2 May meets with U.S. president Grover Cleveland in the White House in Washington, D.C., and presents a document entitled "Statement of Grievances and Protest," which lists injustices committed against the Saints after passage of the Edmunds Law, legislation directed against polygamists in Utah.

1895 Susan B. Anthony attends a woman suffrage convention in Salt Lake City to lend support to the fight for woman suffrage in Utah.

1903 Nephi Pratt, president of the Northwestern States Mission, leads the first missionaries to British Columbia, Canada.

1992 Appearing before the U.S. House Subcommittee on Civil and Constitutional Rights, Elder Dallin H. Oaks argues for the need to restore the freedom of religion damaged by a 1990 Supreme Court decision.

1994 President Ezra Taft Benson is inducted into the University of Idaho alumni hall of fame.

1995 President Gordon B. Hinckley breaks ground for the Vernal Utah Temple.

1999 President Gordon B. Hinckley addresses the Los Angeles World Affairs Council, which includes diplomats from nineteen countries.

MAY 14

1831 Lucy Mack Smith's company of New York Saints from Fayette arrives in Ohio at Fairport Harbor on Lake Erie, en route to Kirtland. The Colesville Saints, under the direction of Newel Knight, arrive at Fairport Harbor, Ohio, eleven miles from Kirtland, while traveling from New York to Kirtland.

President Heber J. Grant, by C. J. Fox, ca. 1945 (see 1945).

1945 President Heber J. Grant dies in Salt Lake City, Utah, at age eighty-eight, having served for more than sixty-two years as a General Authority.

1972 The Tahiti Stake, the first stake in Tahiti, is organized, with Raituia Tehina Tapu as president.

1977 A bishops' central storehouse opens in Colton, California. It is the second such facility in the Church and the first outside Utah.

1994 Church members and leaders across Utah take part in a Church-endorsed clean-up effort in preparation for Utah's centennial in 1996.

1994 The Polish Genealogical Society of America presents the Wiglia Award to the Church for its efforts to microfilm eastern European records in areas that once belonged to the Polish Commonwealth.

1998 Russia grants the Church formal recognition and issues a certificate allowing the Church to continue its missionary and humanitarian efforts in the country.

 MAY 15

1829 John the Baptist confers the Aaronic Priesthood on Joseph Smith and Oliver Cowdery on the banks of the Susquehanna River near Harmony, Pennsylvania, and instructs them to baptize each other and ordain each other to the Aaronic Priesthood. Joseph Smith's account of the experience with John the Baptist is included in Doctrine and Covenants 13 and in Joseph Smith–History 1:68–73. (Joseph Smith is twenty-three years old.)

1830 Lot Smith, later a frontiersmen, Utah War hero, and Church leader in northern Arizona, is born in Williamstown, New York.

1844 Josiah Quincy, a future mayor of Boston (1845–49), visits Joseph Smith in Nauvoo and later states: "It is by no means improbable that some future textbook . . . will contain a question something like this: What historical American of the nineteenth century has exerted the most powerful influence upon the destinies of his countrymen? And it is by no means impossible that the answer . . . may be thus written: Joseph Smith, the Mormon Prophet" (*Figures of the Past*, 376).

1844 Anthon H. Lund, later a member of the Quorum of the Twelve Apostles and a counselor in the First Presidency, is born in Jutland, Denmark.

Nigerian Primary class, ca. 1985 (see 1988).

1858 John W. Taylor, son of John Taylor and later a member of the Quorum of the Twelve Apostles, is born in Provo, Utah.

1880 Helen Mar Whitney begins an important series of articles about early Church history in the *Woman's Exponent*.

1921 Keith W. Wilcox, later a member of the First Quorum of the Seventy, is born in Hyrum, Utah.

1977 The Caracas Venezuela Stake, the first stake in Venezuela, is organized, with Adolfo F. Mayer G. as president.

1988 The Aba Nigeria Stake, the first stake in both Nigeria and West Africa, is organized, with David William Eka as president.

MAY 16

1842 The Prophet Joseph Smith publishes Facsimile 2 and portions of the Book of Abraham in *Times and Seasons,* a Nauvoo publication.

1843 Joseph Smith gives inspired instructions to the Saints in Ramus, Illinois, now included in Doctrine and Covenants 131. A revelation received the following day (17 May) is also included in this section.

The BYU Jerusalem Center for Near Eastern Studies (see 1989).

1855 Elder Orson Hyde leaves Salt Lake City with a company of thirty-five men to settle Carson Valley, on the west side of the Great Basin in what would later become Nevada, making it the first LDS settlement there.

1868 Willard Washington Bean, later a missionary for more than twenty-four years at the Joseph Smith Sr. property in Palmyra, New York, is born in Richfield, Utah.

1951 LaVern Watts Parmley is called as the fifth general president of the Primary, with Arta Matthews Hale and Florence Holbrook Richards as counselors.

1989 On Mount Scopus, overlooking old Jerusalem, President Howard W. Hunter of the Quorum of the Twelve Apostles dedicates the BYU Jerusalem Center for Near Eastern Studies.

1996 President Gordon B. Hinckley begins his historic tour of Asia, during which he will visit Tokyo, Osaka, and Fukuoka, Japan; Naha, Okinawa; Pusan and Seoul, Korea; Taipei, Taiwan; Hong Kong; Phnom Penh, Cambodia; Ho Chi Minh City and Hanoi, Vietnam; and Manila and Cebu City, Philippines.

MAY 17

1834 Angus M. Cannon, later an early stake president in Salt Lake City who served for twenty-eight years, is born in Liverpool, England.

1844 A state convention held in Nauvoo nominates Joseph Smith as a candidate for president of the United States. After James Arlington Bennett is found to be ineligible (being of foreign birth) and Colonel Solomon Copeland declines the offer, Sidney Rigdon is chosen as his running mate.

1869 Ground is broken for the Utah Central Railroad, which is to run from Ogden to Salt Lake City, thereby connecting Salt Lake City to the transcontinental railroad.

1877 President John Young breaks ground for the Logan Temple (later the Logan Utah Temple).

1884 President John Taylor dedicates the Logan (later the Logan Utah Temple) Temple .

1888 During a period of intense persecution, President Wilford Woodruff of the Quorum of the Twelve Apostles privately dedicates the Manti Temple (later the Manti Utah Temple).

1898 Thomas C. Neibaur, later a World War I army private awarded the U.S. Congressional Medal of Honor for defending fellow soldiers from attack and taking eleven enemy soldiers as prisoners, all after being wounded in battle, is born in Sharon, Idaho.

1918 J. Thomas Fyans, later a member of the Presidency of the Seventy, is born in Moreland, Idaho.

1930 The Church participates in the first national/international exposition, when the International Hygiene Exposition at Dresden, Germany, includes an LDS exhibit on the Word of Wisdom.

1959 The Indianapolis Stake, the first stake in Indiana, is organized, with Phillip F. Low as president.

1975 In an announcement regarding a new supervisory program for missions in the United States and Canada, members of the Quorum of the Twelve Apostles are assigned as advisors to the Church's twelve areas throughout the world. Other General Authorities are assigned as supervisors to the twelve areas.

Logan, Utah, *by Christian Eisele, 1892 (see 1884).*

1783 Martin Harris, later one of the Three Witnesses of the Book of Mormon, is born in Easttown, New York.

1838 Joseph Smith, Sidney Rigdon, Thomas B. Marsh, David W. Patten, Bishop Edward Partridge, Elias Higbee, Simeon Carter, Alanson Ripley, and several others leave Far West, Missouri, and travel north to locate possible settlement sites in the face of the imminent expulsion of the Saints from Missouri.

1843 The Prophet Joseph Smith tells Judge Stephen A. Douglas: "Judge, you will aspire to the presidency of the United States; and if ever you turn your hand against me or the Latter-day Saints, you will feel the weight of the hand of [the] Almighty upon you; and you will live to see and know that I have testified the truth to you" (*History of the Church,* 5:394).

1846 Brigham Young establishes Mt. Pisgah on the middle fork of the Grand River as a second temporary way station along the Mormon trail in Iowa.

1918 Glen L. Rudd, later a member of the First Quorum of the Seventy, is born in Salt Lake City, Utah.

1930 Don Lind, later a member of a NASA mission aboard the space shuttle *Challenger* (1985), is born in Midvale, Utah.

1942 Marlin K. Jensen, later a member of the Presidency of the Seventy, is born in Ogden, Utah.

1945 President Heber J. Grant's funeral is held in the Tabernacle in Salt Lake City.

1948 Tom Udall, later a New Mexico representative in the U.S. Congress (1999–), is born in Tucson, Arizona.

1958 The Auckland Stake, the first stake outside of North America and Hawaii, is organized, with George R. Biesinger as president.

1838 Joseph Smith receives Doctrine and Covenants 116, identifying Spring Hill, Daviess County, Missouri, as Adam-ondi-Ahman.

1842 The citizens of Nauvoo elect Joseph Smith as the city's second mayor, replacing John C. Bennett, who had been excommunicated.

1890 The U.S. Supreme Court upholds the constitutionality of the clauses in the Edmunds-Tucker Act that allow the government to confiscate Church property.

The Church Adminstration Building, ca. 1920 (see 1915).

1915 President Charles W. Penrose of the First Presidency dedicates the cornerstone of the new Church Office Building (later known as the Church Administration Building), at 45 East South Temple.

1984 Kenneth Zabriskie, president of the West Indies Mission, visits with the governor of Antigua and receives permission to send missionaries there, thus opening that country for the preaching of the gospel.

1984 President Gordon B. Hinckley breaks ground for the Denver Colorado Temple.

◄ *Martin Harris, ca. 1870 (see 1783).*

1831 Joseph Smith receives Doctrine and Covenants 51 on this day (according to the Kirtland Revelation Book and the Book of Commandments). The revelation contains additional instructions concerning the law of consecration.

1945 Walter William Herger, later a California representative in the U.S. Congress (1987–), is born in Yuba City, California.

1945 David William Eka, later an early pioneer and leader of the Church in Nigeria, is born in Etina, Nigeria.

1947 President George Albert Smith offers the prayer to open the U.S. Senate session, the first Church leader to be so invited.

1951 Michael Dean Crapo, later an Idaho representative in the U.S. Congress (1993–99) and a U.S. Senator (1999–), is born in Idaho Falls, Idaho.

1962 The Boston Stake, the first stake in Massachusetts, is organized, with Wilbur W. Cox as president.

1966 Nearly twenty years after President George Albert Smith offers the prayer at the opening of the U.S. Senate, President Hugh B. Brown of the First Presidency opens the U.S. Senate with prayer.

1969 Elder Marion G. Romney dedicates Spain for the preaching of the gospel.

1973 The Manila Stake, the first stake in the Philippines, is organized, with Augusto Alandy Lim as president.

1993 Elder M. Russell Ballard dedicates the Baltic republic of Lithuania for the preaching of the gospel.

1999 Ground is broken for the Medford Oregon Temple. Elder D. Lee Tobler, a member of the Second Quorum of the Seventy and First Counselor in the North America Northwest Area Presidency, presides over the ceremony.

1838 Elders Heber C. Kimball and Orson Hyde arrive back in Kirtland after introducing the gospel to England.

1844 Elders Brigham Young, Heber C. Kimball, and Lyman Wight of the Twelve leave Nauvoo on a mission to preach and to promote Joseph Smith's candidacy for president of the United States.

1851 Work on the Old Tabernacle in Salt Lake City begins. This tabernacle is located on the site that would later be occupied by the Assembly Hall and serves the Saints until 1870, when it is torn down.

1852 Joseph F. Smith is baptized in City Creek in Salt Lake City, the first of four future Presidents of the Church to be baptized in the same location. (He is thirteen years old.)

1868 President Brigham Young contracts with the Union Pacific Railroad to provide Latter-day Saint labor in constructing a rail line down Echo and Weber Canyons to Ogden, Utah.

The First Presidency, ca. 1945. From left: J. Reuben Clark, President George Albert Smith, and David O. McKay (see 1945).

1888 Elder Lorenzo Snow of the Twelve publicly dedicates the Manti Temple (later the Manti Utah Temple).

1898 Arnold Williams, later Idaho's first LDS governor (1945–47), is born in Fillmore, Utah.

1912 The Young Stake, the first stake in New Mexico, is organized, with David Halls as president.

1913 The National Council of the Boy Scouts of America invites the Church's MIA Scout organization to formally join the BSA, thus beginning a long association between the two groups.

1945 George Albert Smith is ordained and set apart as the eighth President of the Church, with J. Reuben Clark Jr. and David O. McKay as Counselors.

1955 The Church announces the publication of the *New Messenger*, a Braille periodical, which is to contain the best articles from the other Church magazines.

1967 The Guatemala City Stake, the first stake in Guatemala, is organized, with Udine Falabella as president.

1990 The U.S. Supreme Court rules that money given directly to missionaries is not a deductible donation under federal tax law, prompting Church leaders to advise members to follow established procedures of making such donations through their wards.

1995 Eddie Misi, the first convert in the Solomon Islands, is baptized.

▶ *U.S. Liberty Ship* SS Joseph Smith, *22 May 1943.*

1804 Lyman R. Sherman, later one of the First Seven Presidents of the Seventy, is born in Monkton, Vermont.

1874 General Alexander W. Doniphan, a friend to the Mormons during the difficult days of persecution in Missouri, visits Salt Lake City and is greeted warmly by Church leaders.

1893 Wilford C. Wood, later an artifact collector and purchaser of early LDS historical sites, is born in South Bountiful, Utah.

1924 LeGrand R. Curtis, later a member of the Second Quorum of the Seventy, is born in Salt Lake City, Utah.

1935 H. Aldridge Gillespie, later a member of the Second Quorum of the Seventy, is born in Riverside, California.

1940 Kieth Merrill, later an Academy Award–winning filmmaker and director of *The Testaments: Of One Fold and One Shepherd,* is born in Ogden, Utah.

1943 Eugene W. Hilton, representing the Oakland Stake, christens the *SS Joseph Smith,* a U.S. Liberty ship used during World War II to transport troops, freight, and prisoners.

1977 The Oslo Norway Stake, the first stake in Norway, is organized, with Osvald Bjareng as president.

1977 The Church announces the creation of the Church Activities Committee, which is given responsibility for coordinating cultural arts and physical activities. Similar groups are organized at the stake and ward levels.

1843 In Nauvoo Addison Pratt, Noah Rogers, Benjamin F. Grouard, and Knowlton F. Hanks are set apart for the first mission to the South Pacific Islands. It is to Utah, not Illinois, that they return at the conclusion of their mission.

The Salt Lake Temple baptismal font, ca. 1911 (see 1893).

1893 Baptisms for the dead are performed in the Salt Lake Temple for the first time.

1899 Latter-day Saint missionaries arrive in the Cook Islands for the first time.

1926 Colleen Kay Hutchins (Vandeweghe), later the first LDS Miss America (1952), is born in Salt Lake City, Utah.

1932 Julio E. Davila, later a member of the Second Quorum of the Seventy, is born in Bucaramunga, Colombia.

1843 Camilla Clara Meith (Cobb), later the founder of the first Utah kindergarten, is born in Dresden, Germany.

1845 Under the direction of Brigham Young, the Saints lay the capstone of the Nauvoo Temple.

1845 William B. Smith, a son of Joseph and Lucy Mack Smith, is ordained Patriarch to the Church.

1847 The sick detachments of the Mormon Battalion that had wintered at Pueblo leave for Fort Laramie.

1909 Bernard P. Brockbank, later a member of the First Quorum of the Seventy, is born in Salt Lake City, Utah.

1921 Gerald Eldon Melchin, later a member of the First Quorum of the Seventy, is born in Kitchener, Canada.

1944 During World War II, the Church announces that it will restrict the calling of military-age men as bishops, freeing many for service in the war.

Deseret News editorial cartoon, by Jonathan Brown, 26–27 May 1999.

1999 The Church launches its FamilySearch™ Internet Genealogy Service at a news conference. The innovation is considered to be the most significant advance in family history since the invention of microfilm. The site quickly becomes one of the most sought-after sites on the Internet, receiving over forty million hits each day.

1829 Oliver Cowdery baptizes Joseph Smith's younger brother Samuel at Harmony, Pennsylvania. Samuel is the third person baptized in this dispensation, following Oliver Cowdery and Joseph Smith on 15 May.

1856 The ship *Horizon* leaves Liverpool, England, for Boston, carrying 856 Saints led by Edward Martin. Most in the company later become part of the ill-fated Martin and Willie handcart companies, which become stranded in present-day Wyoming during their trek to Utah.

The press purported to have been used to print the Book of Mormon (see 1906).

1906 President Joseph F. Smith purchases the press on which the first edition of the Book of Mormon was printed.

1935 The Brazilian Mission is organized.

1946 More than one thousand Saints gather at the Irmeta Branch chapel, near Mexico City, for a two-day Mexican Mission conference. President George Albert Smith gives one of the first speeches ever made by a Church President in Mexico.

1952 Gordon Harold Smith, later a U.S. Senator from Oregon (1997–), is born in Pendleton, Oregon.

1984 President Gordon B. Hinckley of the First Presidency dedicates the Boise Idaho Temple.

1996 Robert A. Mills receives the National Intelligence Medal of Achievement from the U.S. Central Intelligence Agency.

1844 Joseph Smith addresses the Saints during the last month of his life: "I, like Paul have been in perils, and oftener than anyone in this generation. . . . The Lord has constituted me so curiously that I glory in persecution" (*History of the Church,* 6:408).

1847 The first company of pioneers arrives at a point directly north of Chimney Rock, a distinctive landmark on the journey to Zion.

1848 President Brigham Young leaves Winter Quarters for the second (and last) time to journey to the Salt Lake Valley.

1884 Preston Nibley, later a prominent author, compiler, and assistant Church historian, is born in Logan, Utah.

1946 Twenty-one people are baptized into the Church between sessions of the Mexican Mission conference. President George Albert Smith presides over the conference during his visit to Mexico.

Abel Paez speaking at the Mexican Mission conference, 26 May 1946.

1962 President David O. McKay breaks ground for the Oakland Temple (later the Oakland California Temple).

1972 The Church announces that the Salt Lake Lyric Theater will be renamed the Promised Valley Playhouse and used for Church productions.

1973 President Spencer W. Kimball dedicates the restored Brigham Young home in Nauvoo, Illinois.

1986 Christy Fichtner, a convert of seven months, becomes Miss USA.

1991 The San Francisco de Macoris Dominican Republic Stake, the eighteen thousandth stake of the Church, is organized, with Eric Edison Olivero P. as president.

1996 President Gordon B. Hinckley dedicates the Hong Kong Temple (later the Hong Kong China Temple).

▶ *Louise Yates Robinson, ca. 1928 (see 1866).*

1840 In England, Parley P. Pratt issues the first number of *The Latter-day Saints' Millennial Star*, which would become the longest running publication in the Church (1840–1970).

1849 Crickets appear in the Salt Lake Valley and begin eating the Saints' crops. Several days later, flocks of California seagulls appear and begin eating the crickets, thus saving the pioneers from possible famine.

1850 A tornado demolishes the north wall and weakens the south and east walls of the abandoned Nauvoo Temple so that they must be torn down.

1866 Louise Yates (Robinson), later the seventh general president of the Relief Society, is born in Scipio, Utah.

1893 The first branch in American Samoa is organized in Pago Pago.

1911 Mahonri M. Young's life-size statues of Joseph Smith and his brother Hyrum, *The Prophet* and *The Patriarch,* are placed on Temple Square.

1933 The "Century of Progress" World's Fair opens in Chicago. Avard Fairbanks heads the team that prepares the sculptures, mural paintings, and stained-glass works used in the Church's display.

1934 The first branch in Saskatchewan, Canada, is organized, with G. Gordon Whyte as president.

1978 President Marion G. Romney of the First Presidency breaks ground for the Seattle Washington Temple.

1996 President Gordon B. Hinckley visits Shenzhen, China, becoming the first Church President to visit mainland China.

1997 David A. Bednar is appointed fourteenth president of Ricks College.

1857 Under instructions from President James Buchanan, the United States War Department issues orders for an army to assemble at Fort Leavenworth, Kansas, and march to Utah, beginning the so-called "Utah War."

1878 Rufus K. Hardy, later one of the First Seven Presidents of the Seventy, is born in Salt Lake City, Utah.

1903 O. Leslie Stone, later a member of the First Quorum of the Seventy, is born in Chapin, Idaho.

1944 Gladys Knight, later a member of the 1960s and '70s R&B group Gladys Knight and the Pips and convert to the Church, is born in Atlanta, Georgia.

1988 The First Presidency issues a statement regarding AIDS, emphasizing chastity before marriage, fidelity in marriage, and total abstinence from homosexuality.

▶ *U.S. president Theodore Roosevelt during visit to Salt Lake City, 29 May 1903.*

1781 Emer Harris, brother of Martin Harris and later an early missionary in the Church, is born in Cambridge, New York.

1903 Hundreds of Latter-day Saints gather to greet U.S. president Theodore Roosevelt when he arrives in Salt Lake City.

1903 U.S. president Theodore Roosevelt speaks in the Tabernacle, the first U.S. president to do so, and gives a tribute to the Mormon pioneers.

1946 Five hundred former members who had been part of a group that had left the Church over a dispute regarding native leadership spread flowers along the lane leading to the chapel in Tecako, Mexico, and stand on each side, singing "We Thank Thee, O God, for a Prophet" as President George Albert Smith arrives to address them. He invites them back into the Church, and some twelve hundred eventually return.

1952 President David O. McKay begins a trip to Europe that will include preparatory work for the London and Swiss Temples (later the London England and Bern Switzerland Temples).

1981 The BYU men's golf team wins the NCAA national championship.

1996 President Gordon B. Hinckley dedicates Cambodia for the preaching of the gospel at a meeting held in Phnom Penh and meets with a group of Saints in Ho Chi Minh City, Vietnam, where he dedicates the entire country of Vietnam for the preaching of the gospel.

1999 Ground is broken for three new temples: the Louisville Kentucky, Adelaide Australia, and Veracruz México Temples. Elders John K. Carmack, Vaughn J. Featherstone, and Carl B. Pratt (all of the First Quorum of the Seventy) preside over the respective ceremonies.

MAY 30

1845 Nearly a year after the martyrdom of the Prophet and Patriarch, the nine defendants charged with the murder of Joseph and Hyrum Smith are acquitted.

1878 Two Salt Lake City baseball teams, the Deserets and the Red Stockings, meet in the first game of the season; the Red Stockings with a new second baseman, Heber J. Grant, win 11–3.

1912 At Brigham Young University President Joseph F. Smith dedicates the Maeser Memorial Building, the first building on "Temple Hill," later known as "Upper Campus."

1915 William Paul Daniels, the first black South African convert, is baptized in Salt Lake City; he then returns home to Cape Town.

1916 Devere Harris, later a member of the First Quorum of the Seventy, is born in Portage, Utah.

1927 President Charles W. Nibley of the First Presidency dedicates the Mormon Battalion Monument on the Utah State Capitol grounds.

1977 Poland formally recognizes the Church.

1981 President Spencer W. Kimball breaks ground for the Santiago Chile Temple.

1986 Admiral Paul A. Yost becomes the eighteenth commandant of the U.S. Coast Guard.

1994 President Ezra Taft Benson dies in Salt Lake City at age ninety-four, after serving for more than fifty years as a General Authority.

1999 In Athens, Elder Charles A. Didier, a member of the First Quorum of the Seventy and the Area President of the Europe East Area, dedicates the first chapel in Greece.

MAY 31

1843 Brigham Young moves into a newly built brick home in Nauvoo (later restored and opened to the public).

1933 Henry B. Eyring, later a member of the Quorum of the Twelve Apostles, is born in Princeton, New Jersey.

1934 The Boy Scouts of America awards Elder George Albert Smith the Silver Buffalo, the highest honor awarded by the BSA. Elder Smith is the first Latter-day Saint leader to be so honored.

1942 Stephen D. Nadauld, later a member of the Second Quorum of the Seventy, is born in Idaho Falls, Idaho.

1971 President N. Eldon Tanner of the First Presidency dedicates the new visitors' center in Independence, Missouri.

1996 Elder Dallin H. Oaks represents the Church at the ordination of Carolyn Tanner Irish as the new leader of the Episcopal diocese of Utah.

◀ *Elder Charles A. Didier, his wife, Lucie, and missionaries in the Greece Athens Mission, 30 May 1999.*

⚜ ⚜ ⚜ JUNE *1* ⚜ ⚜ ⚜

1801 Brigham Young, later a member of the Quorum of the Twelve Apostles and second President of the Church, is born in Whitingham, Vermont.

1833 Joseph Smith receives Doctrine and Covenants 95, wherein the Lord chastises the Church for failure to move ahead with building the Kirtland Temple.

1854 Junius F. Wells, later called by President Brigham Young to found the Young Men's program of the Church and an assistant Church historian, is born in Salt Lake City, Utah.

1872 The first issue of the *Woman's Exponent,* a paper owned and published by Latter-day Saint women, is published in Salt Lake City. It is published until 1914.

1896 The first issue of *De Ster,* a monthly Church periodical in Dutch, is published in Rotterdam, Holland.

1915 After being inspired by the Spirit, President Joseph F. Smith dedicates the site for the Laie Hawaii Temple. Upon his return to the mainland, he advises other Church leaders of his action and asks for their support.

1919 General conference is held after being postponed for two months because of the influenza pandemic that swept the world in 1918 and 1919.

1950 President George Albert Smith attends ceremonies in Washington, D.C., during which a life-size Brigham Young statue is placed on display in the U.S. Capitol Building.

1969 The Arkansas Stake, the first stake in Arkansas, is organized, with Dean C. Andrew as president.

President George Albert Smith standing next to the Brigham Young statue in the United States Capitol Building, 1 June 1950.

1976 Elder John and Patricia Albrect, the first full-time Church Educational System (CES) missionaries specifically called to help expand religious education throughout the world, are called to serve at the Church's Nephi High School in the Marshall Islands.

1983 President Gordon B. Hinckley of the First Presidency dedicates the Atlanta Georgia Temple.

1997 President Gordon B. Hinckley dedicates the St. Louis Missouri Temple.

JUNE 2

1833 Martha Jane Knowlton (Coray), later a friend of Joseph Smith and scribe who helps record Lucy Mack Smith's history of her son Joseph Smith, is born in Covington, Kentucky.

1843 Mary Goble (Pay), later a pioneer handcart diarist, is born in Brighton, England.

1846 U.S. president James K. Polk's cabinet authorizes him to ask the Latter-day Saints to provide several hundred men in the war against Mexico. This was an important milestone on the road to enlisting the Mormon Battalion.

1864 Heber J. Grant is baptized in City Creek in Salt Lake City, the second of four future Presidents of the Church to be baptized in the same location. (He is seven years and six months old.)

1874 In one of the largest baptismal services among Native Americans in North America, William Lee and three other elders baptize one hundred Goshute Indians in Utah.

1902 William E. Berrett, later an author, educator, and head of seminaries and institutes of religion, is born in Union, Utah.

JUNE 3

1831 At the fourth conference of the Church, convened in Kirtland, the office of high priest is instituted and nineteen men are ordained to this office. Joseph Smith is ordained a high priest on 7 June.

1846 Jesse Little, a representative of the Church, meets with U.S. president James K. Polk in Washington, D.C., to discuss plans for establishing the Mormon Battalion.

1863 William H. King, later a Utah member of the U.S. Senate (1916–40), is born in Fillmore, Utah.

1887 Charles Ora Card, leading a group of eight families, encamps on Lee's Creek in southern Alberta, Canada, marking the beginning of the LDS settlement in western Canada. Under instructions from President John Taylor, a gathering place for Latter-day Saints in Canada is selected, and on 17 June a site is chosen for what later becomes Cardston.

1890 In preparation for the completion of the interior of the Salt Lake Temple, the First Presidency sets apart John B. Fairbanks, John Hafen, and Lorus Pratt as "art missionaries" to study in Paris, France. Later, Edwin Evans and Herman H. Haag are also sent to Paris to study.

1973 The first stake in El Salvador (San Salvador) is created with Mario Edumundo Scheel as president.

1994 The U.S. National Genealogy Society posthumously elects Archibald F. Bennett, who pioneered acquisition of genealogical materials for the Church, to their Hall of Fame; Bennett is the first Latter-day Saint so honored.

1802 Joshua Seixas, later a teacher in the Kirtland Hebrew School, is born in New York City, New York.

1831 The Prophet Joseph Smith, during a four-day Church conference held at a schoolhouse on the hill above the Isaac Morley farmhouse in Kirtland, sees the Father and the Son and declares, "I now see God, and Jesus Christ at his right hand, let them kill me, I should not feel death as I am now" (in Levi W. Hancock, "The Life of Levi Ward Hancock," 33).

1833 Joseph Smith receives Doctrine and Covenants 96, containing instructions concerning some of the Church property in Kirtland.

1837 Joseph Smith calls Elder Heber C. Kimball to go on a mission to England, the first call to an overseas mission in the Church.

Heber C. Kimball, ca. 1853 (see 1837).

1925 Sylvester Q. Cannon is sustained as the sixth Presiding Bishop of the Church.

1944 Elder Joseph Fielding Smith begins a new radio program *The Restoration of All Things* on Sunday evenings. Later the talks are published in a book under the same title.

1967 A new visitors' center opens at the Joseph Smith birthplace in South Royalton, Vermont.

1805 Albert P. Rockwood, later one of the First Seven Presidents of the Seventy, is born in Holliston, Massachusetts.

Truman O. and Susan Savage Angell and child, ca. 1861 (see 1810).

1810 Truman O. Angell, later the architect of many public and private buildings in Salt Lake City, including the Salt Lake Temple, is born in North Providence, Rhode Island.

1834 Zion's Camp crosses the Mississippi River and enters Missouri on its way to help the Saints who had been driven out of Jackson County.

1846 U.S. president James K. Polk agrees to enlist the services of five hundred to one thousand LDS men during the Mexican War.

1847 The first group of the second pioneer company (sometimes referred to as the "Big Company"), led by Parley P. Pratt and John Taylor, leaves Winter Quarters for the journey to the Rocky Mountains.

1861 Gustave Chaprix arrives in Brussels as the first missionary to Belgium.

1887 The Colonia Juárez Ward, the first ward in Mexico, is organized, with George W. Sevey as bishop.

1956 Richard A. Searfoss, later a U.S. astronaut and member of three space shuttle missions (1993, 1996, 1998), is born in Mount Clemens, Michigan.

1970 The Church sends six thousand pounds of supplies to earthquake victims in Peru.

1976 The First Presidency publishes an official statement to reiterate Church policy opposing abortion.

1976 The Teton Dam in Idaho bursts, flooding Rexburg and surrounding areas. Ricks College president Henry B. Eyring turns the campus into a center of relief and refuge for the two thousand people who are rendered homeless by the flood. Some 386,000 free meals are served in the campus cafeteria.

1980 The Port of Spain Branch, the first branch on the islands of Trinidad and Tobago, is organized.

1994 President Howard W. Hunter is ordained and set apart as the fourteenth President of the Church, with Gordon B. Hinckley and Thomas S. Monson as Counselors; Elder Boyd K. Packer of the Twelve is set apart as acting President of the Twelve.

1997 The Children's Miracle Network (established in 1983 by Marie Osmond and John Schneider), hosts the world's largest annual television fund-raiser to date, raising $152 million. The telethon fund-raiser continues to be aired each year.

JUNE

1806 Philo Dibble, later a close friend of Joseph Smith and painter of early Church historical sites and events, is born in Peru, Massachusetts.

1831 Joseph Smith receives Doctrine and Covenants 52, calling for twenty-eight elders (including Joseph Smith and Sidney Rigdon) to travel to Missouri to hold a conference. The Lord promises that, upon their arrival, he would reveal where Zion is to be located. Although the section heading states that the receipt of the revelation is 7 June, several journal sources indicate that the revelation was actually received on 6 June.

1833 The Prophet Joseph Smith appoints Hyrum Smith, Reynolds Cahoon, and Jared Carter, the Church's building committee, to oversee the construction of the Kirtland Temple.

1840 Forty-one Saints set sail from Liverpool, England, on the ship *Britannia,* en route to Nauvoo; these are the first Saints to gather from Europe.

The ship Britannia *(see 1840).*

1848 LDS pioneer James Brown purchases Fort Buenaventura (at present-day Ogden, Utah) from trader Miles M. Goodyear for $3,000.

Little Soldier (see 1874).

1874 Little Soldier and his tribe of Native Americans from the Ogden area are baptized; this is one of the earliest tribes to join the Church.

1878 George Albert Smith is baptized in City Creek in Salt Lake City, the third of four future Presidents of the Church to be baptized in the same location. (He is eight years old.)

1897 For the first time since the Saints were expelled from Jackson County, Missouri, in November 1833, a branch of the Church is organized in Independence, Missouri, with Richard Preator as branch president.

1979 The Vision of the Celestial Kingdom, given to Joseph Smith Jr., and the Vision of the Redemption of the Dead, given to Joseph F. Smith, are transferred from the Pearl of Great Price to the Doctrine and Covenants, becoming sections 137 and 138.

1994 President Howard W. Hunter, during his first news conference after becoming President, encourages members of the Church to live more Christlike lives and to increase temple attendance.

JUNE 7

1794 Simeon Carter, later a prominent and faithful member of the Church, a missionary, and one of the founders of Brigham City, Utah, is born in Killingworth, Connecticut.

1846 Elder Jesse Little and Thomas L. Kane, a friend of the Latter-day Saints, meet with U.S. president James K. Polk and finalize the agreement for the establishment of the Mormon Battalion.

1870 Milton Bennion, later superintendent of the LDS Sunday School (1943–49), is born in Salt Lake City, Utah.

1925 Sam K. Shimabukuro, later a member of the Second Quorum of the Seventy, is born in Waipahu, Hawaii.

1933 Janette Callister (Hales Beckham), later the tenth general president of the Young Women, is born in Springville, Utah.

1981 The Milan Italy Stake, the first stake in Italy, is organized, with Mario Vaira as president.

1998 President Gordon B. Hinckley dedicates the Preston England Temple.

1834 On the Salt River in eastern Missouri, the main company of Zion's Camp, headed by Joseph Smith, meets the company of volunteers from Michigan recruited by Hyrum Smith and Lyman Wight.

1864 Mary Jane "May" Anderson, later the second general president of the Primary, is born in Liverpool, England.

1888 All stake leaders are instructed to establish an academy for secondary education.

1900 The First Presidency announces the beginning of missionary training classes, one of the foundation stones of future missionary training programs.

1918 William G. Bangerter, later a member of the Presidency of the Seventy, is born in Granger, Utah.

1947 Andrew W. Peterson, later a member of the First Quorum of the Seventy, is born in San Francisco, California.

1978 The First Presidency issues a letter announcing that "all worthy male members of the Church may be ordained to the priesthood without regard for race or color" (D&C Official Declaration 2).

1991 The Mormon Tabernacle Choir begins a twenty-one-day tour of eight European countries, including five countries in which the choir had never performed: Hungary, Austria, Czechoslovakia, Poland, and the Soviet Union.

1804 Henry Harriman, later one of the First Seven Presidents of the Seventy, is born in Rowley, Massachusetts.

1830 The Church gathers in Fayette, New York, to hold its first conference. They accept the Articles and Covenants of the Church of Christ, now Doctrine and Covenants 20.

1853 J. Golden Kimball, later a colorful folk hero and one of the First Seven Presidents of the Seventy, is born in Salt Lake City, Utah.

J. Golden Kimball, ca. 1910 (see 1853).

1874 Samuel O. Bennion, later one of the First Seven Presidents of the Seventy, is born in Taylorsville, Utah.

1878 Orrin Porter Rockwell, bodyguard of Joseph Smith and a Utah folk hero, dies in Salt Lake City at the age of 65. At the time of his death, he had been a member of the Church longer than anyone to that time, having been baptized shortly after the Church was organized.

1895 The Alberta Stake, the first stake in Canada and the first stake outside of the United States, is organized, with Charles Ora Card as president.

1901 The Union Stake, the first stake in Oregon, is organized, with Franklin S. Bramwell as president.

1907 Harold B. Lee is baptized in Bybee Pond near Clifton, Idaho. (He is eight years and two months old.)

1929 During the June general conference of the Young Women's Mutual Improvement Association, leaders announce the creation of a summer camping program for all MIA girls and the merging of the *Young Woman's Journal* with the *Improvement Era.*

1974 The Belfast Ireland Stake, the first stake in Ireland, is organized, with Andrew Renfrew as president.

1978 The first missionaries to the Dominican Republic arrive.

1979 President Spencer W. Kimball breaks ground for the Jordan River Temple (later the Jordan River Utah Temple).

1992 At the site of the historic Social Hall, President Gordon B. Hinckley of the First Presidency dedicates the new Social Hall Memorial and walkway in Salt Lake City.

JUNE 10

1787 Vienna Jacques, later mentioned in Doctrine and Covenants 90, is born in Beverly, Massachusetts. One of only two women mentioned by name in the Doctrine and Covenants, Vienna gave liberally of her means to the Church and was a stalwart friend of Joseph Smith.

1844 The Nauvoo City Council declares the *Nauvoo Expositor,* published by dissidents, a public nuisance. Under the direction of the mayor and the city council, the marshal destroys the type and press. These actions begin the process that eventually leads to the murder of Joseph and Hyrum Smith.

The Nauvoo Expositor *Building, May 1907 (see 1844).*

1868 Resolutions in favor of helping the Union Pacific Railroad build through Utah are passed during a mass meeting in Salt Lake City.

1875 Brigham Young organizes the Young Men's Mutual Improvement Association (forerunner of the current Young Men program) in Salt Lake City.

1877 Sylvester Q. Cannon, later the sixth Presiding Bishop of the Church and a member of the Quorum of the Twelve Apostles, is born in Salt Lake City, Utah.

1883 The San Louis Stake, the first stake in Colorado, is organized, with Silas S. Smith as president.

1956 The Northern Mexican Mission is organized.

1981 The Lisbon Portugal Stake, the first stake in Portugal, is organized, with José Manuel da Costa Santos as president.

▶ *Joseph B. Wirthlin, ca. 1986 (see 1917).*

1829 Joseph Smith deposits the title page of the Book of Mormon in the office of R. R. Lansing, clerk of the Northern District of New York, and obtains a copyright.

1865 Schuyler Colfax, a representative from Indiana and the speaker of the House (later to become the vice president of the United States), and J. M. Ashley, chairman of the House Committee on Territories, arrive in Salt Lake City on a fact-finding mission for the U.S. government. They are to obtain information on the Saints' practice of plural marriage and the Church's attitude toward the federal government.

1889 The Church sponsors a concert in the Tabernacle to raise money to help the victims of the Johnstown, Pennsylvania, flood. This is one of the Church's first major humanitarian efforts directed toward nonmembers.

1895 In St. Petersburg, Russia, Elder August J. Hoglund baptizes Johan M. Lindelof, the first convert in Russia.

1917 Joseph B. Wirthlin, later a member of the Quorum of the Twelve Apostles, is born in Salt Lake City, Utah.

1934 Earl C. Tingey, later a member of the Presidency of the Seventy, is born in Bountiful, Utah.

1939 Monte J. Brough, later a member of the Presidency of the Seventy, is born in Randolph, Utah.

1966 Mark E. Littman and Joel Izatt of the Hansen Planetarium assist artists Sydney E. King and V. Russell Capson in their efforts to place the stars in the heavens on a mural on the rotunda ceiling above where the *Christus* will be placed in the North Visitors' Center on Temple Square. The stars are painted to appear as they would have on 6 April 1830, the day the Church was organized.

Baptisms in the Liberia Monrovia Mission (see 1988).

1978 The Guayaquil Ecuador Stake, the first stake in Ecuador, is organized, with Lorenzo A. Garaycoa as president.

1988 The first baptisms in Sierra Leone, part of the Liberia Monrovia Mission, take place.

1996 President Gordon B. Hinckley breaks ground for the Madrid Spain Temple.

1999 The Perth Australia Temple is announced by the First Presidency in a letter to local priesthood leaders. When completed, it will be the farthest temple from Church headquarters, located some 10,500 miles from Salt Lake City.

JUNE 12

1831 John Whitmer, Church historian, begins the *Book of John Whitmer,* the earliest history of the Church.

1872 The First Presidency issues a general circular letter asking the Saints in Utah to provide funds to facilitate the gathering of the Saints from abroad.

1926 Carlos E. Asay, later a member of the Presidency of the Seventy, is born in Sutherland, Utah.

1926 Durrel A. Woolsey, later a member of the Second Quorum of the Seventy, is born in Escalante, Utah.

1930 Loren C. Dunn, later a member of the First Quorum of the Seventy, is born in Tooele, Utah.

1983 The Suva Fiji Stake, the first stake in Fiji, is organized, with Inosi Naga as president.

1994 President Gordon B. Hinckley breaks ground for the Preston England Temple.

1999 Ground is broken for the Guadalajara México Temple. Elder Eran A. Call, a member of the Second Quorum of the Seventy and President of the Mexico North Area presides over the ceremony.

JUNE 13

1834 Orson Hyde and Parley P. Pratt meet with Missouri governor Daniel Dunklin in Jefferson City to discuss the governor's commitment to assist in restoring the Saints to Jackson County. The governor refuses to honor his previous pledge of help. With Dunklin's refusal to assist the Saints, the principal objective of Zion's Camp—to protect the Saints once they were restored to their lands—is lost.

1837 Elders Heber C. Kimball and Orson Hyde leave Kirtland, Ohio, with Willard Richards, Joseph Fielding, John Goodson, John Snyder, and Isaac Russell to begin the first mission to Great Britain.

1840 Don Carlos Smith is born to Joseph Smith Jr. and Emma Hale Smith in Nauvoo, Illinois.

An artist's rendition of the proposed Salt Lake Temple (see 1857).

1857 The *Illustrated London News* publishes a drawing of the proposed Salt Lake Temple, a sketch that will be reproduced for decades as the temple slowly moves toward completion in 1893.

1963 President David O. McKay sets apart Ernest J. Wilkins as the president of the Language Training Mission (LTM), the forerunner of the Missionary Training Center (MTC). Spanish and Portuguese language missionaries attend as early as 16 June, with German (1964), Navajo and French (1967), and Italian (1969) added later.

1978 President Spencer W. Kimball rededicates the Laie Hawaii Temple, which had undergone extensive remodeling.

1979 The first converts on the Canary Islands are baptized.

1988 The Church celebrates one hundred years of growth in Samoa.

1997 Elder Richard G. Scott breaks ground for the Boston Massachusetts Temple.

1998 Ground is broken for the Houston Texas Temple. Elder Lynn A. Mickelsen, President of the North America Southwest Area, presides over the ceremony.

JUNE 14

1801 Heber C. Kimball, later a member of the Quorum of the Twelve Apostles and First Presidency, is born in Sheldon, Vermont.

1820 Feramorz Little, later an early Salt Lake City mayor, businessman, and philanthropist, is born in Aurelius, New York.

1828 Joseph Smith completes the translation of the Book of Lehi and allows Martin Harris to take the 116-page manuscript of the translation to show his family in Palmyra. The manuscript is subsequently lost.

1846 On the ship *Brooklyn,* filled with Latter-day Saints bound for California, a baby girl is born to Phebe and John Robbins and is named Georgiana Pacific Robbins.

1847 The first pioneer company begins crossing the North Platte River at present-day Casper, Wyoming, taking three days to get the entire company across.

1850 Elder Erastus Snow and his companion arrive in Copenhagen, Denmark, where they join Peter O. Hansen as the first missionaries to Denmark and Scandinavia.

1856 The ship *Thornton* arrives in New York City with 764 Saints led by James G. Willie. Most in the company are those who later make up the ill-fated Martin and Willie handcart companies, which become stranded on their way to Utah later that year.

1860 Latter-day Saints arrive in present-day Franklin, Idaho, and establish the first town in Idaho.

1900 The Scandinavian Jubilee—the fiftieth anniversary of the introduction of the gospel in Scandinavian countries—is celebrated in the Tabernacle in Salt Lake City.

Florence Hansen, ca. 1980 (see 1920).

1920 Florence Lambert Peterson (Hansen), later the sculptress who created many well-known works, including *Joseph and Emma* and *Teaching with Love,* and creator of Hansen Classic porcelain sculptures, is born in Salt Lake City, Utah.

1932 Athos M. Amorim, later a member of the Second Quorum of the Seventy, is born in Rio de Janeiro, Brazil.

1969 The Germany Dresden Mission is organized.

1985 President Gordon B. Hinckley of the First Presidency rededicates the remodeled Manti Temple (later the Manti Utah Temple).

1998 The Mormon Tabernacle Choir begins a seven-nation tour of Europe.

1999 The First Presidency announces plans to build a temple adjacent to the Winter Quarters burial ground, in Omaha, Nebraska.

~*~ ~*~ ~*~ **JUNE** ~*~ ~*~ ~*~
15

1828 Emma Smith gives birth to her and Joseph's first son, Alvin. The child dies the same day.

1850 The first edition of the *Deseret News,* the Church newspaper, is published in Salt Lake City.

Printing of the First Deseret News, *by Paul Clowes (see 1850).*

1855 Thomas S. Smith and his company of settlers found Fort Limhi, on the Salmon River in Idaho. The fort becomes the headquarters for missionaries laboring among the Native Americans in the area.

1901 Ezra Christiansen Dalby is appointed the fifth president of Ricks College.

1905 The Swedish Mission is organized.

1922 Morris K. Udall, later an Arizona representative in the U.S. Congress (1961–89) and a U.S. presidential candidate, is born in St. Johns, Arizona.

1929 The Mormon Tabernacle Choir begins radio broadcasts.

1969 The Pago Pago Stake, the first stake in American Samoa, is organized, with Patrick Peters as president.

1989 Elder Russell M. Nelson breaks ground in Warsaw for the first Latter-day Saint meetinghouse in Poland.

JUNE 16

1834 Joseph Smith leads Zion's Camp across the Grand River in northern Missouri.

1844 Joseph Smith addresses the Saints in Nauvoo once in the morning and once in the afternoon, preaching on the nature of God and asking citizens from the state and nation to support Saints in their constitutional rights.

1854 Workmen begin to lay the foundation for the Salt Lake Temple.

1894 The first Maori Saints to immigrate to Utah leave Auckland, New Zealand.

1962 Wally Joyner, later a professional baseball player and the first rookie ever to be voted to start in the all-star game, is born in Atlanta, Georgia.

1974 The Copenhagen Denmark Stake, the first stake in Denmark, is organized, with Johan Helge Benthin as president.

1985 A site is dedicated for the first meetinghouse in the Carribean islands of St. Vincent and the Grenadines.

JUNE 17

1854 John Bernhisel gives a public address in Salt Lake City reporting that Senator Chase of Ohio said of Brigham Young, "No governor had ever done so well by the Indians since William Penn, as Governor Young" (in B. H. Roberts, *Comprehensive History of the Church,* 4:52).

1883 Elbert D. Thomas, later a Utah member of the U.S. Senate (1932–50), is born in Salt Lake City, Utah.

1888 The Samoan Mission is organized.

1934 John H. Groberg, later a member of the First Quorum of the Seventy, is born in Idaho Falls, Idaho.

Mark H. Willes, ca. 1999 (see 1941).

1941 Mark H. Willes, later chairman, president, and chief executive officer of Times Mirror, is born in Salt Lake City, Utah.

1978 The first area conference in the United States is held in Hawaii.

1996 *Time* magazine publishes its list of the twenty-five most influential Americans. Among those noted is Steven R. Covey (a former BYU professor, author of *7 Habits of Highly Effective People,* and founder of the Covey Leadership Center).

1844 Because of serious threats made by the enemies of the Church, Joseph Smith orders the Nauvoo Legion to protect Nauvoo and addresses the men, giving his last public discourse.

1850 Elder John Taylor and other missionaries arrive in Boulogne-sur-mer, France, to open the French Mission.

1879 Stephen L Richards, later a member of the Quorum of the Twelve Apostles and First Presidency, is born in Mendon, Utah.

1937 L. Edward Brown, later a member of the Second Quorum of the Seventy, is born in Preston, Idaho.

Carl W. Buehner, Joseph L. Wirthlin, and Thorpe B. Isaacson of the Presiding Bishopric at the dedication of the Aaronic Priesthood Restoration Monument (see 1960).

1960 Presiding Bishop Joseph L. Wirthlin dedicates the Aaronic Priesthood Restoration Monument on the banks of the Susquehanna River in Pennsylvania.

1978 The Montreal Quebec Stake, the first stake in Quebec, Canada, is organized, with Gerard C. Pelchat as president.

1983 The first meetinghouse on Prince Edward Island, Canada, is completed.

1995 The Bangkok Thailand Stake, the first stake in Thailand, is organized, with Thipparad Kitsaward as president.

1834 Five Missouri vigilantes visit Zion's Camp, swearing the camp will be destroyed that night. As the men leave, the previously cloudless sky becomes stormy, causing Fishing River and Little Fishing River to rise more than forty feet in one night, deterring the planned attack.

1836 Lorenzo Snow is baptized in the Chargrin River near Kirtland, Ohio. (He is twenty-two years and two months old.)

1853 The first branch in Iceland is organized on Westmann Island.

1880 Louise Bouton Felt is called as the first general president of the Primary, with Matilda Morehouse W. Barratt and Clare Cordelia Moses Cannon as counselors. Elmina Shepherd Taylor is called as the first general president of the Young Women's Mutual Improvement Association (predecessor to the Young Women organization), with Margaret Young Taylor and Martha Horne Tingey as counselors.

1930 James O. Mason, later a member of the Second Quorum of the Seventy, is born in Salt Lake City, Utah.

1936 Merrill J. Bateman, later BYU president, the Presiding Bishop of the Church, and a member of the First Quorum of the Seventy, is born in Lehi, Utah.

1940 Susan Michaelene Packer (Grassli), later the eighth general president of the Primary, is born in Salt Lake City, Utah.

1951 *Look* magazine publishes Gordon B. Hinckley's response to an article "The Mormons: We Are a Peculiar People," one of his earliest exposures in the national media.

1955 The New Orleans Stake, the first stake in Louisiana, is organized, with Clive M. Larson as president.

1959 The First Presidency issues a formal statement urging Latter-day Saints to keep the Sabbath holy and specifically to abstain from shopping on Sunday.

1988 The Church gives the Salt Lake Twenty-Fifth Ward building to the Salvation Army to assist the charitable organization in its work.

1998 The First Presidency directs the bishops of the Church to confirm new converts in a sacrament meeting soon after their baptism.

BYU President Merrill J. Bateman (center) at a university commencement exercise, flanked by Elder Henry B. Eyring (left) and Elder M. Russell Ballard (right) (see 1936).

1846 The ship *Brooklyn,* transporting over two hundred Saints to California, arrives at Honolulu, Sandwich Islands.

1849 Franklin S. Richards, later the first general counsel of the Church (a position created to advise Church leaders on legal matters), is born in Salt Lake City, Utah.

1869 The Paris Stake, the first stake in Idaho, is organized, with David P. Kimball as president.

1917 David S. King, later a Utah representative in the U.S. Congress (1958–62) and U.S. ambassador (Malagasy, 1967; Mauritius, 1968), is born in Salt Lake City, Utah. King was the son of William H. King, a Utah member of the U.S. Senate.

1945 David S. Monson, later a Utah representative in the U.S. Congress (1984–86), is born in Salt Lake City, Utah.

1974 The country of Luxembourg becomes part of the Belgium Brussels Mission.

1982 The Mormon Tabernacle Choir sings in Royal Albert Hall in London, England.

1983 The West Indies Mission is organized.

1985 President Gordon B. Hinckley dedicates the Freiberg Germany Temple, the only temple built in a communist country.

The Freiberg Germany Temple, ca. 1991 (see 1985).

1987 In a letter sent to priesthood leaders, the First Presidency defines the organizational structure of ward Young Women presidencies and requests consistent midweek activities for Young Women.

1992 Elder James E. Faust breaks ground for the Orlando Florida Temple.

1998 Ground is broken for the Albuquerque New Mexico Temple. Elder Lynn A. Mickelsen, a member of the First Quorum of the Seventy and President of the North America Southwest Area, presides over the ceremony.

▶ *Stereoscope with box set of "The Latter Day Saints" tour stereo cards (see 1904).*

1834 Colonel John Sconce and two other leading men of Ray County, Missouri, visit Joseph Smith at Zion's Camp. Sconce relates that he had been on his way to destroy the Mormons but was stopped by the storm on the night of 19 June. He acknowledges the hand of God in the storm and asks Joseph Smith what the intentions of Zion's Camp were. After Joseph relates the tribulations of the Missouri Saints and his intention to assist them and to restore them to their lands, Sconce promises to use his influence to disperse the mobs.

1898 Spencer Dewey Adams, later the first Latter-day Saint in baseball's major leagues (with the 1923 Pittsburgh Pirates) and the first to play in the World Series (1925), is born in Layton, Utah.

1904 Discussions between the First Presidency and promoters begin regarding the feasibility of creating a complete stereo-view set of Mormon history sites. Eventually "The Latter Day Saints' Tour from Palmyra, New York to Salt Lake City, Utah through the Stereoscope" with a booklet written by Elder B. H. Roberts describing Church historical sites and providing historical background is completed and sold nationally and internationally by Underwood & Underwood of Ottawa, Kansas, the largest producer of this popular medium.

1937 Jon M. Huntsman, later an international businessman and philanthropist, is born in Blackfoot, Idaho.

1960 Evan Goulding, a Ricks College student, wins the national calf roping championship at the National Intercollegiate Rodeo Association finals.

JUNE 22

1793 Edward Hunter, later the Presiding Bishop of the Church, is born in Newtown, Pennsylvania.

1806 Aaron Johnson, later a municipal court judge, captain of nearly six hundred pioneers, and founder of Springville, Utah, is born in Haddam, Connecticut.

1834 Joseph Smith receives Doctrine and Covenants 105, calling for the disbanding of Zion's Camp and indicating that Zion would not be redeemed at this time.

The Granite Mountain Records Vault (see 1966).

1844 Illinois Governor Thomas Ford meets with Elder John Taylor and John M. Bernhisel to discuss the destruction of the *Nauvoo Expositor* and the state of affairs in Hancock County. At midnight, Joseph and Hyrum Smith cross the Mississippi River into Iowa, intending to travel to the Rocky Mountains and scout out a place of refuge for the Saints.

1851 Elder George Q. Cannon baptizes the first converts on the island of Maui. Elder Joseph Richards baptizes the first converts in Calcutta, India.

1966 President Hugh B. Brown of the First Presidency dedicates the Granite Mountain Records Vault, a special facility for preserving important genealogical records, located in Little Cottonwood Canyon, east of Salt Lake City, Utah.

1986 President Thomas S. Monson of the First Presidency organizes the sixteen hundredth stake of the Church in Kitchener, Ontario, Canada, with Graeme K. Hingston as president.

1991 President Gordon B. Hinckley of the First Presidency rededicates the renovated Alberta Temple (later the Cardston Alberta Temple).

JUNE 23

1799 John Milton Bernhisel, later Utah's first delegate to the U.S. House of Representatives (1851–59, 1861–63), is born in Pennsylvania.

1844 Joseph and Hyrum Smith return to Nauvoo from Iowa, submit to Illinois authorities, and consent to appear in court at Carthage on a charge of inciting a riot when the press of the *Nauvoo Expositor* was destroyed on 10 June.

President Gordon B. Hinckley, ca. 1995 (see 1910).

1910 Gordon B. Hinckley, later a member of the Quorum of the Twelve Apostles and the fifteenth President of the Church, is born in Salt Lake City, Utah.

1956 Missionary work recommences in Chile, some 104 years after Elder Parley P. Pratt had left the country following an unsuccessful attempt to establish a permanent mission.

1968 The Maine Stake, the first stake in Maine, is organized, with Olie W. Ross as president.

1973 Golfer Johnny Miller wins the U.S. Open.

1974 Modifications are made to the administration of the Aaronic Priesthood and the Young Women programs, and the MIA youth programs are discontinued. Ruth Hardy Funk is called as the seventh general president of the Young Women, with Hortense Hogan Child and Ardeth Greene Kapp as counselors.

1979 The first area conference in the continental United States is held in Houston, Texas.

1994 Jeffrey R. Holland is ordained an Apostle, replacing Marvin J. Ashton, who had died.

▶ *The Willard Richards family, 26 March 1845 (see 1804).*

JUNE 24

1789 Zera Pulsipher, later one of the First Seven Presidents of the Seventy, is born in Rockingham, Vermont.

1804 Willard Richards, later a member of the Quorum of the Twelve Apostles and the First Presidency, is born in Hopkinton, Massachusetts.

1834 Cholera spreads through Zion's Camp, attacking sixty-eight Saints and resulting in fifteen deaths. When Joseph Smith tries to heal the brethren by the laying on of hands, he himself is taken ill and learns that he should not attempt to interfere with a decree from God.

1844 Joseph and Hyrum Smith leave Nauvoo at 6:30 A.M. for Carthage and are met by Captain Dunn, who requests that they return to Nauvoo to encourage the Nauvoo Legion to give up arms loaned to them by the state. They finally arrive in Carthage a few minutes before midnight and spend the night at the Hamilton House Hotel.

1931 William "Billy" Earl Casper, later a professional golfer, PGA champion, and winner of the Masters, is born in San Diego, California.

1984 Members of the First Quorum of the Seventy are grouped into Area Presidencies throughout the thirteen major geographical areas of the Church.

1988 Hungary grants the Church legal recognition.

1990 Missionaries organize a group of Saints in the African nation of Botswana, prior to receiving the legal recognition required to organize a formal branch.

1991 The Russian Republic in the Soviet Union announces its formal recognition of the Church after the Mormon Tabernacle Choir's concert in Moscow's Bolshoi Theater.

JUNE 25

1833 Joseph Smith provides the plat of the "City of Zion," featuring square blocks, large home lots, and streets running in the four cardinal directions. The design is intended to serve a city of up to twenty thousand inhabitants and becomes the basic model for LDS settlements in the Intermountain West.

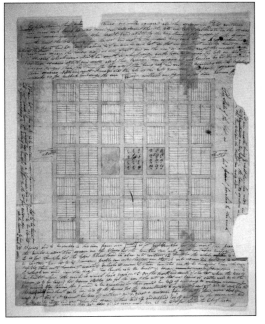

"City of Zion" plat, 1833.

1844 The Prophet Joseph Smith and Hyrum Smith appear in court in Carthage. Through legal manipulation, they are sent to Carthage Jail on a charge of treason. They are first confined to the criminal's cell, but because of crowded conditions, they are later placed in the more comfortable debtor's cell.

1850 Elder Lorenzo Snow of the Quorum of the Twelve Apostles and his companions arrive in Genoa, Italy, opening missionary work in that land.

1869 The first group of LDS immigrants to make the trip to Utah by rail reaches Ogden.

1900 In Rexburg, Idaho, President George Q. Cannon of the First Presidency lays the cornerstone for the Spori Building at the Bannock Stake Academy (later Ricks College).

1966 The Bermuda Branch, the first branch in Bermuda, is organized.

1976 As a goodwill gesture by the state of Missouri to symbolically apologize for past abuse to Latter-day Saints, Missouri governor Christopher S. Bonds signs an executive order rescinding the infamous "extermination order" issued in October 1838 by Governor Lilburn W. Boggs.

1989 The Church creates the Tecalco Stake, the one hundredth stake in Mexico, making Mexico the first country outside the United States to have one hundred stakes.

1817 George A. Smith, later a member of the Quorum of the Twelve Apostles and First Presidency, is born in Potsdam, New York.

1829 The title page of the Book of Mormon appears in print for the first time in the *Wayne Sentinel,* a paper published in Palymra, New York.

1844 Joseph and Hyrum Smith and friends are moved to the jailor's bedroom on the second floor of the Carthage Jail and spend much of the day in conversation with attorneys, visitors to the jail, and Illinois governor Thomas Ford.

1855 The Indian Territory Mission is organized, with headquarters in Independence, Missouri.

1856 The Saints that will make up the Willie handcart company arrive in Iowa City to outfit themselves for their journey west.

Handcart pioneers, ca. 1874 (see 1856).

1858 After having been stopped for the winter by the delay tactics of the Utah territorial milita, General Albert Sidney Johnston's army finally enters the abandoned Salt Lake Valley. There is no conflict, and the army moves on to establish Camp Floyd in Cedar Valley in Utah County.

1880 Latter-day Saint pioneers on their way to settle southern Utah begin taking wagons through Hole-in-the-Rock, a narrow passageway cut by the Saints through the stone wall of Glenn Canyon.

1948 General Mark Clark, commander of the ninth army, attends a memorial service in Garland, Utah, honoring Clyde, LeRoy, and twins Rolon and Rulon Borgstrom—four brothers killed during a six-month period in World War II. President George Albert Smith is the principal speaker.

1961 At the first world seminar for mission presidents, *A Uniform System for Teaching Investigators* is introduced, as is the "every member a missionary" program. The conference in Salt Lake City lasts until 27 July.

1988 The Saint John New Brunswick Stake, the first stake in New Brunswick, Canada, is organized with Blaine E. Hatt as president.

1993 Ground is broken for the Bogotá Colombia Temple (later the Bogotá D.C. Colombia Temple). Elder William R. Bradford, a member of the First Quorum of the Seventy and President of the South America North Area presides over the ceremony.

1994 President Howard W. Hunter, President Gordon B. Hinckley of the First Presidency, and Elder M. Russell Ballard commemorate the sesquicentennial of the martyrdom of Joseph and Hyrum Smith in three separate speeches given during remembrance events in Nauvoo and Carthage, Illinois.

The Martyrdom of Joseph and Hyrum, *by Gary Smith (see 1844).*

1844 A mob kills Joseph and Hyrum Smith at Carthage Jail. John Taylor, in an eyewitness account of the martyrdom now found in Doctrine and Covenants 135, declared: "To seal the testimony of this book [the Doctrine and Covenants] and the Book of Mormon, we announce the martyrdom of Joseph Smith the Prophet, and Hyrum Smith the Patriarch" (v. 1).

1847 The first company of pioneers crosses the Continental Divide at South Pass and meets Moses "Black" Harris, a mountain man who had lived in the West for twenty-five years.

1934 Dennis E. Simmons, later a member of the Second Quorum of the Seventy, is born in Beaver Dam, Utah.

1972 Latter-day Saint missionaries enter the Southeast Asian country of Malaysia for the first time.

1975 During the opening session of the June 1975 auxiliary conference, the Church announces that it is to be the last of such conferences and will be replaced with annual regional meetings for priesthood and auxiliary leaders.

1989 One hundred and forty-five years after the martyrdom of Joseph and Hyrum Smith, President Gordon B. Hinckley of the First Presidency dedicates the restored Carthage Jail complex in Illinois.

1993 President Gordon B. Hinckley of the First Presidency rededicates the refurbished and remodeled Hotel Utah, renaming it the Joseph Smith Memorial Building. Used primarily for Church offices and meeting facilities, it also contains a five-hundred-seat theater for the presentation of full-length Church films, the first of which being the 1993 drama *Legacy* (directed by Academy Award–winning film director Kieth Merrill, with the muscial score by Merrill Jenson).

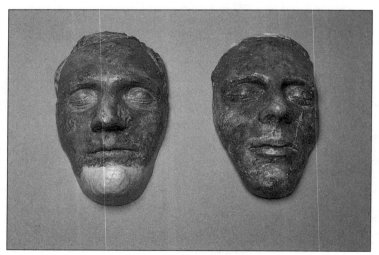

▶ *Death masks of the Prophet Joseph Smith (right) and Hyrum Smith (left), prepared by George Cannon (see 1844).*

JUNE 28

1813 Orrin Porter Rockwell, later a bodyguard of Joseph Smith and Church folk hero, is born in Belcher, Massachusetts.

1830 Emma Smith, Joseph and Polly Knight, and twelve others are baptized in Colesville, New York.

1844 The day after the martyrdom, George Cannon (father of Church leader George Q. Cannon) makes death masks of Joseph and Hyrum Smith, providing historians with a valuable source of information about the two men's facial features.

1847 The first pioneer company leaves the Oregon Trail. Rather than taking the Sublette cut-off on the Oregon Trail, the group veers west towards Fort Bridger. After crossing the Little Sandy, the company meets Jim Bridger and discusses with him the possibility of settlement in the Great Basin.

1854 Evan Stephens, later the Mormon Tabernacle Choir conductor for twenty-six years (1890–1916) and a composer, is born in Pencader, Wales.

1875 John H. Taylor, one of the First Seven Presidents of the Seventy, is born in Salt Lake City, Utah.

1902 The Middle States Mission is organized.

1953 The Butte Stake, the first stake in Montana, is organized, with Edgar T. Henderson as president.

1978 President Spencer W. Kimball dedicates the Monument to Women at the Nauvoo Visitors' Center.

JUNE 29

1836 During a mass meeting in Clay County, Missouri, citizens accuse their Latter-day Saint neighbors of the same charges raised in Jackson County and pass a resolution asking them to leave the county to avoid bloodshed.

1844 Before a public funeral, about ten thousand Saints view the bodies of Joseph and Hyrum Smith at the Mansion House in Nauvoo. Afterwards two decoy coffins are filled with sand and buried. At about midnight the coffins containing the bodies are buried secretly in the basement of the unfinished Nauvoo House.

1890 Henry A. Dixon, later a Utah representative in the U.S. Congress (1954–60), is born in Provo, Utah.

1933 David E. Sorensen, later a member of the Presidency of the Seventy, is born in Aurora, Utah.

1935 Wm. Rolfe Kerr, a member of the First Quorum of the Seventy, is born in Tremonton, Utah.

1936 Harmon Clayton Killebrew, later a professional baseball star and inductee into the National Baseball Hall of Fame, is born in Payette, Idaho.

1960 Elder Bruce R. McConkie sets apart his son, Joseph Fielding McConkie, a nineteen-year-old, for his mission. This begins the policy of extending calls on a regular basis to nineteen-year-old young men as full-time missionaries.

1993 The government of Mexico formally registers the Church, granting it all the rights of a religious organization, including the right to own property.

1995 Elder L. Tom Perry breaks ground for the new John Taylor Religion Building at Ricks College in Rexburg, Idaho.

JUNE 30

1830 Samuel Smith, the first missionary to preach the gospel after the organization of the Church, begins his mission, selling copies of the Book of Mormon in several New York communities.

1847 Samuel Brannan meets Brigham Young and the first pioneer company at the Green River in present-day Wyoming and updates the Church leaders about the Saints who traveled to California on the ship *Brooklyn* the previous year. In an unsuccessful effort to convince Brigham and the others to locate Church headquarters in California, Brannan extols the virtues of the West Coast and relates all that the Saints living there had accomplished.

1916 The First Presidency and the Quorum of the Twelve Apostles issue "The Father and the Son: A Doctrinal Exposition by the First Presidency and the Twelve" on the identity and relationship of God the Father and Jesus Christ.

1931 L. Aldin Porter, later a member of the Presidency of the Seventy, is born in Salt Lake City, Utah.

1935 The Oahu Stake, the first stake outside of North America and the first stake in Hawaii, is organized, with Ralph E. Wooley as president.

1940 The Washington Stake, the first stake in the District of Columbia, is organized, with Ezra Taft Benson as president. At this time, Benson is serving as the executive secretary of the National Council of Farmer Cooperatives.

1941 Kwok Yuen Tai, later a member of the Second Quorum of the Seventy and the first Chinese General Authority, is born in Hong Kong.

1947 W. Craig Zwick, later a member of the First Quorum of the Seventy, is born in Salt Lake City, Utah.

1957 The Virginia Stake, the first stake in Virginia, is organized, with Cashell Donahoe Sr. as president.

1970 The BYU's men's track and field team wins the NCAA national championship; it is the first time a BYU athletic team has won a national title.

Shawn Bradley, ca. 1990 (see 1993).

1977 Alexandre Mourra, the first Haitian convert, is baptized.

1993 Shawn Bradley, a returned missionary and former BYU basketball player is drafted second overall by the Philadelphia 76ers in the first round of the NBA draft, the highest any LDS basketball player has ever been drafted. Josh Grant, a returned missionary and former University of Utah player, is drafted in the second round by the Denver Nuggets.

JULY 1

1829 Joseph Smith completes the translation of the Book of Mormon.

1837 Elders Heber C. Kimball, Orson Hyde, Willard Richards, Joseph Fielding, and three Canadian converts, John Goodson, Isaac Russell, and John Snyder, set sail on the ship *Garrick* for Liverpool, where they will begin the first proselyting mission to England.

1846 At Mosquito Creek (near Council Bluffs, Iowa) Captain James Allen of the U.S. Army discusses with Brigham Young the government's proposal to enlist five hundred Mormon volunteers for the war with Mexico.

1850 The first regular overland mail service west of the Missouri River begins, running between Independence, Missouri, and Salt Lake City, Utah.

1855 Orson F. Whitney, later a member of the Quorum of the Twelve Apostles, is born in Salt Lake City, Utah.

1857 Martha Maria Hughes (Cannon), later a women's rights activist, medical school graduate, and the first woman in the United States to be elected to a state senate (Utah), is born in Llandudno, Wales.

1866 President Brigham Young ordains Joseph F. Smith an Apostle. He serves as an additional counselor to Brigham Young until 1877 but is not set apart as a member of the Quorum of the Twelve Apostles until 8 October 1867, when he fills the vacancy created by the excommunication of Amasa M. Lyman.

1880 Martha Hughes Cannon receives a medical degree from Michigan Medical School. In August 1878, she had been set apart by President John Taylor to obtain this training.

1919 The Canadian Mission is organized.

1921 Franklin S. Harris begins his term as the fourth president of BYU.

1943 Coleen K. Kent (Menlove), later the tenth general president of the Primary, is born in Salt Lake City, Utah.

1945 Howard S. McDonald begins his term as the fifth president of BYU.

1948 Finland grants the Church legal status.

1954 Michael D. Reid, later a BYU all-American in golf (1974–75) and a PGA player (winning victories in 1987 and 1988), is born in Bainbridge, Maryland.

1967–99 Reflecting the growth of missionary work throughout the world, 209 missions are organized on this date between 1967–99. With the exceptions of 1972, 1973, 1981, and 1982, there was at least one mission created every year during this period, and there were several organized in many of the years. The largest number of new missions created was in 1990, with twenty-eight new missions organized. Among the missions organized on this day during this thirty-three-year period are the Chile Concepcion (1975), Ghana Accra (1985), Zaire Kinshasa (1987), Hungary Budapest (1990), Poland Warsaw (1990), Albania Tirana (1996), Madagascar Antananarivo (1998), and Armenia Yeredevan (1999) Missions.

1971 Henry B. Eyring is appointed tenth president of Ricks College.

1989 Rex E. Lee begins his term as the ninth president of BYU.

JULY 2

1833 Joseph Smith completes the translation of the Old Testament, finishing his revision of the Bible.

1834 Joseph Smith meets with a number of men from Zion's Camp and promises them that if they will humble themselves, covenant to keep the commandments, and obey the counsel of the Lord, the cholera will be stayed the same hour. The men heed Joseph's words, and the plague ends.

Memorial marker to Zion's Camp cholera victims in Mound Grove Cemetery, Independence, Missouri (see 1834).

1839 While instructing the Twelve, Joseph Smith teaches for the first time that the angel Gabriel was the ancient prophet Noah.

1849 In Salt Lake City, the general assembly of the provisional state of Deseret meets for the first time.

1899 Following Lorenzo Snow's 8 May revelation on tithing, General Authorities and stake and ward leaders gather for a solemn assembly held in the Salt Lake Temple and resolve to accept and keep the law of tithing as a commandment of the Lord.

1917 Leonard J. Arrington, later a prominent LDS historian whose works include books on Idaho history, Brigham Young, and Church economics, is born near Twin Falls, Idaho.

1947 Sterling VanWagenen, director of the first U.S. film festival (it would later become known as the Sundance Film Festival) and producer of *The Trip to Bountiful* (1985), is born.

1964 For the first time, Latter-day Saint missionaries enter Macao, an enclave administered by Portugal near the mouth of China's Canton River.

1972 President Joseph Fielding Smith dies at age ninety-five in Salt Lake City, after serving for more than sixty-two years as a General Authority.

1985 President Gordon B. Hinckley of the First Presidency dedicates the Stockholm Sweden Temple.

1994 The Church participates in relief efforts in the aftermath of the worst recorded flooding in Georgia.

✦✦✦ JULY 3 ✦✦✦

1834 Joseph Smith authorizes General Lyman Wight to give a discharge to every man of Zion's Camp who had proved faithful. Joseph Smith also organizes the Clay-Caldwell Stake, the first stake in Missouri, with David Whitmer as president and William W. Phelps and John Whitmer as assistant presidents. Members of the Missouri high council were Christian Whitmer, Newel Knight, Lyman Wight, Calvin Beebe, William E. McLellin, Solomon Hancock, Thomas B. Marsh, Simeon Carter, Parley P. Pratt, Orson Pratt, John Murdock, and Levi Jackman.

1835 Michael H. Chandler arrives in Kirtland to display four Egyptian mummies and some scrolls of papyrus containing hieroglyphics. These are later purchased, and by revelation Joseph translates the Book of Abraham from the preserved items.

1870 Albert Carrington is ordained an Apostle, replacing Ezra T. Benson, who had died.

1955 The South Australian Mission is organized.

1973 The Michigan Mission is organized.

1976 The Spain Seville and the Texas Houston Missions are organized.

1999 Ground is broken for the Oklahoma City Oklahoma Temple. Elder Rex D. Pinegar, a member of the First Quorum of the Seventy and President of the North America Southwest Area, presides over the ceremonies.

1838 The Saints celebrate the national holiday by laying the cornerstone for the Far West Temple in Far West, Missouri, and participate in meetings which include Sidney Rigdon's fiery speech later known as the "Mormon Declaration of Independence."

1839 Having been imprisoned since November 1838, Parley P. Pratt and Morris Phelps escape from jail in Columbia, Missouri, while the community is involved in a patriotic celebration.

1845 Jennetta Richards, wife of Elder Willard Richard, dies in Nauvoo and is buried the following day; she is apparently the first woman to be dressed in her temple clothing for burial.

1852 A wagon train carrying machinery that John Taylor had purchased in France for a sugar factory in Utah leaves Ft. Leavenworth, Kansas. Although the machinery arrives safely in Utah, a combination of events prevents the Saints from manufacturing sugar in Utah at this time.

1887 Fireworks at Temple Square set the roof of the Tabernacle on fire, but little damage is done.

1919 William Harrison "Jack" Dempsey, the first Latter-day Saint world boxing champion, wins the Heavyweight Boxing World Championship, maintaining his hold on the title until 1926.

1975 The Iran Tehran Mission is organized.

1976 President Spencer W. Kimball addresses over twenty-three thousand people attending the Church-sponsored U.S. bicentennial devotional at the Capitol Centre in Landover, Maryland.

1988 The Mormon Tabernacle Choir returns home from a tour of Hawaii, Australia, and New Zealand, during which the choir performed nineteen times in twenty-one days.

1866 Charles H. Hart, later one of the First Seven Presidents of the Seventy and the first General Authority to have received a law degree, is born in Bloomington, Idaho.

1873 Zion's Savings Bank and Trust is organized, with Brigham Young serving as president.

1940 Kenneth Johnson, later a member of the First Quorum of the Seventy, is born in Norwich, England.

1976 The New Zealand Christchurch Mission is organized.

◄ *The Far West Temple cornerstone (see 1838).*

1838 The last group of Saints in Kirtland, known as the Kirtland Camp or the poor camp, leaves for Missouri.

1851 The Saints gather in a sycamore grove and organize the San Bernardino Stake, the first stake in California, with David Seely as president.

1926 Neal A. Maxwell, later the Church commissioner of education and a member of the Quorum of the Twelve Apostles, is born in Salt Lake City, Utah

1971 The Italy North Mission is organized.

1986 New missionary discussions are issued for use in the English-speaking missions of the Church.

1992 Latter-day Saint career scouter Rees A. Falkner is named national director of the Boy Scouts of America.

San Bernardino sketch, ca. 1853 (see 1851).

1803 David Fullmer, an early Church and civic leader in Salt Lake City, is born in Chillisquaque, Pennsylvania.

1852 The temple endowment is performed in Salt Lake City in the newly completed "Council House." This is the first time the endowment is available to the general Church membership since the exodus of the Saints from Nauvoo.

1854 Rulon S. Wells, later one of the First Seven Presidents of the Seventy, is born in Salt Lake City, Utah.

1904 Charles W. Penrose is ordained a member of the Twelve, replacing Abraham O. Woodruff, who had died.

1906 Abraham Fernanadez baptizes ex-Queen Liliuokalani of Hawaii, the first monarch to join the Church.

1946 LDS military servicemen baptize Tatsui, Chiyo, and Yasuo Sato, the first converts in Japan in twenty years. This ushers in a new period of Church activity in Japan.

1967 Ted E. Brewerton, president of the Guatemala–El Salvador Mission, sends Elders Neil Gruwell, David Bell, Fred Podlesny, and Floyd Baum to Venezuela as that country's first missionaries.

1968 The Brazilian North Mission is organized.

1969 The California East Mission is organized.

1972 Harold B. Lee is ordained and set apart as the eleventh President of the Church, with N. Eldon Tanner and Marion G. Romney as Counselors.

1979 The Puerto Rico San Juan Mission is organized.

1988 Vance Law is named to the National League's all-star baseball team after a very successful year in the majors.

JULY 8

1776 Lucy Mack (Smith), later the mother of Joseph and Hyrum Smith, is born in Gilsum, New Hampshire.

1808 Alexander Doniphan, later a military leader, legal council to Joseph Smith, and friend to the Latter-day Saints in Missouri, is born in Mason County, Kentucky.

1838 Joseph Smith receives four revelations: Doctrine and Covenants 117, instructing William Marks and Newel K. Whitney to move to Missouri; Doctrine and Covenants 118, calling John Taylor, John E. Page, Wilford Woodruff, and Willard Richards to the Quorum of the Twelve Apostles and instructing the Twelve to conduct a mission to Great Britain and to leave from Far West, Missouri, on 26 April 1839; Doctrine and Covenants 119, instructing the Saints on the law of tithing; and Doctrine and Covenants 120, appointing the council on the disposition of tithes to consist of the First Presidency, the Quorum of the Twelve, and the Presiding Bishopric.

1856 The Saints that later make up the Martin handcart company arrive at Iowa City to outfit themselves for their journey west.

1879 Hyrum Gibbs Smith, son of Hyrum Fisher and Annie Maria Gibbs Smith and later the fifth Patriarch of the Church, is born in South Jordan, Utah.

1907 George Romney, later the president of American Motors, governor of Michigan, U.S. presidential candidate, and secretary of housing and urban development, is born in Colonia Dublan, Mexico.

1912 Representing the United States, Alma Richards wins the gold medal in the high jump at the Olympic Games held in Sweden. He is the first Latter-day Saint to win an Olympic medal.

Coach E. L. "Gene" Roberts and Alma Richards, ca. 1912 (see 1912).

1916 The Tongan Mission is organized.

1921 Spencer H. Osborn, later a member of the First Quorum of the Seventy, is born in Salt Lake City, Utah.

1956 Elder Henry D. Moyle organizes the first branch in Peru.

1962 The Irish and Korean Missions are organized.

1978 Missionaries arrive for the first time in the west Pacific country of Palau.

1981 Latter-day Saint Church services are held for the first time in the northern South American country of French Guiana.

JULY 9

1834 With Zion's Camp march concluded, Joseph Smith, Hyrum Smith, Frederick G. Williams, and William E. McLellin leave Clay County, Missouri, for Kirtland.

1841 Joseph Smith receives Doctrine and Covenants 126, informing Brigham Young that his missionary service has been acceptable to the Lord and that he will no longer be required to journey away from his family.

1875 Martin Harris, one of the Three Witnesses of the Book of Mormon, bears testimony of the book while on his deathbed.

1953 The Church announces the organization of the United Church School System (the forerunner to the Church Educational System), with Ernest L. Wilkinson as administrator.

1976 The Japan Okayama Mission is organized.

JULY 10

1804 Emma Hale Smith, wife of the Prophet Joseph Smith and first president of the Nauvoo Female Relief Society, is born in Harmony, Pennsylvania.

1875 At age ninety-two Martin Harris, one of the Three Witnesses of the Book of Mormon, dies in Clarkston, Utah, and is buried with a copy of the Book of Mormon in his right hand and a copy of the Doctrine and Covenants in his left.

1879 The Sunday School Union issues the *Deseret Sunday School Reader* for children.

1949 The Chinese Mission is organized; it is discontinued in 1953.

Emma Hale Smith, ca. 1844 (see 1804).

1966 The California South Mission is organized.

1977 The Italy Catania Mission is organized.

1993 In Laie, Oahu, King Taufa'ahau Tupou IV of Tonga attends the Polynesian Cultural Center's thirtieth anniversary festivities.

JULY 11

1851 Thomas L. Kane, a nonmember friend of the Saints with connections in Washington, D.C., writes a letter to U.S. president Millard Fillmore, defending the character of Brigham Young.

1931 Ray H. Wood, later a member of the Second Quorum of the Seventy, is born in Salt Lake City, Utah.

1933 Cree-L Kofford, later a member of the First Quorum of the Seventy, is born in Santaquin, Utah.

1970 The Spain Mission is organized.

1996 President Gordon B. Hinckley begins a tour of early Church history sites.

Thomas L. Kane (see 1851).

JULY 12

1771 Joseph Smith Sr., later father of the Prophet Joseph Smith, the first Patriarch to the Church, one of the Eight Witnesses of the Book of Mormon, and Assistant Counselor to the First Presidency, is born in Topsfield, Massachusetts.

1797 John Gaylord, later one of the First Seven Presidents of the Seventy, is born in Pennsylvania.

1843 At the request of his brother Hyrum, Joseph Smith dictates to William Clayton the revelation on the power of the priesthood to seal husbands and wives for time and eternity, later known as Doctrine and Covenants 132.

1925 The North Central States Mission is organized.

1943 John B. Dickson, later a member of the First Quorum of the Seventy, is born in Tacoma, Washington.

1978 Elaine Anderson Cannon is called as the eighth general president of the Young Women, with Arlene Barlow Darger and Norma Broadbent Smith as counselors.

The general presidency of the Young Women, ca. 1978. From left: Arlene Barlow Darger, President Elaine Anderson Cannon, and Norma Broadbent Smith (see 1978).

1847 An advance party of the first pioneer company, headed by Orson Pratt and consisting of forty-two men and twenty-three wagons, camps at the head of Echo Canyon.

1859 Horace Greeley, editor of the *New York Tribune,* conducts a two-hour interview with Brigham Young. The interview captures national attention when it is published in New York in August, becoming what is considered by some to be the first such interview printed in an American newspaper.

Depiction of Horace Greeley's interview with Brigham Young (see 1859).

1897 ElRay LaVar Christiansen, later an Assistant to the Quorum of the Twelve Apostles, is born in Mayfield, Utah.

1921 Phillip T. Sonntag, later a member of the First and Second Quorums of the Seventy, is born in Salt Lake City, Utah.

1993 Madagascar officially recognizes the Church.

1996 President Gordon B. Hinckley holds a press conference at Council Bluffs, Iowa, and thanks all who supported the Church celebrations and activities surrounding the sesquicentennial anniversary of the exodus of the Latter-day Saints to the West. The same day, President Hinckley dedicates the reconstructed Kanesville Tabernacle in Council Bluffs, Iowa, where Brigham Young had been sustained as the second President of the Church on 27 December 1847.

1997 A parade commemorating the Church's pioneer sesquicentennial takes place in Rome, Italy.

1849 Following the discovery of gold in California, Latter-day Saints at the site send gold dust to Salt Lake City as tithing.

1933 W. Don Ladd, later a member of the Second Quorum of the Seventy, is born in San Mateo, Florida.

1961 The Berlin Mission is organized.

1969 President N. Eldon Tanner of the First Presidency dedicates the Salt Palace in Salt Lake City.

1972 The Quebec Mission is organized.

1992 The Lusaka Branch, the first branch in Zambia, is organized.

▶ *The Mormon Tabernacle Choir, ca. 1999 (see 1929).*

JULY 15

1792 John Murdock, later a close friend of Joseph Smith and the father of the twins Joseph and Emma adopted in 1831, is born in Kortwright, New York.

1856 The Willie handcart company leaves Iowa City for Florence (Winter Quarters), Nebraska.

1891 Brigham Smoot and Alva J. Butler arrive in Tonga as the first Latter-day Saint missionaries to those islands. Exactly one year later they baptize Tonga's first convert.

1916 Ferril A. Kay, later a member of the First Quorum of the Seventy, is born in Annabella, Utah.

1929 The Mormon Tabernacle Choir, with Ted Kimball as announcer, Anthon Lund as conductor, and Edward P. Kimball as organist, has its first broadcast on NBC radio, later switching to KSL radio, on the CBS network.

1968 Latter-day Saint missionaries enter the South Pacific Islands of New Caledonia for the first time.

1973 The Port Vila Branch, the first branch in the southwest Pacific archipelago of Vanuatu, is organized, with Lanipoto Fehoko as president.

1987 The Genealogical Library celebrates the completion of transferring information from the card catalog system to a computer system.

1999 The American Society of Landscape Architects awards the Church a "once-in-a-century" medallion for its landscaping and gardens at Church headquarters in Salt Lake City.

JULY 16

1781 John Smith, Joseph Smith's uncle and the third Patriarch to the Church and first stake president in the Salt Lake Valley, is born in Derryfield, New Hampshire.

1831 The Colesville Branch, the first significant group of Latter-day Saints to locate in Missouri, arrives in Jackson County and settles in Kaw Township (later part of Kansas City).

1846 Ezra T. Benson is ordained an Apostle at Council Bluffs, Iowa, replacing John E. Page, who had apostatized.

1846 The first four companies of the Mormon Battalion begin service in western Iowa.

1847 The Mormon Battalion is formally discharged at Los Angeles.

1852 The first branch in Norway is organized in Osterrisor.

1931 Wayne M. Hancock, later a member of the Second Quorum of the Seventy, is born in Safford, Arizona.

1946 On a hill near Larsmo, Elder Ezra Taft Benson dedicates Finland for the preaching of the gospel.

1975 The Belgium Antwerp Mission is organized.

1988 A monument commemorating the Mormon Battalion is dedicated near Council Bluffs, Iowa; another monument, honoring the Latter-day Saint pioneers who established Nebraska's first community is dedicated in Florence, Nebraska.

1989 The Mormon Tabernacle Choir celebrates sixty years of continuous network radio broadcasting on its Sunday morning program, *Music and the Spoken Word*.

1995 The International Olympic Committee votes to hold the 2002 winter games in Salt Lake City.

1814 William Clayton, later secretary to Joseph Smith and hymn composer ("Come, Come, Ye Saints"), is born in Penwortham, England.

The Deseret Hospital board of directors, ca. 1882 (see 1882).

1882 The Deseret Hospital, the third hospital in Utah and the first Church hospital, is opened by the Relief Society in Salt Lake City.

1894 U.S. president Grover Cleveland signs the Utah Statehood Bill, authorizing Utah to hold a constitutional convention.

1956 Lloyd D. Newell, later the voice for *Music and the Spoken Word*, is born in Provo, Utah.

1992 U.S. president George Bush meets with the First Presidency and members of the Quorum of the Twelve Apostles and in the evening makes a surprise appearance at the Mormon Tabernacle Choir's concert on Temple Square.

1833 A number of prominent men in Independence, Missouri, prepare the "Secret Constitution," in which they state their accusations against the Mormons. The Saints later refer to it as the "Manifesto of the Mob."

1846 Prior to the departure of the Mormon Battalion, a grand ball is held near Council Bluffs, with music supplied by William Pitt's brass band.

1853 The Walker War, a conflict between the Latter-day Saint settlers and local Native Americans, begins near Payson, Utah.

1857 Abraham Smoot, Porter Rockwell, and Judson Stoddard leave Ft. Laramie for Salt Lake City, carrying news of the approach of Johnston's army.

1893 Orrice Abram "Abe" Murdock Jr., later a Utah representative in the U.S. Congress (1933–41) and a U.S. Senator (1940–46), is born in Austin, Nevada.

BYU president Rex E. Lee with U.S. president George Bush in Provo, Utah, 18 July 1992.

1944 Lino Alvarez, later a member of the Second Quorum of the Seventy, is born in Arteaga, Mexico.

1973 The North Carolina Mission is organized.

1976 Amy Steele (Gant), later a BYU volleyball player, a first-team all-American, a first-team academic all-American, and one of the top ten NCAA women athletes of the year (1997), is born in Provo, Utah.

1992 While campaigning in Utah, U.S. president George Bush visits Brigham Young University.

1993 The first meetinghouse in Swaziland is dedicated by Elder Richard P. Lindsay, a member of the Second Quorum of the Seventy and the President of the Africa Area.

▸ *President Joseph Fielding Smith, ca. 1970 (see 1876).*

1778 Samuel Bent, later a member of the Nauvoo high council and the Council of Fifty, is born in Barre, Massachusetts.

1847 From the top of Big Mountain, Orson Pratt and John Brown become the first in Brigham Young's company to see the Salt Lake Valley.

1851 Zerubbabel Snow, Broughton D. Harris, Stephen B. Rose, and Henry R. Day, the first federally appointed officials to the territory of Utah, arrive in the territory.

1867 Swarms of grasshoppers are first sighted in the Salt Lake Valley. The insects quickly begin to devour the settlers' crops.

1876 Joseph Fielding Smith, later a member of the Quorum of the Twelve Apostles and tenth President of the Church, is born in Salt Lake City, Utah.

1884 Joseph Fielding Smith is baptized in City Creek in Salt Lake City, the fourth of four future Presidents to be baptized in this location. (He is eight years old.)

1909 President Joseph F. Smith arrives in Europe to attend the annual Netherlands Mission conference in Rotterdam. To date, this is the largest Church meeting ever held outside the stakes of Zion with members, missionaries, and mission presidents from the Netherlands, Germany, and other European missions attending.

1997 Some three million hours of community service are contributed Churchwide as part of Worldwide Pioneer Heritage Service Day.

JULY 20

1831 Joseph Smith receives Doctrine and Covenants 57, indicating that Jackson County "is the land of promise, and the place for the city of Zion" (v. 2). The revelation also specifies a location for a temple to be built.

1833 Several hundred Jackson County citizens meet and demand that the Saints leave the county. A mob destroys the Church's printing press, which was being used to publish Joseph Smith's revelations, and tars and feathers Bishop Edward Partridge and Charles Allen.

1837 Heber C. Kimball, Orson Hyde, Willard Richards, Joseph Fielding, John Goodson, Isaac Russell, and John Snyder arrive in Liverpool on the ship *Garrick* and organize the first mission in the British Isles, with Heber C. Kimball as president.

1837 Twenty-three converts from Quebec, Canada, emigrate to join the Saints in the United States.

1897 At the beginning of the six-day celebration commemorating the fiftieth anniversary of the pioneers' arrival in the Salt Lake Valley, President Wilford Woodruff dedicates the Brigham Young Monument.

1951 Because the Korean War reduces the number of young elders available to serve as full-time missionaries, the First Presidency issues a call for seventies to help with missionary work.

1985 One hundred thousand people attend a Church dance festival at the Rose Bowl in southern California.

1995 The Presbyterian General Assembly of the United States adopts a resolution that the Church is "a new and emerging religion that expresses allegiance to Jesus Christ in terms used within the Christian tradition." Although it rejects the Church's claim as the only true church, the document does much to heal wounds.

1998 The First Presidency announces that temples will be built in Brisbane, Australia; Hermosillo, Sonora, Mexico; Tampico, Tamaulipas, Mexico; and Kiev, Ukraine.

The Brigham Young Monument (see 1897).

1801 Mary Fielding (Smith), later the wife of Hyrum Smith and mother of Joseph F. Smith, is born in Bedfordshire, England.

1846 The Mormon Battalion begins its march from Trader's Point (near Council Bluffs, Iowa) to California.

Cover of Time *magazine featuring President George Albert Smith, 21 July 1947.*

1847 Orson Pratt and Erastus Snow, members of Brigham Young's pioneer company, enter the Salt Lake Valley. After making a twelve-mile circuit through the valley, they return to their camp in Emigration Canyon.

1849 Addison Pratt receives the first endowment given in the Salt Lake Valley. The sacred ordinances are performed on Ensign Peak.

1851 Acting in his capacity as U.S. Indian Agent for the territory of Utah, Brigham Young organizes three Indian agencies.

1879 Elder Joseph Standing, a missionary laboring in Georgia, is shot and killed by an anti-Mormon mob near Varnell's Station, Georgia. This is the first murder of a Latter-day Saint missionary since the death of Parley P. Pratt in 1857 and marks the beginning of a period of violence against missionaries in the South.

1898 George Dewey Clyde, later the governor of Utah (1956–65), is born in Mapleton, Utah.

1905 David Matthew Kennedy, later the U.S. secretary of the treasury (1969–71) and a special representative of the First Presidency, is born in Argyle, Utah.

1929 Joe J. Christensen, later a member of the Presidency of the Seventy, is born in Banida, Idaho.

1931 Gene Fullmer, later the Boxing Middleweight Champion (1957), is born in West Jordan, Utah.

1935 President Heber J. Grant dedicates Torlief Knaphus's Angel Moroni Monument at the top of the Hill Cumorah.

1935 Lynn A. Mickelsen, later a member of the First Quorum of the Seventy, is born in Idaho Falls, Idaho.

1947 *Time* magazine features President George Albert Smith on its cover and highlights the centennial of the arrival of the Mormon pioneers in the Great Basin.

1954 The First Presidency announces plans to build the Church College of Hawaii, later known as BYU–Hawaii.

JULY 22

1828 Clarissa Decker (Young), later a wife of Brigham Young and one of three women in the vanguard pioneer company of 1847, is born in Freedom, New York.

1839 In the course of a malaria epidemic in Commerce (later Nauvoo), Illinois, and Montrose, Iowa, a number of Saints are miraculously healed through the priesthood administrations of the Prophet Joseph Smith.

1915 President Joseph F. Smith and nearly 250 dignitaries from Utah leave Salt Lake City for San Francisco to participate in the International Congress of Genealogy and the Congress of Religious Philosophies, both of which were scheduled to coincide with the Panama-Pacific International Exposition being held at the same time.

President Joseph F. Smith (front row, third from right) and party at the International Congress of Genealogy in San Francisco (see 1915).

1934 Samuel P. Cowley, a member of the Church and head of the Bureau of Investigation's antigangster unit, supervises the capture of John Dillinger, a notorious gangster in Chicago. In the process, Dillinger is killed during a gun battle. Tragically, four months later Cowley is killed in a shootout with "Baby Face Nelson," another infamous gangster of the period.

1952 The First Presidency announces the purchase of a site in Bern, Switzerland, for the first European temple of the Church.

1974 The Argentina Buenos Aires South Mission is organized.

The Sesquicentennial Mormon Trail Wagon Train, 22 July 1997.

1978 The U.S. Senate passes a bill that had been earlier approved by the House of Representatives, designating the Mormon Trail from Nauvoo, Illinois, to Salt Lake City, Utah, as a national historic trail.

1997 President Gordon B. Hinckley, representatives of the national and international press, and more than fifty thousand others gather at the mouth of Emigration Canyon to welcome the Sesquicentennial Mormon Trail Wagon Train at the conclusion of its ninety-three-day journey from Nauvoo to the Salt Lake Valley.

JULY 23

1772 Daniel S. Miles, later one of the First Seven Presidents of the Seventy, is born in Sanbornton, New Hampshire.

1818 Benjamin F. Johnson, later a friend of Joseph Smith and an important colonizer in Utah, Arizona, and Mexico, is born in Pomfret, New York.

1833 Under mounting pressure from the mob, Church leaders in Missouri sign a memorandum agreeing that at least one-half of the Mormons would leave Jackson County by 1 January 1834 and all of the Saints would leave by 1 April 1834.

1833 Joseph Smith presides at the laying of the cornerstone for the Kirtland Temple, the first temple completed in this dispensation.

1837 Joseph Smith receives Doctrine and Covenants 112, containing instructions to Thomas B. Marsh.

1837 Elders Heber C. Kimball and Orson Hyde preach in the Vauxhall Chapel in Preston, England, giving the first Latter-day Saint sermon ever preached in that country.

1847 Brigham Young ascends Big Mountain, where he views the Salt Lake Valley for the first time.

1877 Before three hundred spectators, the Salt Lake City baseball team, the Deserets, hosts the Cheyenne Red Stockings in the first game with an out-of-territory club; the Deserets win 3–2. The following year, Heber J. Grant begins playing second base for the Deserets.

1899 Samuel P. Cowley, later one of the first Latter-day Saints to join the Bureau of Investigation (the precursor to the FBI) and a law enforcement legend, is born in Franklin, Idaho.

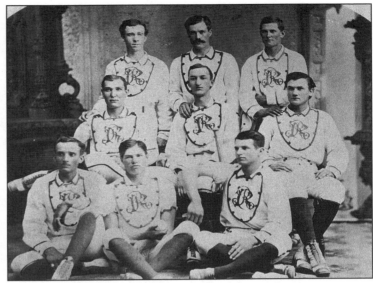

The Deserets (Heber J. Grant in center), ca. 1878 (see 1877).

1937 Church members are counseled to receive patriarchal blessings from stake patriarchs, not from the Church Patriarch, whose main assignment is to bless those where no stake patriarch is called.

1971 The Fiji Mission is organized.

1981 Elder Gordon B. Hinckley is set apart as a Counselor to President Spencer W. Kimball, the first time since the administration of President David O. McKay that a Church President has more than two Counselors. Neal A. Maxwell is ordained an Apostle, replacing Gordon B. Hinckley.

1994 President Gordon B. Hinckley of the First Presidency dedicates a monument and burial site to fifteen handcart pioneers of the Willie company who died of exposure and starvation during their trek on the high plains of Wyoming at Rock Creek.

1998 Youth from Serbia, Croatia, Bosnia, and Slovenia attend a youth conference in the Balkan states. The conference continues through 26 July.

1847 Brigham Young enters the Salt Lake Valley, the journey from Winter Quarters having taken him 111 days. Having been ill with Colorado Tick Fever, he is one of the last of the pioneer company to enter the valley. That same day, those who had arrived on 22 July begin planting crops.

1849 The first celebration commemorating the entrance of the pioneers into the Salt Lake Valley is held, with a number of the original 1847 pioneers in attendance.

1857 While celebrating the tenth anniversary of the Saints' arrival in the Salt Lake Valley, Brigham Young receives word from Abraham Smoot, Porter Rockwell, and Judson Stoddard that U.S. president James Buchanan is sending an army against the Saints in Utah.

1897 The fiftieth anniversary of Brigham Young's entrance into the Salt Lake Valley is celebrated with a grand parade.

1929 The Czechoslovak Mission is organized.

1938 Dallas N. Archibald, later a member of the First Quorum of the Seventy, is born in Logan, Utah.

1975 President Spencer W. Kimball dedicates the new twenty-eight-story Church Office Building in Salt Lake City.

1997 President Gordon B. Hinckley breaks ground for a twenty-one-thousand-seat assembly building just north of Temple Square in Salt Lake City.

1999 Ground is broken for the Reno Nevada Temple. Elder Rex D. Pinegar, a member of the First Quorum of the Seventy and President of the North America Southwest Area, presides over the ceremony.

1810 Elijah Abel, later an early black convert, pioneer, and faithful missionary, is born in Frederick, Maryland.

1831 The Colesville Saints, the first body of Saints to settle in Missouri, arrive in Independence, Missouri.

1836 Joseph Smith, Sidney Rigdon, Hyrum Smith, and Oliver Cowdery leave Kirtland on a trip to Salem, Massachusetts, seeking funds to relieve the financial challenges which had beset the Church.

1847 Elders George A. Smith, Heber C. Kimball, and Ezra T. Benson speak at the first Church service held in the Salt Lake Valley.

1887 President John Taylor dies in hiding in Kaysville, Utah, at age seventy-eight, after serving for more than forty-eight years as a General Authority.

1897 Celebrations commemorating the fiftieth anniversary of the Saints' arrival in the Salt Lake Valley end with memorial services in the Tabernacle honoring the deceased pioneers.

President John Taylor, by A. Westwood, 1882 (see 1887).

Pioneers of 1847 at a fiftieth anniversary celebration of their arrival in the Salt Lake Valley, 24 July 1897 (see 24–25 July 1897).

1933 D. Lee Tobler, later a member of the Second Quorum of the Seventy, is born in Provo, Utah.

1941 Yoshihiko Kikuchi, later a member of the First Quorum of the Seventy and the first native-born Japanese General Authority, is born in Hokkaido, Japan.

1992 Gunars Kavals, the first convert in the Baltic republic of Latvia, is baptized.

1994 In the rotunda of the Utah Capitol, President Gordon B. Hinckley of the First Presidency speaks at the unveiling ceremonies of a heroic-sized statue of Utah territorial governor Brigham Young.

1994 Brigham Young University and the University of Jordan announce plans to develop links of cooperation between the two institutions.

1999 President Gordon B. Hinckley dedicates the Pony Express Monument, created and placed in Salt Lake City by the National Pony Express Association.

1847 Brigham Young, Heber C. Kimball, Wilford Woodruff, George A. Smith, Ezra T. Benson, Willard Richards, Albert Carrington, William Clayton, and Lorenzo Dow Young climb a hill at the north of the Salt Lake Valley and name it Ensign Peak.

1850 Peter Forsgren, the first convert in Sweden, is baptized.

1897 The Northwestern States Mission is organized.

1908 Lowell L. Bennion, later a philosopher, educator, and humanitarian, is born in Salt Lake City, Utah.

Ensign Peak, ca. 1980 (see 1847).

1912 Church leaders in northern Mexico order the Saints to evacuate to El Paso, Texas, as a result of civil strife within Mexico, which displaces some forty-eight thousand Latter-day Saints from the Mexican colonies.

1932 Earl M. Monson, later a member of the Second Quorum of the Seventy, is born in Salt Lake City, Utah.

1954 *Life* magazine highlights the Mormon Tabernacle Choir's twenty-five years of broadcasting.

1973 The Australia Northeast Mission is organized.

1976 The Sweden Goteborg Mission is organized.

1987 Church members celebrate 150 years in the British Isles.

1998 President Gordon B. Hinckley dedicates the Monticello Utah Temple, the first of the new smaller temples.

1820 Lorin Farr, later a friend of Joseph Smith, pioneer, and civic and Church leader in Ogden, Utah, is born in Waterford, Vermont.

1847 Brigham Young and fifteen others cross the Jordan River and travel to Black Rock at the southern end of the Great Salt Lake. There they take their first swim in the lake and comment on the buoyancy of the salt water.

1913 President Joseph F. Smith dedicates the site for the Alberta Temple (later the Cardston Alberta Temple).

1930 Helvécio Martins, later a member of the Second Quorum of the Seventy and the first General Authority of African descent, is born in Rio de Janeiro, Brazil.

1949 Donald L. Hallstrom, later a member of the First Quorum of the Seventy, is born in Honolulu, Hawaii.

1963 Jason Buck, later a BYU football player, winner of the Outland Trophy (given to the best defensive lineman in the NCAA), and a professional football player, is born in Moses Lake, Washington.

1973 The Canada-Maritimes Mission is organized.

1847 Brigham Young identifies the site where the Salt Lake Temple is to be built.

1856 The Martin handcart company leaves Iowa City for Florence (Winter Quarters), Nebraska.

1955 The Northern Far East Mission is organized.

1985 President Gordon B. Hinckley speaks at the commemoration of the fiftieth anniversary of the Angel Moroni Monument at the Hill Cumorah.

1994 The First Presidency announces sending a relief package worth $760,000 to Rwanda, including emergency supplies and funds to deliver the supplies.

Elder Neal A. Maxwell following an interview with Hugh Hewitt for the PBS series Searching for God in America, *28 July 1996.*

1996 The PBS series *Searching for God in America* features an interview with Elder Neal A. Maxwell of the Quorum of the Twelve Apostles.

1847 The sick detachments of the Mormon Battalion and the Mississippi Saints, who had wintered at Pueblo, Colorado, arrive in the Salt Lake Valley.

1887 President John Taylor's funeral is held in Salt Lake City.

1912 During civil unrest in Mexico, thousands of Latter-day Saints flee the LDS settlements in northern Mexico.

Funeral of President John Taylor, 29 July 1887.

1915 Elder James E. Talmage addresses the Congress of Religious Philosophies in San Francisco (held in conjunction with the Panama-Pacific International Exposition) and later publishes his talk as *Philosophical Basis of Mormonism.*

1915 Bruce Redd McConkie, later a member of the Quorum of the Twelve Apostles, is born in Ann Arbor, Michigan.

1943 Adele Cannon Howells is called as the fourth general president of the Primary, with LaVern Watts Parmley and Dessie Grant Boyle as counselors.

1996 In San Fransico, California, Church members and others gather to commemorate the sesquicentennial of the arrival of the Saints on the *Brooklyn,* which docked in San Francisco Bay on 31 July 1846.

1998 The First Presidency announces plans to build temples in Bismarck, North Dakota, and St. Paul, Minnesota.

1837 Having outrun other baptismal candidates to the River Ribble, George D. Watt becomes the first convert in Great Britain when he is baptized by Elder Heber C. Kimball.

1844 Samuel Smith dies of "bilious fever" just over a month after the martyrdom of his brothers Hyrum and Joseph.

1849 Elder Thomas Howells baptizes Augustus Saint d'Anna, the first convert in France.

1887 Under provisions of the Edmunds-Tucker Act, suits are filed against the Church and its Perpetual Emigrating Fund Company, and the federal government begins confiscating Church property.

1965 Having traveled nearly eight thousand miles, 131 adults and 29 children from Japan attend the Laie Hawaii Temple to participate in all-Japanese temple work, the first time a group had traveled from Japan to have their temple work done.

1972 The Argentina East Mission is organized.

1977 The Church Educational System is placed under an Education Executive Committee of the Quorum of the Twelve Apostles.

1993 The annual *City of Joseph* pageant in Nauvoo, Illinois, is canceled because of the flooding of the Mississippi River.

1994 Hundreds celebrate the naming of Melissa Coray Peak in eastern California. The peak is named after a Mormon Battalion soldier's wife who had accompanied the battalion on its two-thousand-mile trek.

JULY 31

1846 The ship *Brooklyn,* with over two hundred Latter-day Saints aboard, arrives at Yerba Buena (San Francisco), California. These are the first Saints to set foot in California.

1846 The California Mission is organized.

1901 Alexander Schreiner, later a Mormon Tabernacle Choir organist (1924–77) and composer, is born in Nürnberg, Germany.

1914 Victor Lee Brown, later the tenth Presiding Bishop of the Church, is born in Cardston, Alberta, Canada.

1920 James E. Faust, later a member of the Quorum of the Twelve Apostles and First Presidency, is born in Delta, Utah.

1938 The Seattle Stake, the first stake in Washington, is organized, with Alex Brown as president.

President James E. Faust, by Knud Ebsberg, 1990 (see 1920).

1949 Joseph A. Cannon, later a member of the Environmental Protection Agency (1981–85) and Utah businessman, is born in Salt Lake City, Utah.

1967 The Ohio Mission is organized.

1979 U.S. secretary of defense Harold Brown awards Kermith H. Speierman of the National Security Agency the Distinguished Civilian Service Award for his work in the field of cryptology.

1985 Li Xiannian, president of the People's Republic of China, and his wife, Madame Lin Jiamei, tour the Church's Polynesian Cultural Center in Hawaii as part of their tour of the United States and Canada.

1998 President Gordon B. Hinckley embarks on a twelve-city tour of Canada.

~ ~ ~ AUGUST 1 ~ ~ ~

1831 Joseph Smith receives Doctrine and Covenants 58, instructing the Missouri Saints concerning the principles upon which Zion would be established.

1846 President Brigham Young and the Quorum of the Twelve Apostles determine that the Saints should winter at the Missouri River and not attempt to cross the plains that year.

1875 George W. Hill baptizes over three hundred Shoshone Indians in the Malad River in Idaho and participates in giving blessings to many sick members of that tribe.

1888 Moroni Timbimboo, a member of the Northwestern Shoshone nation and the first Native American bishop in the Church, is born at Washakie, a Church-sponsored farming community in Utah.

1941 Cecil O. Samuelson, later a member of the First Quorum of the Seventy, is born in Salt Lake City, Utah.

1965 The Guatemala–El Salvador Mission is organized.

1969 The Arizona Mission is organized.

1970 The Ecuador Mission is organized.

1971 Dallin H. Oaks begins his term as the seventh president of BYU.

1973 The Japan Nagoya and the Thailand Missions are organized.

1974 The California San Diego Mission is organized.

Elder Jeffery R. Holland, ca. 1994 (see 1980).

1980 Jeffrey R. Holland begins his term as the ninth president of BYU.

1984 The Haiti Port-au-Prince Mission is organized.

1989 The Kingdom of Jordan approves a Latter-day Saint center for culture and education to be established in Amman.

1999 President Gordon B. Hinckley dedicates the Guayaquil Ecuador Temple.

~~~ AUGUST 2 ~~~

1831 The Prophet Joseph Smith and eleven other men lay the first log for the first house constructed by the Colesville Saints in Kaw Township, Missouri.

1833 Doctrine and Covenants 94 and 97 are received. Section 94 reiterates the commandment to build the Kirtland Temple and calls for the building of a house for the First Presidency and a printing house. Section 97 warns the Saints in Missouri of impending judgments.

1854 President Brigham Young advises the British Mission presidency to stop sending immigrants through New Orleans, as many had become sick at that port. Immigrants after this time enter the United States through ports in New York and Boston.

1897 Matthew Cowley, later a member of the Quorum of the Twelve Apostles, is born in Preston, Idaho.

1923 Adney Yoshio Komatsu, later a member of the First Quorum of the Seventy, is born in Honolulu, Hawaii.

Matthew Cowley standing outside a Maori carved house in New Zealand, ca. 1939 (see 1897).

1985 The Church announces the release of the first new Church hymnal in thirty-seven years.

~~~ AUGUST 3 ~~~

1804 John C. Bennett, later an Assistant President to the First Presidency, is born in East Marlborough, Virginia.

1831 In the presence of Sidney Rigdon, Edward Partridge, W. W. Phelps, Oliver Cowdery, Martin Harris, and Joseph Coe, Joseph Smith dedicates the location for a temple west of Independence, Missouri.

Joseph F. Smith and party during visit to Copenhagen, Denmark, in 1910.

1852 Workers begin to construct a wall around Temple Square in Salt Lake City. Work on the temple itself begins in April 1853.

1910 During his second trip to Europe, President Joseph F. Smith meets with Saints in Denmark, becoming the first Church President in that country.

1926 Orvil Hansen, later an Idaho representative in the U.S. Congress (1969–75), is born in Firth, Idaho.

1932 Richard D. Allred, later a member of the Second Quorum of the Seventy, is born in Salt Lake City, Utah.

1945 Christine Meader (Durham), later the first Latter-day Saint woman and the first woman in Utah to be appointed as a state supreme court justice (1982), is born in Los Angeles, California.

1952 Kim Ho Jik, having converted to the Church while attending graduate school in the United States, participates in the first baptisms in Korea, which include those of his children, Tai Whan and Young Sook.

1956 Todd Christensen, later a BYU fullback (1974–77), a five-time all-pro tight end with the Oakland Raiders and Seattle Seahawks of the NFL, and NBC Sports color commentator, is born in Bellafonte, Pennsylvania.

Todd Christensen (see 1956).

1969 Sponsored by the Church's Genealogical Society, the eight-day World Conference on Records opens, attracting numerous genealogists and genealogical societies and giving the society international recognition as a leader in genealogical endeavors.

1976 The Taiwan Kaohsiung Mission is organized.

1998 The First Presidency announces that a temple will be built in Regina, Saskatchewan, Canada.

▶ *Charles W. Carter's photographic studio, ca. 1868 (see 1832).*

1810 Dan Jones, later a friend of Joseph Smith and successful missionary in Wales, where he baptized some 2,000 converts, is born in Halkyn, Wales.

1831 As called for in Doctrine and Covenants 52, a conference of the Church is held at the home of Joshua Lewis in Kaw Township, Missouri.

1832 Charles W. Carter, later a nineteenth-century Utah photographer who took pictures of important Church history sites, events, and people is born in London, England.

1899 Ezra Taft Benson, later a member of the Quorum of the Twelve Apostles and thirteenth President of the Church, is born in Whitney, Idaho.

1902 The Bureau of Information and Church Literature (the forerunner to the visitors' center) opens on Temple Square in Salt Lake City.

1907 Ezra Taft Benson is baptized in the Logan River Canal. (He is eight years old.)

1969 The South Central States Mission is organized.

1991 The newly renovated Smith Family Cemetery in Nauvoo, Illinois, is dedicated. The cemetery contains the graves of Joseph, Emma, and Hyrum Smith, among others. A site of interest to both the RLDS and the LDS Church, the dedication is performed under the joint direction of President Wallace Smith, president of the RLDS Church, and Elder M. Russell Ballard of the LDS Church.

1997 *Time* magazine features the progress and material wealth of the Church in an article entitled "Kingdom Come."

1998 President Gordon B. Hinckley speaks to fifteen hundred members at a Church conference in Manitoba, Canada.

1844 Sidney Rigdon meets with Elders Parley P. Pratt, Willard Richards, George A. Smith, John Taylor, and Amasa Lyman and argues that a guardian must be appointed over the Church.

1861 Latter-day Saint missionaries arrive in the Netherlands for the first time.

1922 L. Tom Perry, later a member of the Quorum of the Twelve Apostles, is born in Logan, Utah.

The Swiss Temple, ca. 1955 (see 1953).

1926 Agricol Lozano, later a prominent member of the Church in Mexico City, a Church legal representative, and an author, is born in Tula de Allende, Mexico.

1934 Ned B. Roueche, later a member of the Second Quorum of the Seventy, is born in Salt Lake City, Utah.

1953 President David O. McKay breaks ground for the Swiss Temple (later the Bern Switzerland Temple), the first temple to be built on the European continent.

1968 The Mexico North Central Mission is organized.

1983 President Gordon B. Hinckley of the First Presidency dedicates the Apia Samoa Temple. Within a week he dedicates the Nuku'alofa Tonga Temple; this is the first time two temples have been dedicated within a week of each other.

1830 Daniel W. Jones, later a heroic rescuer of the 1856 Martin handcart company and the translator of the first portions of the Book of Mormon in Spanish, is born in Booneslick, Missouri.

1831 Polly Knight, wife of Joseph Knight Sr., dies in Jackson County, Missouri. Her death likely led to the receipt of Doctrine and Covenants section 59 the following day.

1833 Joseph Smith receives Doctrine and Covenants 98, instructing the Saints on how they should react to persecution.

1836 Joseph Smith receives Doctrine and Covenants 111 while in Salem, Massachusetts, where he is seeking funds to help get the Church out of debt. The revelation contains instructions concerning his activities in the Salem area.

1838 Fifty to one hundred Missourians attack approximately thirty Mormons who had come to Gallatin, Missouri, to vote in the state and county elections. This famous "Election Day Battle" becomes one of the factors leading to the Mormon War in Missouri and the Saints' expulsion from the state.

1842 Joseph Smith prophesies that the Saints would later flee to the Rocky Mountains and there become a mighty people.

1851 The Kula Branch, the first branch in Hawaii, is organized on the island of Maui.

1993 Tomas Tomasson, the ambassador of Iceland, presents Iceland's highest honor, the Order of the Falcon, to Byron T. Geslison, who served three missions to the country and reopened missionary work there in 1975.

1994 The Missionary Department of the Church announces that over one-third of the population of the United States has been visited by Church representatives, with approximately 36 percent having friends or relatives who are Church members.

1998 The First Presidency announces plans to build a temple in Montreal, Quebec, Canada.

▶ *A member in Sierra Leone copies his testimony into copies of the Book of Mormon, ca. 1980 (see 1988).*

1831 Joseph Smith receives Doctrine and Covenants 59, giving additional instructions and commandments to the Jackson County Saints concerning the principles upon which Zion would be established. Among these instructions is a special emphasis on keeping the Sabbath day holy.

1846 A company of Saints from Mississippi, under the leadership of John Brown, arrives at Pueblo, Colorado, and remains there until the spring of 1847, waiting for the advance company of pioneers.

1956 Less than one month after the organization of the first branch in Peru (8 July), Elders Darwin Thomas, Edward T. Hall, Donald L. Hokanson, and Shirrel M. Plowman arrive to begin preaching the gospel among the people there.

1968 The Australian West Mission is organized.

1977 The Fargo North Dakota Stake, the first stake in North Dakota, is organized, with John R. Price as president.

1979 The BYU Young Ambassadors perform in the People's Republic of China.

1988 The first branch in the African republic of Sierra Leone is organized in Goderich.

AUGUST 8

1831 Joseph Smith receives Doctrine and Covenants 60, instructing the Prophet's party to travel from Independence to St. Louis via the Missouri River and to preach the gospel en route.

1838 Worried about effects of the election-day scuffle at Gallatin two days earlier, Joseph Smith, along with a large party of men, visits Judge Adam Black of Daviess County and secures from him a signed statement declaring he (Black) was not associated with any mob in the county. After their visit, the judge files a misdemeanor charge against Joseph Smith, charging him and his party with intimidation.

1839 Romania Bunnell (Pratt Penrose), later a pioneer, physician, and women's advocate, is born in Washington, Indiana.

1842 John Morgan, later one of the First Seven Presidents of the Seventy, is born in Greensburg, Indiana.

1844 While addressing the Saints in a public meeting held in Nauvoo to settle Sidney Rigdon's claims to leadership, Brigham Young is transfigured and has the appearance of Joseph Smith. During an afternoon meeting, the Saints vote to sustain the Quorum of the Twelve Apostles, rather than Sidney Rigdon, as the rightful leaders of the Church.

1915 Robert L. Simpson, later a member of the First Quorum of the Seventy, is born in Salt Lake City, Utah.

1924 George E. Wahlen, later a World War II marine medic and U.S. Congressional Medal of Honor recipient (1944) for rescuing fourteen wounded marines while seriously wounded himself during the battle of Iwo Jima, is born in Ogden, Utah.

1938 President J. Reuben Clark Jr. of the First Presidency delivers his influential address *The Charted Course of the Church in Education* at a summer gathering of CES teachers at Aspen Grove in Provo Canyon.

Judge John J. Sirica and D. Todd Christofferson, his law clerk, 2 August 1974.

1974 U.S. president Richard M. Nixon announces his resignation, which was a result of the Watergate investigation, in which several Latter-day Saints played a significant role. Among those involved in the investigation was future member of the Seventy D. Todd Christofferson, law clerk to Judge John J. Sirica. Christofferson and Sirica were the first to hear the Nixon tapes, which ultimately brought about the president's resignation.

1976 A branch is organized in Reykjavik, Iceland, the first Icelandic branch to be organized since the Church withdrew missionaries in 1914.

1994 Richard W. Henderson, Jamie T. Hipwell, John T. Smith, and Brian W. Strong, the first four Cambodian-speaking missionaries from the United States, arrive in Cambodia.

1998 President Gordon B. Hinckley speaks to 12,000 people in Hamilton, Ontario, Canada, at the largest Church meeting ever held in that province.

❧❧❧ AUGUST 9 ❧❧❧

1831 Having dedicated the land of Zion and the temple lot in Jackson County, Missouri, Joseph Smith and his party begin their return trip to Kirtland.

1847 Catharine C. Steele, wife of John Steele, gives birth to a daughter they name Young Elizabeth Steele; she is the first white child born in the Salt Lake Valley.

1877 Mahonri Mackintosh Young, later an artist and sculptor of many significant works, including a sculpture of his grandfather Brigham Young (located in the U.S. Capitol) and the *This Is the Place Monument,* is born in Salt Lake City.

1903 Near the Kremlin in Moscow, President Francis M. Lyman of the Quorum of the Twelve Apostles dedicates Russia for the preaching of the gospel.

1924 Nathan K. Van Noy Jr., later a private in the U.S. Army and a posthumous Congressional Medal of Honor recipient for protecting fellow soldiers despite being mortally wounded, is born in Grace, Idaho.

1951 Neil L. Andersen, later a member of the First Quorum of the Seventy, is born in Logan, Utah.

1975 At an area conference in Tokyo, Japan, President Spencer W. Kimball announces that the Church's eighteenth temple will be built in Tokyo. Overjoyed, the Japanese Saints burst into applause at the announcement.

1983 President Gordon B. Hinckley of the First Presidency dedicates the Nuku'alofa Tonga Temple. Four days earlier he had dedicated the Apia Samoa Temple. This is the first time two temples are dedicated within a week of each other.

1985 President Gordon B. Hinckley of the First Presidency dedicates the Chicago Illinois Temple.

❧❧❧ AUGUST 10 ❧❧❧

1817 Warren Foote, later an important journalist and chronicler of early Church history, is born in Dryden, New York.

1847 The Saints in the Salt Lake Valley begin construction of the "Old Fort."

1953 President David O. McKay dedicates the site for the London Temple (later the London England Temple).

1954 The First Presidency issues a letter counseling members involved in the Indian student placement program to provide Indian children with all spiritual and cultural opportunities possible in addition to their education at public schools.

1996 Elder Richard G. Scott breaks ground for the Guayaquil Ecuador Temple.

1997 President Gordon B. Hinckley becomes the first Church President to visit Paraguay and addresses seven thousand members, some of whom had traveled up to nine hours to attend the meeting.

1997 Lee Groberg's *Trail of Hope: The Story of the Mormon Trail* makes its world premiere on PBS.

1998 The First Presidency announces plans to build a temple in Detroit, Michigan.

1807 David Rice Atchison, later a non-Mormon military and political leader in Missouri and a legal counselor and friend to Joseph Smith, is born in Frogtown, Kentucky.

1831 As Joseph Smith and those with him set up camp at McIlwaine's bend on the Missouri River en route from Jackson County to Kirtland, W. W. Phelps sees Satan riding upon the waters. The Lord explains the vision the following day.

1848 The Saints in the Salt Lake Valley celebrate their first harvest with a feast.

1856 The Willie handcart company arrives in Florence, Nebraska.

1859 Heber Manning Wells, later the first governor of the state of Utah (1896–1904), is born in Salt Lake City.

Heber M. Wells, the first LDS state governor and the first governor of Utah (see 1859).

1935 Darwin B. Christenson, later a member of the Second Quorum of Seventy, is born in Firth, Idaho.

1970 The government of the Asian archipelago Indonesia officially recognizes the Church.

1993 More than a hundred Latter-day Saint volunteers help at the Catholic World Youth Day during Pope John Paul II's visit to Denver, Colorado.

1996 The Tarawa Kiribati Stake, the first stake in Kiribati, is organized, with Atunibeia Mote as president.

1998 The First Presidency announces plans to a build temple in Edmonton, Alberta, Canada.

1831 Joseph Smith receives Doctrine and Covenants 61, where the Lord explains W. W. Phelps's vision of Satan riding upon the waters.

1841 Joseph Smith preaches to about one hundred Sac and Fox Indians during their visit to Nauvoo. The group includes Chiefs Keokuk, Kiskuhosh, and Appenoose.

1850 Erastus Snow baptizes the first fifteen converts to the Church in Copenhagen, Denmark.

1901 The Japan Mission is organized by Elder Heber J. Grant. It is discontinued in 1924 and reopened in 1948.

1920 Gardner H. Russell, later a member of the First Quorum of the Seventy, is born in Salt Lake City, Utah.

1932 Dallin H. Oaks, later BYU president and a member of the Quorum of the Twelve Apostles, is born in Provo, Utah.

1991 The first group of the Church on Gibraltar since 1854 is organized, with Keven Paul Wahnon as its leader.

Elder Dallin H. Oaks, ca. 1986 (see 1932).

AUGUST 13

1827 Paul Schettler, later president of the Netherlands Mission and an interpreter who accompanied President George A. Smith on his trip to Palestine in 1872, is born in Prussia.

The Sacred Grove, 13 August 1907.

1831 While traveling to Kirtland, Joseph Smith and his company meet with Hyrum Smith, John Murdock, Harvey Whitlock, and David Whitmer, who are on their way to Jackson County, and Joseph receives Doctrine and Covenants 62 in their behalf.

1853 Augustus Farnham publishes a periodical called *Zion's Watchman* in Sydney, Australia.

1907 Utah landscape and portrait photographer George Edward Anderson takes his famous and moving photograph of the Sacred Grove in New York. Anderson is the first professional Latter-day Saint photographer to capture images of LDS historical sites in Missouri, Illinois, Ohio, New York, Pennsylvania, and Vermont.

1961 The Alaska Stake, the first stake in Alaska, is organized, with Orson P. Millett as president.

1982 Elder Bruce R. McConkie of the Quorum of the Twelve breaks ground for the Sydney Australia Temple.

1983 President Gordon B. Hinckley breaks ground for the Chicago Illinois Temple.

1985 Joe J. Christensen is appointed twelfth president of Ricks College.

1986 The first branch is organized on the Netherlands island of Aruba, located off the coast of Venezuela.

1991 Tonga observes the centennial of the founding of the Church on that Pacific Island.

1998 The First Presidency announces plans to build a temple in Spokane, Washington.

1866 J. Wilford Booth, later a long-term mission president in the Near East, is born in Alpine, Utah. Following service as a missionary to Turkey (1898–1902), he is twice called to serve as the president of the mission covering most of the Near East (1904–09, 1921–28).

1892 The Star Valley Stake, the first stake in Wyoming, is organized, with George Osmond as president.

1893 Joseph L. Wirthlin, later the eighth Presiding Bishop of the Church, is born in Salt Lake City, Utah.

1932 James V. Hansen, later a Utah representative in the U.S. Congress (1980–), is born in Salt Lake City, Utah.

1935 The Argentine Mission is organized.

Woman with Deseret Industries bag (see 1938).

1938 The first Deseret Industries store opens in Salt Lake City, Utah.

1960 The Toronto Ontario Stake, the first stake in Ontario, Canada, is organized, with William M. Davies as president.

1988 Kay Wildcat, a Shoshone Church member, is chosen as Miss Indian America during a competition held in Bismarck, North Dakota.

1998 The first annual PEARL awards show, sponsored by Faith Centered Music Association and the LDS Booksellers Association, is held at Kingsbury Hall in Salt Lake City. The awards honor excellence in faith-centered music.

1778 John Tanner, later a friend of Joseph Smith and Church financial benefactor, is born in Hopkinton, Rhode Island.

1840 Joseph Smith preaches the funeral sermon of Seymour Brunson. During the course of his remarks the Prophet reveals for the first time the doctrine of baptism for the dead.

1854 The wall around Temple Square in Salt Lake City is completed.

1889 The Church buys a ranch in Skull Valley, Utah, for immigrating Saints from Hawaii to settle on. The Hawaiian Saints later name their settlement *Iosepa* (Joseph in Hawaiian), in honor of both Joseph Smith and Joseph F. Smith, an early missionary to Hawaii.

1943 Eni Fa'aua'a Hunkin Faleomavaega Jr., a delegate to the U.S. Congress from American Samoa (1989–), is born in Vailoatai Village, American Samoa.

1962 Elder Richard L. Evans speaks and the Mormon Tabernacle Choir sings at the Century 21 Exposition in Seattle, Washington.

1987 The First Presidency announces the renaming of the Church Genealogical Department as the Family History Department.

1992 President Gordon B. Hinckley of the First Presidency dedicates three monuments to the pioneers of the Willie and Martin handcart companies near South Pass, Wyoming.

1813 William Pitt, later a musician and leader of the Nauvoo Brass Band, is born in Dymock, England.

Charles R. Savage & George M. Ottinger Studio in Salt Lake City, ca. 1864–70 (see 1832).

1832 Charles R. Savage, later an internationally recognized, award-winning Utah portrait and landscape photographer, is born in Southampton, England.

1847 With autumn coming on, seventy-two men leave the Salt Lake Valley for Winter Quarters to rejoin their families and help others make the move west. Another company, led by Brigham Young, leaves ten days later.

1866 *Harper's Weekly* includes a double-page spread featuring Mormon-related illustrations, including depictions of Salt Lake City, important buildings, the First Presidency, the Quorum of the Twelve Apostles, the Patriarch, and the Presiding Bishop.

1878 Lightning strikes the tower of the St. George Temple (later the St. George Utah Temple) and damages it slightly.

1996 The First Presidency announces plans to build a temple in Billings, Montana.

1999 The First Presidency announces The Hague Netherlands Temple in a letter to local priesthood leaders.

1999 BYU athletics unveils its new look, which includes new colors, a new logo, and new uniforms.

1829 Joseph Smith and Martin Harris secure a contract with E. B. Grandin to print five thousand copies of the Book of Mormon at a cost of $3,000.

1835 Oliver Cowdery presents the *Book of Doctrine and Covenants of the Church of the Latter-day Saints* to the Church in a general assembly at Kirtland along with "The Testimony of the Twelve Apostles to the Truth of the Book of Doctrine and Covenants" and a document entitled "Of Governments and Laws in General" (later section 134 of the Doctrine and Covenants).

1942 Lucy Gates Bowen, a granddaughter of Brigham Young, christens the *SS Brigham Young,* a U.S. liberty ship used during World War II to transport troops, freight, and prisoners.

1955 The Southern Far East Mission is organized.

1997 The Abidjan Ivory Coast Stake, the first stake in the West African country of Ivory Coast, is organized, with Cyr Philippe Assard as president.

The Grandin Building, where the Book of Mormon was first published, ca. 25 August 1988 (see 1829).

AUGUST 18

1856 The Willie handcart company leaves Florence (Winter Quarters), Nebraska, for the Salt Lake Valley.

1882 The Utah Commission, created by the antipolygamy Edmunds Law, arrives in the territory to begin supervising election procedures in Utah and to enforce the disenfranchisement of much of the Mormon population.

1941 Keith B. McMullin, later the Second Counselor in the Presiding Bishopric, is born in St. George, Utah.

1985 Elder Neal A. Maxwell dedicates the first building built specifically as an LDS meetinghouse in the West African country of Ghana.

1996 Elder Richard G. Scott breaks ground for the Santo Domingo Dominican Republic Temple.

AUGUST 19

1814 Benjamin L. Clapp, later one of the First Seven Presidents of the Seventy, is born in West Huntsville, Alabama.

1906 Philo T. Farnsworth, later a scientist and the inventor who is credited as being the "father of television," is born near Beaver, Utah.

1933 Mary Ellen Wood (Smoot), later the thirteenth general president of the Relief Society, is born in Ogden, Utah.

1977 The first annual Church Educational System Religious Educators Symposium (later known as CES Conference), a multiday conference for seminary and institute faculty highlighting the upcoming course of study, is held at BYU.

1988 Benjamin and Ruth Hudson arrive in Guyana, a republic on the northern coast of South America, to begin missionary work.

1989 President Gordon B. Hinckley of the First Presidency dedicates the Portland Oregon Temple.

1999 The First Presidency announces that the massive new assembly building located north of Temple Square will be called the Conference Center.

1842 Amasa M. Lyman is ordained an Apostle, replacing Orson Pratt, who had been excommunicated (he returns to the Church and the Quorum of the Twelve Apostles a year later).

1859 Horace Greeley, the *New York Tribune* editor, publishes his 13 July 1859 interview with Brigham Young, which is reported to be the first such interview published in an American newspaper.

1924 Hartman Rector Jr., later a member of the First Quorum of the Seventy, is born in Moberly, Missouri.

1932 The First Presidency announces plans to erect a monument on the summit of the Hill Cumorah.

1992 Elder Richard G. Scott begins a five-day tour of Africa, during which he dedicates Zambia, Botswana, Namibia, and Congo for the preaching of the gospel.

The Angel Moroni Statue on the Hill Cumorah (see 1932).

1809 Charles C. Rich, later a member of the Quorum of the Twelve Apostles, is born in Campbell County, Kentucky.

1892 William James Critchlow Jr., later an Assistant to the Quorum of the Twelve Apostles, is born in Brigham City, Utah.

1927 Thomas S. Monson, later a member of the Quorum of the Twelve Apostles and First Presidency, is born in Salt Lake City, Utah.

1951 Michael L. Ballam, later a gifted tenor, a professor of music at Utah State University, and founder and president of the Utah Festival Opera Company, is born in Logan, Utah.

1959 Richard Zokol, later a member of BYU's 1981 NCAA championship golf team and a PGA champion, is born in Kitimat, British Columbia, Canada.

Thomas S. Monson, by Knud Ebsberg, 1990 (see 1927).

1999 President Gordon B. Hinckley dedicates the Spokane Washington Temple.

1828 Helen Mar Kimball (Whitney), later an important author and writer, is born in Mendon, New York.

1847 The choir that would later become the Mormon Tabernacle Choir sings at a special conference held in the Salt Lake Valley. During this same conference, the Saints choose the name "Great Salt Lake City" for the city they are building and name the river running north and south through the valley the Jordan River.

1967 The Mormon Tabernacle Choir participates at the Expo '67 in Montreal, Canada (22–23 August).

1987 John Tarsnoh, the first convert to the Church in the southwest African country of Liberia, is baptized.

Helen Mar Kimball Whitney, ca. 1880 (see 1828).

1842 Lucy Hannah White (Flake), later an important Arizona pioneer and diarist, is born in Knox County, Illinois.

1910 G. Carlos Smith, later the general superintendent of the Young Men's Mutual Improvement Association (1967–69), is born in Salt Lake City, Utah.

Poster announcing the world premiere of Brigham Young (see 1940).

1928 Warren E. Hansen, later a member of the Presidency of the Seventy, is born in Tremonton, Utah.

1940 The largest world premiere of any Hollywood movie to date is held in Salt Lake City with the release of Darryl F. Zanuck's production of *Brigham Young,* one of the first motion pictures to portray the Church in a positive way. It stars Dean Jagger, who later joins the Church.

1970 The West Virginia Stake, the first stake in West Virginia, is organized, with David L. Atkinson as president.

1981 President Gordon B. Hinckley of the First Presidency dedicates the national headquarters of Sons of Utah Pioneers in Salt Lake City, Utah.

1868 Joseph Francis Merrill, later a member of the Quorum of the Twelve Apostles, is born in Richmond, Utah.

1898 George H. Hudson is killed in the Philippines during the Spanish-American War, the first member of the Church to die in combat in a U.S. war.

1932 Robert D. Hales, later a member of the Quorum of the Twelve Apostles, is born in New York City, New York.

1954 Orson Scott Card, later an award-winning science-fiction, fantasy, and religious writer, is born in Richland, Washington.

Robert D. Hales, ca. 1998 (see 1932).

1977 While in Warsaw, President Spencer W. Kimball dedicates Poland for the preaching of the gospel.

1985 President Gordon B. Hinckley of the First Presidency dedicates the Johannesburg South Africa Temple.

1991 President Howard W. Hunter of the Quorum of the Twelve Apostles dedicates Panama for the preaching of the gospel.

1829 Martin Harris agrees to mortgage his farm to cover the printing costs of the Book of Mormon.

1856 The Martin handcart company and the Hodgett wagon train leave Florence (Winter Quarters), Nebraska, for the Salt Lake Valley.

1858 Matthias F. Cowley, later a member of the Quorum of the Twelve Apostles, is born in Salt Lake City, Utah.

Founding of the Primary Association, by Lynn Fausett, 1941 (see 1878).

1878 In Farmington, Utah, Aurelia Rogers holds the first meeting of the Primary.

1914 The First Presidency instructs missionaries serving in France and Germany to evacuate their missions because of the outbreak of war in Europe a few weeks earlier.

1939 President M. Douglas Wood, president of the West German Mission, telegraphs missionaries serving in Germany to immediately leave the country for Holland, just a week before the outbreak of World War II.

1955 President Joseph Fielding Smith of the Quorum of the Twelve Apostles dedicates Guam for the preaching of the gospel, and the first LDS missionaries arrive in Guam.

1982 President Gordon B. Hinckley of the First Presidency breaks ground for the Manila Philippines Temple.

1990 President Gordon B. Hinckley of the First Presidency dedicates the Toronto Ontario Temple.

1990 Mugisa James Collins, the first convert to the Church in the central African country of Uganda, is baptized.

▶ *George Q. Cannon, ca. 1900 (see 1860).*

AUGUST

1817 Richard Ballantyne, later the founder of the LDS Sunday School program, is born in Whitridgebog, Roxburghshire, Scotland.

1860 George Q. Cannon is ordained an Apostle, replacing Parley P. Pratt, who had been assassinated in 1857.

1883 The first permanent branch of the Church among the Maori people in New Zealand is organized at Papawai.

1923 President Heber J. Grant dedicates the Alberta Temple (later the Cardston Alberta Temple) in Cardston after years of delay caused by World War I and economic setback in western Canada.

1962 The Glasgow Stake, the first stake in Scotland, is organized, with Archibald R. Richardson as president.

▶ *Minerva Teichert (see 28 August 1888)*

AUGUST 27

1778 Mary Musselman (Whitmer), later the wife of Peter Whitmer Sr., mother of five Book of Mormon witnesses, and the only woman to be shown the Book of Mormon plates, is born in Strausburg, Pennsylvania.

1793 Edward Partridge, later the first bishop of the Church, is born in Pittsfield, Massachusetts.

1802 John Whitmer, one of the Eight Witnesses of the Book of Mormon, is born in Harrisburg, Pennsylvania.

1895 A star representing Utah is added to the United States flag, bringing the total number of stars on the flag to forty-five.

1937 L. Jay Sylvester, later a world-class discus thrower, holder of six world records and six national championships, and an Olympic silver medalist (1968), is born in Tremonton, Utah.

1940 Spencer J. Condie, later a member of the First Quorum of the Seventy, is born in Preston, Idaho.

1955 President David O. McKay breaks ground for the London Temple (later the London England Temple).

1961 The North Carolina Stake, the first stake in North Carolina, is organized, with Cecil E. Reese as president.

1971 President Joseph Fielding Smith presides at the first Church area conference. The historic meeting is held in Manchester, England, not far from where missionaries first arrived in England in 1837.

1982 President Gordon B. Hinckley breaks ground for the Taipei Taiwan Temple.

AUGUST 28

1815 Henry W. Bigler, later a Mormon Battalion member and journal keeper who recorded the discovery of gold at Sutter's Mill in 1848, is born in Shinnston, West Virgina.

1852 During a special conference in Salt Lake City, Church leaders announce the expansion of the missionary effort, including new fields of service in India, Siam, and Hong Kong.

1880 George Reynolds, incarcerated for plural marriage, decides to prepare a concordance to the Book of Mormon while in prison. Over the course of the project, Reynolds prepares and transcribes as many as 350 passages per day from the Book of Mormon and completes 25,000 entries by the time he is released in January 1881. The concordance is completed in 1899.

1888 Minerva Bernetta Kohlhepp (Teichert), later a gifted artist and the first woman to paint a mural in a temple (the world room in the Manti Temple), is born in Ogden, Utah.

1889 A group of Hawaiian Saints arrives at the Church-owned ranch in Skull Valley, Utah, and names the settlement *Iosepa* (Joseph in Hawaiian) in honor of Joseph Smith and Joseph F. Smith, who had served in Hawaii as a missionary.

1962 Rick Fehr, later a member of BYU's 1981 NCAA championship golf team and a PGA champion, is born in Seattle, Washington.

1987 President Ezra Taft Benson dedicates the Frankfurt Germany Temple.

1993 Elder Russell M. Nelson attends the Parliament of the World's Religions in Chicago, Illinois, exactly 100 years after the body rejected a Latter-day Saint delegation headed by Elder B. H. Roberts.

❧❧❧ AUGUST 29 ❧❧❧

1832 Historical sources indicate that Doctrine and Covenants 99 was received on this date. The revelation contains instructions to John Murdock and appoints him to serve a short-term mission.

1839 Elders Parley P. Pratt and Orson Pratt leave Nauvoo to embark on the mission of the Quorum of the Twelve Apostles to England.

1842 Having been in hiding since 8 August (after being falsely accused of the attempted assassination of ex-Governor Lilburn W. Boggs), Joseph Smith makes a surprise appearance at a meeting of the Saints in the grove in Nauvoo, Illinois.

1852 At a special conference in Salt Lake City, the doctrine of plural marriage is first publicly announced by Orson Pratt under the direction of Brigham Young. Several Church leaders had been practicing the principle privately since learning of it from Joseph Smith in Nauvoo.

1877 President Brigham Young dies in Salt Lake City at age seventy-six, after serving the Church for more than forty-two years.

1886 In Haifa, Elder Jacob Spori baptizes Johan George Grau, the first convert in Palestine.

Stereoscope image of Brigham Young's grave (see 1877).

❧❧❧ AUGUST 30 ❧❧❧

1830 In Harmony, Pennsylvania, Joseph Smith is threatened by mobs. Later, at the request of Oliver Cowdery, David Whitmer moves Joseph and his family to Fayette, New York.

1831 According to several early historical sources, Doctrine and Covenants 63 is received on this date. The revelation reproves a number of Kirtland Saints for their disobedience and gives further instructions concerning the establishment of the Church in Missouri.

1870 Martin Harris, one of the Three Witnesses of the Book of Mormon, arrives in Salt Lake City at the age of eighty-eight, after having been separated from the Church for nearly thirty-three years.

1911 Stanley "Stan" Howard Watts, later a respected BYU basketball coach and a member of the Basketball Hall of Fame, is born in Murray, Utah.

1949 Gregory J. Newell, later the U.S. ambassador to Sweden (1985), is born in Geneseo, Illinois.

1987 Elder Marvin J. Ashton dedicates the Democratic Republic of Congo (Zaire) for the preaching of the gospel.

1992 Elder Neal A. Maxwell organizes the Orlando Florida South Stake, the Church's nineteen hundredth stake, with Carl E. Reynolds Jr. as president.

1994 The First Presidency issues a statement reaffirming the Lord's blessings to families that hold family home evenings.

1830 Hyrum Smith introduces Parley P. Pratt, who had borrowed a copy of the Book of Mormon from a Baptist deacon, to the Prophet Joseph Smith in Fayette, New York.

1843 Joseph Smith and his family begin moving into the Mansion House in Nauvoo.

1844 Illinois governor Thomas Ford appoints Brigham Young lieutenant-general of the Nauvoo Legion, replacing Joseph Smith, who had been martyred earlier that year.

1854 Colonel Edward J. Steptoe arrives in Salt Lake City to take his appointed position as governor of the territory of Utah. When he sees how well Brigham Young is administering the territory, he petitions U.S. president Franklin Pierce to reappoint Brigham Young as governor; the president eventually follows this counsel.

1861 Mormon convert and pioneer George Ottinger begins his famous painting of Green River, one of only three paintings of the Mormon Trail done by a Latter-day Saint while on the trek.

1947 The Uruguay Mission is organized.

1954 The First Presidency adapts the age for ordaining young men to the priesthood, making it 14 for teachers and 16 for priests (the previous ages having been 15 and 17).

Green River, by George Ottinger, 31 August 1861.

1830 Oliver Cowdery baptizes Parley P. Pratt a day after Parley meets the Prophet Joseph Smith in Fayette, New York.

1842 Joseph Smith addresses a letter to the Saints, now found in Doctrine and Covenants 127, containing information on procedures associated with the practice of baptism for the dead. At this time the Prophet is hiding at Edward Hunter's home from Missouri officials who are bent on returning him to stand trial in Missouri.

1871 J. Reuben Clark Jr., later a member of the Quorum of the Twelve Apostles and the First Presidency, is born in Grantsville, Utah.

1896 In Denver, Colorado, the Mormon Tabernacle Choir competes in the Great Western Eisteddfod, a Welsh-style music and literature contest.

Home of Bishop Edward Hunter in Nauvoo, ca. 1900 (see 1842).

1901 On a wooded hill located south of Yokohama, Elder Heber J. Grant dedicates Japan for the preaching of the gospel. Of this event Alma O. Taylor states: "His tongue was loosed and the Spirit rested mightily upon him; so much that we felt the angels of God were near for our hearts burned within us as the words fell from his lips" (Britsch, *From the East*, 50).

1906 J. Reuben Clark is appointed to be the U.S. State Department's assistant solicitor, becoming the first Latter-day Saint appointed to this legal position in the federal government. He later serves as the department's solicitor (1910–13).

1934 Harold G. Hillam, later a member of the Presidency of the Seventy, is born in Sugar City, Idaho.

1941 Gene R. Cook, later a member of the First Quorum of the Seventy, is born in Lehi, Utah.

1947 The Finnish Mission is organized.

1958 The New Zealand South Mission is organized.

1959 Keith Clearwater, later a member of BYU's 1981 NCAA national championship golf team and the 1987 PGA Rookie of the Year, is born in Long Beach, California.

1962 The Northeast British Mission is organized.

1968 The Japan and Japan-Okinawa Missions are organized.

1974 The Church College of Hawaii is made a branch of Brigham Young University and is renamed Brigham Young University—Hawaii Campus.

1990 The Philippines Ilagan Mission is organized.

1991 Membership in the Church reaches eight million approximately two years after reaching seven million.

❧❧❧ SEPTEMBER 2 ❧❧❧

1856 The John A. Hunt company, the last wagon train of the season, leaves Florence, Nebraska, for Salt Lake City, following the Willie and Martin handcart companies.

1877 President Brigham Young's funeral is held in the Tabernacle in Salt Lake City.

President Wilford Woodruff, by H. E. Peterson, 1889 (see 1898).

1898 President Wilford Woodruff dies in San Francisco, California, at age ninety-one, after serving for more than fifty-nine years as a General Authority. After hearing of the death and praying for guidance, President Lorenzo Snow of the Quorum of the Twelve Apostles sees Jesus Christ in the Salt Lake Temple and is instructed to organize the First Presidency again immediately.

1906 David B. Haight, later a member of the Quorum of the Twelve Apostles, is born in Oakley, Idaho.

1932 Elder J. Golden Kimball is killed in an automobile accident while returning to Salt Lake City from a vacation in California.

1996 During its national convention held in Salt Lake City, the American Legion awards President Gordon B. Hinckley the "Good Guy Award."

SEPTEMBER 3

1793 John P. Greene, later a missionary and close friend of Joseph Smith, is born in Herkimer County, New York. A copy of the Book of Mormon left with the Greene family eventually converts Brigham Young and the entire Young family.

1837 At a conference of the Church in Kirtland, Ohio, Oliver Cowdery, Joseph Smith Sr., Hyrum Smith, and John Smith are appointed Assistant Counselors to the Prophet Joseph Smith.

1985 The first branch is established in the Caribbean island country of Grenada.

1998 The First Presidency announces plans to build a temple in Raleigh, North Carolina.

SEPTEMBER 4

1837 Joseph Smith receives a revelation at Kirtland, Ohio, warning Church historian John Whitmer and stake presidency member W. W. Phelps that if they did not repent they would be removed from their places. Both eventually leave the Church, although William W. Phelps later returns to full activity. This revelation is not included in the Doctrine and Covenants.

1947 Missionaries from the Mexican Mission arrive in Guatemala to begin preaching the gospel in that Central American nation.

1950 Latter-day Saint car racer Ab Jenkins shatters twenty-six world and American records on the Bonneville Salt Flats in his *Mormon Meteor III*.

Ab Jenkins in his Mormon Meteor III *(see 1950).*

1950 The first early-morning seminary, with 198 students, is organized in southern California under the direction of Ray L. Jones.

1983 The first branch is organized on the Azores Islands, located eight hundred miles off the coast of Portugal.

1999 President Gordon B. Hinckley dedicates the Columbus Ohio Temple.

SEPTEMBER 5

1858 Joseph W. McMurrin, later one of the First Seven Presidents of the Seventy, is born in Tooele, Utah.

1880 U.S. president Rutherford B. Hayes and his wife visit Salt Lake City.

1954 The Suva Branch, the first branch in the South Pacific republic of Fiji, is organized.

1968 The Nuku'alofa Stake, the first stake in Tonga, is organized, with Orson Hyde White as president.

1973 Leonard Myles-Mills, later a BYU track star, the NCAA 100-meter dash champion (1998 and 1999), and African National Champion (1999), is born in Accra, Ghana.

1982 U.S. president Ronald Reagan honors the Mormon Tabernacle Choir on its fiftieth anniversary of continuous weekly broadcasts with the CBS Radio Network.

Leonard Myles-Mills, ca. 1998 (see 1973).

SEPTEMBER 6

1842 Joseph Smith addresses a second letter containing further instructions regarding the practice of baptism for the dead, now found in Doctrine and Covenants 128: "Let us, therefore, as a church and a people, and as Latter-day Saints, offer unto the Lord an offering in righteousness; and let us present in his holy temple, when it is finished, a book containing the records of our dead, which shall be worthy of all acceptation" (v. 24).

1845 Jesse Knight, later a businessman, entrepreneur, and benefactor of Brigham Young University, is born in Nauvoo, Illinois.

1857 Thomas B. Marsh, a former president of the Quorum of the Twelve Apostles, speaks to a group of Saints shortly after his return to the Church, apologizing for his previous behavior and asking for the Saints' fellowship.

1888 Edward Stevenson, Joseph S. Black, and assistant Church historian Andrew Jenson leave Salt Lake City to visit various Church history sites in the East. This was one of the first Church-sponsored attempts to collect historical information about the Church on site following the Saints' removal to Utah.

1898 Henry Thorpe Beal Isaacson, later an Assistant to the Quorum of the Twelve Apostles and Counselor in the First Presidency, is born in Ephraim, Utah.

1954 Elder Harold B. Lee speaks at a servicemen's conference in Korea.

1965 The U.S. government designates Nauvoo, Illinois, as a National Historical Landmark.

1980 Latter-day Saint missionaries enter the African nation of Kenya for the first time.

SEPTEMBER 7

1803 Harriet Page Wheeler Young, later one of three women in the original pioneer company of 1847, is born in Hillsboro, New Hampshire.

1804 Zebedee Coltrin, later one of the First Seven Presidents of the Seventy, is born in Ovid, New York.

1814 John Van Cott, later one of the First Seven Presidents of the Seventy, is born in Canaan, New York.

1878 Elders Joseph F. Smith and Orson Pratt visit David Whitmer in Richmond, Missouri, and interview him about his involvement in the early events of the Church.

1897 Seymour D. Young, later a member of the First Quorum of the Seventy, is born in Salt Lake City, Utah.

1905 Ivy Baker (Priest), later the treasurer of the United States, is born in Kimberly, Utah.

1915 Royden G. Derrick, later a member of the Presidency of the Seventy, is born in Salt Lake City, Utah.

1927 Philo T. Farnsworth makes the first electronic television transmission at his laboratory in San Francisco, California.

1930 Richard E. Cook, later a member of the Second Quorum of the Seventy, is born in Pleasant Grove, Utah.

1958 President David O. McKay dedicates the London Temple (later the London England Temple).

SEPTEMBER 8

1809 William Law, later a member of the First Presidency and one of the ringleaders of the Nauvoo apostates seeking Joseph's life in 1844, is born in Tyrone, Ireland.

1857 Captain Stewart Van Vliet, quartermaster for Johnston's army, arrives in Salt Lake City to speak with Brigham Young. After being favorably impressed with the Saints, he later leaves for Washington to use his influence in favor of the Saints.

1873 David O. McKay, later a member of the Quorum of the Twelve Apostles and the ninth President of the Church, is born in Huntsville, Utah.

1876 Amanda Inez Knight (Allen), later one of the first single women missionaries called by the Church, is born in Payson, Utah.

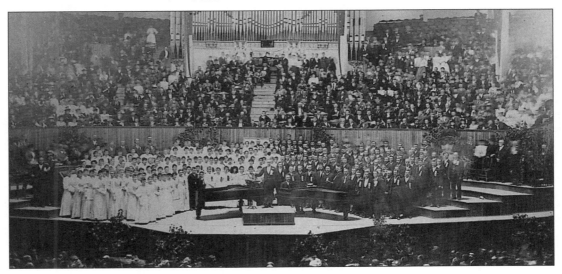

▶ *Mormon Tabernacle Choir in Festival Hall, World's Fair, September 1893 (see 1893).*

1881 David O. McKay is baptized in Spring Creek near Huntsville, Utah; he is the first future President of the Church to be baptized on his eighth birthday.

1893 The Mormon Tabernacle Choir wins the $1,000 second prize at the singing contest held at the World's Fair in Chicago.

1898 President Wilford Woodruff's funeral is held in the Tabernacle in Salt Lake City, Utah.

1940 Quentin L. Cook, later a member of the First Quorum of the Seventy, is born in Logan, Utah.

1950 Michael K. Simpson, an Idaho representative in the U.S. Congress (1999–), is born in Burley, Idaho.

1951 Colleen Kay Hutchins (Vandeweghe), a BYU graduate and master's degree student at the University of Utah, wins the Silver Anniversary Miss America Pageant, becoming the first Latter-day Saint Miss America.

1955 Terry Tempest (Williams), later the author of several works and considered by *Newsweek* as one of the most influential persons on economic, political, and environmental issues in the western United States, is born in Corona, California.

1969 President Hugh B. Brown breaks ground for the Ogden Temple (later the Ogden Utah Temple).

1980 In a ceremony in Jerusalem, Yitzhak Navon, president of Israel, presents Dr. Henry Eyring the Wolf Prize, considered by some as second only to the Nobel Prize, for his contributions to the field of chemistry.

1998 President Gordon B. Hinckley appears on CNN's popular *Larry King Live* television program. In the interview, President Hinckley declares, "My role is to declare a doctrine. My role is to stand as an example before the people. My role is to be a voice in defense of the truth" (http://www.cnn.com/TRAN-SCRIPTS/9809/08/114.00.html).

SEPTEMBER 9

1850 Congress approves an act creating the territory of Utah.

1858 The Bank of Deseret issues the first engraved Deseret Currency Association notes. The notes are printed and issued in Salt Lake City in denominations of $1, $2, and $3 and are backed by livestock.

Three-dollar Deseret Currency Association note (see 1858).

1924 Russell M. Nelson, later a heart surgeon and a member of the Quorum of the Twelve Apostles, is born in Salt Lake City, Utah.

1929 Ralph Harding, an Idaho representative in the U.S. Congress (1961–65), is born in Malad City, Idaho.

1938 Howard P. "Buck" McKeon, a California representative in the U.S. Congress (1993–), is born in Los Angeles, California.

1978 A new missionary training program is announced, requiring English-speaking missionaries to receive four weeks of training and missionaries learning other languages to receive the standard eight weeks of training at the new Missionary Training Center in Provo, Utah.

1993 The African nation of Cameroon officially recognizes the Church.

❧ ❧ ❧ SEPTEMBER 10 ❧ ❧ ❧

1845 A mob attacks and kills Edmund Durfee in Morley's Settlement, Hancock County, Illinois, and sets fire to the buildings in the settlement. The event marks an escalation of the mob's efforts to force the Saints from Illinois following the death of Joseph Smith.

1846 In an incident later known as the Battle of Nauvoo, anti-Mormon forces converge on Nauvoo and open fire on the city, intending to drive out the remaining Mormons.

1896 The Montana Mission is organized.

1924 Boyd K. Packer, later a member of the Quorum of the Twelve Apostles, is born in Brigham City, Utah.

1933 Sponsored by funds provided by industrialist Henry Ford, the Mormon Tabernacle Choir arrives at the "Century of Progress" fair in Chicago. The choir sang in the Ford Symphony Gardens during a week of open-air concerts, two of which were broadcast nationally by CBS.

President Boyd K. Packer, by Knud Ebsberg, ca. 1990 (see 1924).

1946 The first missionaries to Costa Rica arrive in the country.

1961 The Berlin Stake, the first stake in Germany, is organized, with Rudi Seehagen as president.

1982 President Gordon B. Hinckley, Counselor to President Spencer W. Kimball, hosts U.S. president Ronald Reagan for a tour of a cannery at the Ogden Area Welfare Services Center. President Reagan praises the volunteerism embodied in the center's operation.

1985 The first branch of the Church on the Caribbean islands of St. Kitts and Nevis is organized, with Reuel Lambourn as president.

1990 Missionaries arrive in the Balkan nation of Bulgaria for the first time.

SEPTEMBER 11

1790 Artemus Millet, later the superintendent and head mason for the Kirtland Temple, is born in Westmoreland, New Hampshire.

1813 Joatana H. Napela, later an early Hawaiian convert who assisted George Q. Cannon in translating the Book of Mormon into Hawaiian, is born on the island of Maui, Hawaii.

1831 Joseph Smith receives Doctrine and Covenants 64, which gives instructions to the Saints concerning forgiveness and the future of Zion.

1833 Joseph Smith, Sidney Rigdon, Frederick G. Williams, Oliver Cowdery, and Newel K. Whitney announce that, as a result of the destruction of the Church press in Independence, Missouri, Oliver Cowdery will publish *The Evening and Morning Star* and the *Latter-day Saints' Messenger and Advocate* from Kirtland, Ohio.

1846 President Brigham Young and the Quorum of the Twelve Apostles formally select the site for Winter Quarters (later Florence, Nebraska), the main winter encampment of the Saints. This is the first city in Nebraska.

1851 Hans F. Peterson arrives in Riisør, becoming the first Latter-day Saint missionary to Norway.

1853 William W. Taylor, one of the First Seven Presidents of the Seventy, is born in Salt Lake City, Utah.

1857 The Mountain Meadows Massacre takes place in southern Utah.

1884 Harvey Fletcher, later an internationally recognized research scientist and the "father of stereophonic sound," is born in Provo, Utah.

1935 F. David Stanley, later a member of the Second Quorum of the Seventy, is born in Salt Lake City, Utah.

1955 President David O. McKay dedicates the Swiss Temple (later the Bern Switzerland Temple) in Bern, Switzerland.

1982 Elder Boyd K. Packer breaks ground for the Lima Peru Temple.

1998 The First Presidency announces plans to build temples in Birmingham, Alabama, and Columbia, South Carolina.

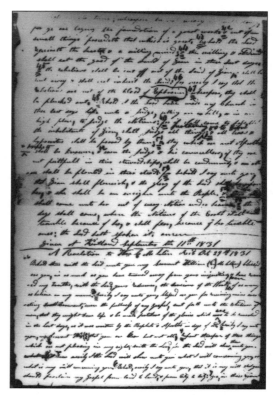

Manuscript of the Book of Commandments marked by W. W. Phelps where he had finished setting type before a mob broke in and destroyed the press in 1833.

～～～ SEPTEMBER *12* ～～～

1830 Elmina Shepard (Taylor), later the first general president of the Young Women's Mutual Improvement Association (predecessor to the Young Women organization), is born in Middlefield, New York.

1831 Joseph Smith and his family move to the John Johnson home in Hiram, Ohio, where the Prophet continues his translation of the Bible.

1852 The first branch is organized in British India at Poonah.

1906 Rose Marie Yancey (Reid), later an internationally renowned swimsuit designer, businesswoman, and author, is born in Cardston, Alberta, Canada.

1924 Howard C. Nielson, later a Utah representative in the U.S. Congress (1983–91), is born in Richfield, Utah.

1951 James E. Talmage's classic book *The Articles of Faith* is published in Spanish.

1974 Elder Gordon B. Hinckley offers an invocation at the U.S. Congress.

1979 The Mormon Tabernacle Choir commences a four-day tour of Japan and Korea.

1981 The First Presidency announces a smaller, less-expensive ward meetinghouse design called the Sage Plan.

1982 Elder Richard G. Scott breaks ground for the Guatemala City Temple (later the Guatemala City Guatemala Temple).

1991 Elder Boyd K. Packer dedicates the republic of the Ukraine in the former Soviet Union for the preaching of the gospel.

1998 Ground is broken for the Columbus Ohio Temple. Elder John K. Carmack, a member of the Quorum of the Seventy and President of the North America East Area presides over the ceremony.

The Ukraine dedication site, which overlooks the Dnieper River in Kiev and is near the monument honoring Prince Vladimir, who introduced Christianity to the land just over a millennium ago, ca. 1995 (see 1991).

✦ ✦ ✦ SEPTEMBER *13* ✦ ✦ ✦

1800 Newel Knight, later a close friend of Joseph Smith and president of the Colesville Branch, is born in Marlborough, Vermont.

1855 The Horticultural Society is organized in Salt Lake City with Wilford Woodruff as president. Other societies organized that year include the Universal Scientific Society, the Polysophical Society, the Deseret Philharmonic Society, and the Deseret Typographical Association.

1856 Under the direction of President Brigham Young, President Jedediah M. Grant of the First Presidency institutes the "Mormon Reformation" at a conference in Kaysville. The purpose of the reformation was to remind the Saints of their blessings and to call them to repentance for being lax in keeping the commandments.

1898 Lorenzo Snow is ordained as the fifth President of the Church, with George Q. Cannon and Joseph F. Smith as Counselors.

1914 A. B. Christensen is appointed sixth president of Ricks College.

1933 Angel Abrea, later a member of the First Quorum of the Seventy and the first Argentine General Authority, is born in Buenos Aires, Argentina.

1937 Don Bluth, later a Disney animator for such classics as *Sleeping Beauty* (1955) and *Pete's Dragon* (1977) and director of *An American Tail* (1987) and *Land Before Time* (1987) is born in El Paso, Texas.

1970 The Chesapeake Stake, the first stake in Maryland, is organized, with June B. Thayn as president.

President Lorenzo Snow, by Lewis A. Ramsey, ca. 1898 (see 1898).

1993 The Council of Religious Affairs of the Council of Ministers in the Soviet Union approves the registration of the Leningrad Branch of the Church. The approval marks formal recognition in the Soviet Union for the first time.

1994 President Howard W. Hunter addresses full-time missionaries over the satellite system, the first-ever satellite address to missionaries.

1840 Joseph Smith Sr., Patriarch to the Church and one of the Eight Witnesses of the Book of Mormon, dies in Nauvoo, Illinois.

1850 The government of the provisional state of Deseret approves the incorporation of the Perpetual Emigrating Company, which facilitates the immigration of thousands of converts to Utah until 1887.

1930 George Hansen, an Idaho representative in the U.S. Congress (1965–69, 1975–85), is born in Tetonia, Idaho.

1935 The *Deseret News* announces the appointment of Elder John A. Widtsoe to teach a religion class at the University of Southern California (USC). This becomes the first institute of religion outside the Intermountain West.

1963 President David O. McKay dedicates a monument in Kansas City, Missouri, commemorating the establishment of the city's first school, which was erected by the Colesville Saints in 1831.

A monument commemorating the establishment of the first school in present-day Kansas City, Missouri, in 1831, ca. 1963 (see 1963).

1993 Elder Joseph B. Wirthlin dedicates the Mediterranean island of Cyprus for the preaching of the gospel.

1994 Elder Dallin H. Oaks dedicates the Republic of Cape Verde, located four hundred miles west of Senegal on the African coast, for the preaching of the gospel.

1843 Joseph Smith opens the Nauvoo Mansion as a hotel.

1850 The first branch of the Church in Denmark is organized in Copenhagen.

1851 The first two converts in Germany are baptized.

1857 Having recently learned that U.S. president James Buchanan is sending an army to Utah to quell an alleged rebellion, Governor Brigham Young declares martial law in the territory and orders the militia to prevent Johnston's army from entering the Salt Lake Valley.

1876 Don Byron Colton, later a Utah representative in the U.S. Congress (1920–32), is born in Mona, Utah.

1940 Merlin Jay Olsen, later a consensus all-American defensive tackle, Outland Trophy winner at Utah State University, NFL Hall of Fame inductee, and TV and movie star, is born in Logan, Utah.

1941 The Western Canadian Mission is organized.

Interior of the Liberty Jail Visitors' Center, ca. 1963 (see 1963).

1963 President Joseph Fielding Smith of the Quorum of the Twelve Apostles dedicates the new Liberty Jail Visitors' Center on the site where his grandfather Hyrum Smith and great-uncle Joseph Smith were incarcerated with others during the winter of 1838–39.

1969 President Hugh B. Brown of the First Presidency breaks ground for the Provo Temple (later the Provo Utah Temple).

1978 Ronnie Oei and family, the first converts in the west Pacific island republic of Palau, are baptized.

1983 President Gordon B. Hinckley of the First Presidency dedicates the Santiago Chile Temple.

1985 Miss Utah, Church member Sharlene Wells, is chosen as the new Miss America.

1990 At a memorial service at the site of the Mountain Meadows Massacre of 1857 in Cedar City, Utah, President Gordon B. Hinckley of the First Presidency addresses a gathering composed of descendants of those involved on both sides of the tragedy. President Hinckley also dedicates a newly completed commemorative monument at the site.

Miss America Sharlene Wells (see 1985).

1993 Elder Matjaz Juhart, the first missionary called from the republic of Slovenia, enters the Missionary Training Center in Provo.

SEPTEMBER 16

1845 A mob in Hancock County, Illinois, attempts to kill Sheriff Jacob Backenstos (a nonmember) for his efforts to bring mob members to justice. While defending Backenstos, Orrin Porter Rockwell shoots and kills Frank A. Worrell, one of the leaders of the mob.

1852 Anthony Woodward Ivins, later a member of the Quorum of the Twelve Apostles and First Presidency, is born in Toms River, New Jersey.

1962 The North Argentine Mission is organized.

1978 President Spencer W. Kimball addresses the first closed-circuit Churchwide meeting for women ages twelve and older in the Tabernacle on Temple Square. The meeting is broadcast via satellite to meetinghouses throughout the world, as are general priesthood meetings.

1991 Monroe G. McKay, a former J. Reuben Clark Law School faculty member, is invested as chief judge of the U.S. Tenth Circuit Court of Appeals.

1993 The government of the central African nation of Ethiopia recognizes the Church.

1995 Canadian government officials name the Alberta Temple (later the Cardston Alberta Temple) a Canadian Historic Site at a ceremony in Cardston.

SEPTEMBER 17

1846 Following the Battle of Nauvoo—a week-long anti-Mormon assault against the Saints remaining in the city—several hundred Church members are forced across the Mississippi River to Iowa, where they await help from those already on the trail.

1858 James H. Moyle, later an attorney, politician, and Church leader, is born in Salt Lake City, Utah.

1870 Edward Stevenson rebaptizes Martin Harris, one of the Three Witnesses of the Book of Mormon.

1888 George Q. Cannon turns himself in to federal authorities and is sentenced to 175 days in the penitentiary for violating antipolygamy laws.

1900 J. Willard Marriott, later a Church leader, international businessman, and founder of Marriott Hotels, is born in Marriott, Utah.

1920 Lloyd P. George Jr., later a member of the First Quorum of the Seventy, is born in Kanosh, Utah.

1978 The first episode of the TV series *Battlestar Gallactica,* created, written, and produced by Church member Glen A. Larson, airs on ABC. The story line of the series incorporates many LDS beliefs and doctrines.

1988 The Church joins VISN, an interfaith cable television network sponsored by eighteen religious organizations.

1988 The BYU Folk Dancers perform at the opening ceremonies of the 1988 Olympic Games in Seoul, Korea.

1998 The First Presidency announces plans to build the Memphis Tennessee Temple.

SEPTEMBER 18

1810 Hosea Stout, later a diary recorder, police officer, lawyer and missionary, is born in Pleasant Hill, Kentucky.

1839 Apostles Brigham Young and Heber C. Kimball leave Nauvoo, embarking on a mission to England.

1848 John Henry Smith, later a member of the Quorum of the Twelve Apostles and Counselor in the First Presidency, is born near Kanesville, Iowa.

The First Presidency, ca. 1907. From left: Anthon H. Lund, President Joseph F. Smith, and John Henry Smith (see 1848).

1931 Rex D. Pinegar, later a member of the Presidency of the Seventy, is born in Orem, Utah.

1933 Robert F. Bennett, later a successful businessman and, like his father, Wallace F. Bennett, a Utah member of the U.S. Senate (1992–), is born in Salt Lake City, Utah.

1941 Gary J. Coleman, later a member of the the First Quorum of the Seventy, is born in Wenatchee, Washington.

1952 Bruce D. Porter, later a member of the Second Quorum of the Seventy, is born in Albuquerque, New Mexico.

1960 The Austrian Mission is organized.

1966 The Hartford Stake, the first stake in Connecticut, is organized, with Hugh S. West as president.

SEPTEMBER  19

1811 Orson Pratt, later a member of the Quorum of the Twelve Apostles, is born in Hartford, New York.

1830 Orson Pratt is baptized by his brother Parley P. Pratt in Canaan, New York.

The Orson Pratt family, ca. 1853 (see 1830).

1888 Jacob Spori is selected to be the first principal of the newly created Bannock Stake Academy (later Ricks College).

1897 Marion G. Romney, later a member of the Quorum of the Twelve Apostles and First Presidency, is born in Colonia Juárez, Mexico.

1923 H. Burke Peterson, later a member of the First Quorum of the Seventy, is born in Salt Lake City, Utah.

1931 L. Lionel Kendrick, later a member of the First Quorum of the Seventy, is born in Baton Rouge, Louisiana.

1968 Troy Dalbey, later an Olympic gold medalist in swimming at the 1988 Seoul games, is born in St. Louis, Missouri.

1972 Elder Gordon B. Hinckley offers a prayer at Mars Hill in Athens, Greece. President Harold B. Lee later states that the prayer stands as a rededication of Greece for the preaching of the gospel.

1992 Twenty converts to the Church are baptized in Central Africa Republic, and the first two branches in that country are organized, with Celestin N'Gakondou as president of the Bangui 1st Branch and Gaspard Lapet as president of the Bangui 2nd Branch.

1999 President Gordon B. Hinckley dedicates the Bismarck North Dakota Temple.

SEPTEMBER 20

1811 John F. Boynton, later a member of the Quorum of the Twelve Apostles, is born in Bradford, Massachusetts.

1850 U.S. president Millard Fillmore appoints the first territorial officials for the newly created territory of Utah; Brigham Young is appointed as its first governor.

1910 The Deseret Gymnasium, owned by the Church, opens in a building on the Church Administration Block.

1917 U.S. president Woodrow Wilson appoints James H. Moyle, the first Latter-day Saint to serve in a subcabinet position in the United States, as assistant secretary of the U.S. Treasury.

The Tragedy of Winter Quarters, *by Avard T. Fairbanks (see 1936).*

1936 President Heber J. Grant dedicates the Winter Quarters Cemetery Monument in Florence, Nebraska, with the *Tragedy of Winter Quarters* statue by Avard T. Fairbanks as the central sculpture. The monument honors the Saints who perished there during the winter of 1846–47.

1959 The Brazilian South Mission is organized.

1984 President Gordon B. Hinckley of the First Presidency dedicates the Sydney Australia Temple.

1986 President Gordon B. Hinckley breaks ground for the Portland Oregon Temple.

1990 Bookcraft, Inc., releases Gerald N. Lund's first volume in the historical novel series *The Work and the Glory.* The series sells more than one million copies, becoming one of the most successful ventures in Church publication history.

1994 David W. Checketts is named president and chief executive officer of Madison Square Garden.

1997 Ground is broken for the first meetinghouse in Greece.

SEPTEMBER 21

1823 During the night, the angel Moroni visits Joseph Smith for the first time and tells him about the gold plates. Doctrine and Covenants 2 is taken from Moroni's message.

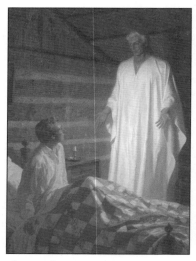

The Angel Moroni Appears to Joseph Smith, *by Tom Lovell, ca. 1987* (*see 1823*).

1839 George A. Smith leaves Nauvoo to embark on the mission of the Quorum of the Twelve Apostles to England.

1851 The First Presidency issues an epistle to the Saints still living in Iowa, urging them to continue on to Utah.

1862 James E. Talmage, later a member of the Quorum of the Twelve Apostles, is born in Hungerford, England.

1952 The El Paso Stake, the first stake in Texas, is organized, with Edward V. Turley Sr. as president.

1965 The First Presidency establishes a missionary quota in the United States, limiting the number of those serving to two per ward to comply with U.S. Selective Service rules during the Vietnam War.

1997 The Port-au-Prince Haiti Stake, the first stake in Haiti, is organized, with Reynolds Antoine Saint-Louis as president.

1998 Brother and sister Donny and Marie Osmond make their return to TV as hosts of a talk show called *The Donny and Marie Show.* They had starred in a one-hour variety show from 1976 to 1979.

SEPTEMBER 22

1823 Moroni appears to Joseph Smith at the Hill Cumorah and shows him the gold plates for the first time. He visits Joseph on the same date for the next four years at this location.

1827 Joseph Smith receives the plates, the Urim and Thummim, and the breastplate from the angel Moroni at the Hill Cumorah.

1828 Moroni returns the gold plates to Joseph Smith, having taken them from the Prophet after Martin Harris lost 116 manuscript pages of the translated record.

1832 Beginning on this day, Joseph Smith receives Doctrine and Covenants 84, a revelation on priesthood. Portions of the revelation were received the following day.

Aerial view (looking north) of the Hill Cumorah (lower right), ca. 1988 (see 1823 and 1827).

1832 John Smith, son of Hyrum and Jerusha Barden Smith and later the fourth Patriarch to the Church, is born in Kirtland, Ohio.

1841 A company of men leaves Nauvoo for the pine forests of Wisconsin to procure lumber for the Nauvoo Temple.

1851 Elder Amasa M. Lyman and others purchase the San Bernardino ranch in southern California for a Latter-day Saint colonization. The ranch consists of about 100,000 acres.

1897 Elder Janne M. Sjødahl presents King Oscar of Sweden with a Book of Mormon in an onyx box on behalf of Scandinavian Saints in Utah.

1948 William (Bill) H. Orton, a Utah representative in the U.S. Congress (1990–96), is born in Ogden, Utah.

1951 President David O. McKay breaks ground for the Los Angeles Temple (later the Los Angeles California Temple).

1965 J. Averil Jesperson, president of the Andes Mission, receives a letter from Elder Spencer W. Kimball suggesting that he begin missionary work in Ecuador. Missionaries first arrive in Ecuador two weeks later.

SEPTEMBER 23

1886 Federal deputy marshals search the Gardo House in Salt Lake City in an unsuccessful attempt to find and arrest President John Taylor for violation of antipolygamy laws.

1911 Frank E. "Ted" Moss, a Utah member of the U.S. Senate (1959–77), is born in Holladay, Utah.

1945 President George Albert Smith dedicates the Idaho Falls Temple (later the Idaho Falls Idaho Temple).

1995 President Gordon B. Hinckley reads the Proclamation on the Family in a general Relief Society meeting. The proclamation, issued by the First Presidency and the Quorum of the Twelve Apostles, declares gospel standards, doctrines, and practices relative to the family.

Idaho Falls Temple (see 1945).

SEPTEMBER 24

1839 George Careless, later a pioneer musician and composer of nine hymn settings found in the LDS hymnal (1985), is born in London, England.

1860 The Stoddard handcart company, consisting of 126 people and twenty-two handcarts, enters Salt Lake City, the last of the ten handcart companies to cross the plains.

1864 Annie Clark (Tanner), later the author of *A Biography of Ezra T. Clark* and *A Mormon Mother,* is born in Farmington, Utah.

1890 President Wilford Woodruff issues the Manifesto, marking the end of Church-sanctioned plural marriages. In 1914 it is added to the Doctrine and Covenants and is later known as Official Declaration 1.

U.S. president William Howard Taft standing to the right of Reed Smoot (at the pulpit) in the Provo Tabernacle, 24 September 1909.

1909 U.S. president William Howard Taft visits Utah and tours the communities south of Salt Lake City with Elder Reed Smoot, a U.S. senator from Utah.

1922 Douglas Stringfellow, later a Utah representative in the U.S. Congress (1953–55), is born in Draper, Utah.

1937 The New England Mission is organized.

SEPTEMBER 25

1835 Marriner W. Merrill, later a member of the Quorum of the Twelve Apostles, is born in Sackville, New Brunswick, Canada.

1919 Lynn A. Sorensen, later a member of the First Quorum of the Seventy, is born in Salt Lake City, Utah.

1928 President Charles W. Nibley of the First Presidency dedicates the Moscow Institute Building, which is located adjacent to the University of Idaho campus. It is the first institute building in the Church. A year earlier, J. Wyley Sessions began the program with fifty-seven students.

1944 Carlos H. Amado, later a member of the First Quorum of the Seventy, is born in Guatemala City, Guatemala.

1951 Jackson Stewart Horsley, later an Olympic bronze medalist in swimming at the 1968 Mexico City games, is born in Salt Lake City, Utah.

1958 Greg Olsen, later the artist of such paintings as *O Jerusalem* and *A Light to the Gentiles,* is born in Iona, Idaho.

Couple in front of the Manila Philippines Temple (see 1984).

1984 President Gordon B. Hinckley of the First Presidency dedicates the Manila Philippines Temple.

1998 The First Presidency announces plans to build the Mérida México Temple.

SEPTEMBER 26

1815 Jesse Little, later a pioneer and president in the Eastern States Mission in the 1840s and '50s, is born in Belmont, Maine.

1830 Joseph Smith receives Doctrine and Covenants 29, a revelation containing information about the Second Coming.

1835 The Quorum of the Twelve Apostles returns to Kirtland from its first organized mission, having preached the gospel in the eastern United States for nearly five months.

1856 The first two handcart companies, the Ellsworth and McArthur companies, arrive in Salt Lake City amidst great celebration.

1942 James C. Christensen, later an internationally recognized fantasy painter, is born in Culver City, California.

1963 U.S. president John F. Kennedy speaks for ninety minutes in the Tabernacle in Salt Lake City on foreign policy. (He is assassinated two months later on 27 November 1963.)

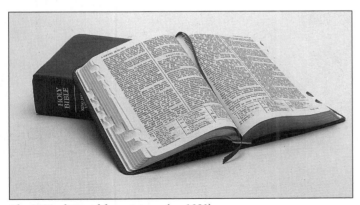

The 1981 edition of the scriptures (see 1981).

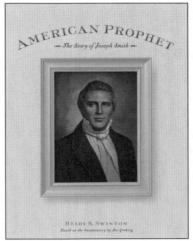

Book cover of American Prophet: The Story of Joseph Smith, *a companion volume to the Lee Groberg film by the same name (see 1999).*

1981 The Church publishes a new version of the triple combination (Book of Mormon, Doctrine and Covenants, and Pearl of Great Price) that includes extensive cross-references and an index.

1992 The First Presidency authorizes the use of humanitarian relief funds for the aid of drought victims in Somalia and other African nations and later sends one million pounds of food in the first shipment.

1998 Ground is broken for the St. Paul Minnesota Temple. Elder Hugh W. Pinnock, a member of the First Quorum of the Seventy and a counselor in the North American Central Area Presidency, presides over the ceremonies.

1999 Residents of Utah preview Lee Groberg's *American Prophet: The Story of Joseph Smith,* which is narrated by Gregory Peck and includes the voice talent of Megan Follows as Emma Smith. The film later premieres nationally on PBS on 26 November.

SEPTEMBER 27

1809 Peter Whitmer Jr., later one of the Eight Witnesses of the Book of Mormon, is born in Fayette, New York.

1850 The First Presidency issues the Fourth General Epistle to the Church. The epistle addresses the lack of communication between the state of Deseret and the rest of the Union.

1935 Val R. Christensen, later a member of the Second Quorum of the Seventy, is born in Hooper, Utah.

1940 Jorge A. Rojas Ornelas, later a member of the Second Quorum of the Seventy, is born in Delicias, Mexico.

Architect's rendering of the Missionary Training Center in Provo, Utah (see 1976).

1943 Randall (Randy) Charles Bachman, later a rock superstar and member of the popular 1960s and '70s bands Guess Who and Bachman-Turner Overdrive, is born in Winnipeg, Canada.

1976 President Spencer W. Kimball dedicates the first buildings of the new Language Training Mission (LTM), later known as the Missionary Training Center (MTC), in Provo.

SEPTEMBER 28

1847 The second or "big company" of pioneers, led by Elders Parley P. Pratt and John Taylor, begins arriving in the Salt Lake Valley.

1848 Addison Pratt arrives in the Salt Lake Valley after serving a five-year mission to the South Pacific, where he baptized approximately twelve hundred people.

1850 U.S. president Millard Fillmore signs papers appointing Brigham Young as governor of the territory of Utah.

1860 George Edward Anderson, later a famous landscape and portrait photographer and the first professional photographer to systematically collect images of LDS Church history sites, is born in Salt Lake City, Utah.

1877 The cornerstones for the Assembly Hall on Temple Square are laid.

1857 General Daniel H. Wells leaves Salt Lake City to establish military headquarters in Echo Canyon in an effort to defend Utah against the approaching army commanded by Colonel Albert Sidney Johnston. The army had been sent to Utah to quell the Saints' alleged rebellion against the United States government.

1954 Bo Gustafsson, later an Olympic silver medalist in the 50-kilometer walk at the 1984 Los Angeles games, is born in Skee, Sweden.

1967 The new administrative position of regional representative of the Quorum of the Twelve Apostles is announced, and sixty-nine regional representatives are called and trained.

1979 The Church publishes the LDS edition of the King James Version of the Bible, which includes a topical guide, a Bible dictionary, and extensive footnotes.

1801 James Brown, later a missionary, pioneer, and founder of Ogden, Utah, is born in Rowan County, North Carolina.

1901 David Lawrence McKay, later the general superintendent of the Deseret Sunday School (1966–71), is born in Ogden, Utah.

1949 General conference is broadcast on television for the first time.

1961 Florence Smith Jacobsen is sustained as the sixth general president of the Young Women's Mutual Improvement Association (predecessor to the Young Women organization), with Margaret R. Jackson and Dorothy Porter Holt as counselors.

During the presidency of David O. McKay (1966), Counselors Hugh B. Brown and N. Eldon Tanner and Elder Gordon B. Hinckley of the Quorum of the Twelve Apostles become the incorporators of Deseret Management Corporation (see 1966).

1961 Elder Harold B. Lee announces the Church's new correlation effort, which includes the creation of an all-Church Coordinating Council. The council is made up of four members of the Quorum of the Twelve Apostles, the Presiding Bishop, the auxiliary heads, and representatives from the Melchizedek Priesthood Committee and the Church Educational System.

1961 John Henry Vandenberg is sustained as Presiding Bishop of the Church.

1966 The Church consolidates all Church-owned businesses under Deseret Management Corporation. Presidents Hugh B. Brown and N. Eldon Tanner of the First Presidency and Elder Gordon B. Hinckley are the three incorporators.

1978 Emeritus status for General Authorities is announced in general conference, designating seven members of the Seventy to the special status.

1989 The first General Authorities called to serve for five years are released.

1995 President Gordon B. Hinckley announces plans to build temples in White Plains, New York; Caracas, Venezuela; New York City; and Boston, Massachusetts. The temple announced for Boston replaces one previously announced for Hartford, Connecticut.

1997 The First Presidency announces plans to build temples in Houston, Texas, and Porto Alegre, Brazil.

❧ ❧ ❧ OCTOBER ❧ ❧ ❧

1812 Almon W. Babbitt, later an attorney, the agent of the Church at the time of the exodus from Nauvoo, and the provisional state of Deseret's delegate to Congress (1849), is born in Cheshire, Massachusetts.

1817 Henry Grow, later the architect and builder of the Tabernacle in Salt Lake City, is born in Norristown, Pennsylvania.

1833 Oliver Cowdery leaves Kirtland for New York to purchase a printing press to replace the Church's press that had been destroyed by mobs in Jackson County, Missouri.

1835 Joseph Smith writes: "This afternoon I labored on the Egyptian alphabet in company with Brother Oliver Cowdery and W. W. Phelps, and during the research, the principles of astronomy as understood by Father Abraham and the ancients unfolded to our understanding" (*History of the Church,* 2:286).

1844 John Willard Young, later a member of the First Presidency, is born in Nauvoo, Illinois.

1861 The first baptisms in the Netherlands take place near the village of Broek-Akkerwoude.

1872 Henry H. Blood, later the governor of Utah (1933–41), is born in Kaysville, Utah.

1913 President Joseph F. Smith dedicates Mahonri Young's Seagull Monument, commemorating the miracle of the gulls that ate crickets threatening to destroy the crops of the Saints in the spring of 1848.

1938 Janice Kapp (Perry), later the composer of several LDS hymns and songs (including "We'll Bring the World His Truth"), is born in Ogden, Utah.

Professional baseball player Vance Law, 7 July 1988 (see 1956).

1956 Vance A. Law, later a professional baseball player and BYU baseball coach, is born in Boise, Idaho.

1963 The Franco-Belgian Mission is organized.

1976 All of the Assistants to the Quorum of the Twelve Apostles and all members of the First Council of the Seventy are released during general conference and called to the First Quorum of the Seventy, which had been created one year earlier.

1977 The Church publishes *A Topical Guide to the Scriptures of The Church of Jesus Christ of Latter-day Saints* as part of a scripture study helps project directed by the First Presidency.

1978 James E. Faust is ordained an Apostle, replacing Delbert L. Stapley, who had died.

1984 The El Salvador San Salvador Mission is created.

1988 President Ezra Taft Benson opens general conference with a challenge for the Saints to flood the earth with the Book of Mormon.

1994 Patricia Peterson Pinegar is called as the ninth general president of the Primary, with Anne G. Wirthlin and Susan L. Warner as counselors.

1838 Joseph Smith, Sidney Rigdon, and others meet at Far West with the "Kirtland Camp," a group of some 500 Church members from Kirtland who had traveled together to Missouri. A few days later they settle at Adam-ondi-Ahman.

1841 Joseph Smith dedicates the Nauvoo House cornerstone with the original manuscript of the Book of Mormon in it.

1856 The Edward Bunker handcart company, the third to leave Iowa City, arrives in the Salt Lake Valley.

1981 Elder Boyd K. Packer addresses a General Authority Training Meeting and bears testimony of the Lord's influence throughout the process of preparing the newly released LDS edition of the scriptures.

Nauvoo House cornerstone, 4 May 1907 (see 1841).

1995 President Gordon B. Hinckley dedicates the Brigham Young Historic Park, east of the Church Office Building block in Salt Lake City.

1999 Coleen K. Menlove is called as the tenth general president of the Primary, with Sydney S. Reynolds and Gayle M. Clegg as counselors.

1999 The 160th Semiannual General Conference marks the last general conference held in the historic Tabernacle on Temple Square. The worldwide conference had been held in the Tabernacle since 1867.

❧❧❧ OCTOBER 3 ❧❧❧

1806 Oliver Cowdery, later one of the Three Witnesses of the Book of Mormon and Assistant President of the Church, is born in Wells, Vermont.

1837 Seymour B. Young, later one of the First Seven Presidents of the Seventy, is born in Kirtland, Ohio.

1847 The Salt Lake Stake, the first stake in Utah, is organized, with John Smith (an uncle of the Prophet Joseph Smith) as president.

1875 U.S. president Ulysses S. Grant arrives in Salt Lake City, becoming the first U.S. president to visit Utah.

1910 Emmeline B. Wells is called as the fifth general president of the Relief Society, with Clarissa Smith Williams and Julina Lambson Smith as counselors.

Oliver Cowdery monument, ca. 1991 (see 1806).

1918 Just weeks before his passing, President Joseph F. Smith receives the Vision of the Redemption of the Dead, later known as Doctrine and Covenants 138.

1922 Naomi Maxfield (Shumway), later the sixth general president of the Primary, is born in Provo, Utah.

1924 The Church broadcasts general conference for the first time on a Church-owned radio station.

1930 J. Reuben Clark is appointed as U.S. ambassador to Mexico, becoming the first Church member to be appointed as an ambassador.

1956 President David O. McKay dedicates the Relief Society Building in Salt Lake City.

1974 Barbara B. Smith is called as the tenth general president of the Relief Society, with Janath Russell Cannon and Marian Richards Boyer as counselors.

1974 In a talk entitled "Lengthening Our Stride" at a regional representatives' seminar, President Spencer W. Kimball issues a call to help the Church fulfill its worldwide mission.

1975 President Spencer W. Kimball announces the organization of the First Quorum of the Seventy, and Charles Didier, William R. Bradford, and George P. Lee are sustained as the first members of that quorum.

1981 The Church announces the creation of a network of 500 satellite dishes to be placed at stake centers outside of Utah, linking Church headquarters in Salt Lake City with members in the United States and Canada.

1982 Elder Boyd K. Packer, a member of the Scriptures Publication Committee, announces in general conference the addition of the subtitle "Another Testament of Jesus Christ" to the Book of Mormon.

1834 Aurelia Spencer (Rogers), later founder of the Primary and a women's advocate, is born in Deep River, Connecticut.

1855 The ship *Julia Ann,* with twenty-eight members of the Church from Australia on board, wrecks on a coral reef near the Scilly Islands. Five Latter-day Saints die, but all others are eventually rescued and complete their journey to San Francisco.

1856 The Carson Valley Stake, the first stake in Nevada, is organized, with Orson Hyde as president.

1877 Charles Rendell Mabey, later the governor of Utah (1921–25), is born in Bountiful, Utah.

1879 The first edition of the *Contributor,* the official publication of the Young Men's Mutual Improvement Association, is issued. The *Contributor* continues until 1896.

1953 General conference is televised live from Salt Lake City to locations outside the Intermountain West for the first time.

1959 The South German Mission is organized.

1986 The Church announces the discontinuation of stake seventies quorums, reassigning seventies to elders quorums or ordaining them high priests.

1997 Margaret D. Nadauld is sustained as the eleventh general president of the Young Women, with Carol Burdett Thomas and Sharon Greene Larsen as counselors.

1997 The First Presidency announces plans to build temples in Anchorage, Alaska; Colonia Juárez, Chihuahua, Mexico; and Monticello, Utah.

1833 Joseph Smith, Sidney Rigdon, and Freeman Nickerson leave Kirtland, embarking on a one-month proselyting mission to Ontario Province in "upper Canada."

1839 At a general conference held at Commerce (later Nauvoo), Illinois, William Marks is appointed president of the Nauvoo Stake, Bishops Edward Partridge and Vinson Knight are assigned congregations, and the high council is organized.

1839 The Iowa Stake, the first stake in Iowa, is organized, with John Smith as president.

1845 Approximately five thousand Saints attend general conference in the unfinished Nauvoo Temple, the only general conference ever held there.

1851 In Calcutta, Elder Maurice White baptizes a woman named Anna, the first native of India to join the Church.

1854 Joseph Standing, later a missionary and martyr, is born in Salt Lake City, Utah.

1856 President Brigham Young organizes the effort to rescue the Martin and Willie handcart companies, both of which are still east of South Pass in Wyoming.

◄ *The general Young Women presidency, ca. 1997. From left: Carol B. Thomas, President Margaret D. Nadauld, and Sharon G. Larsen (see 1997).*

1857 During the Utah War, a small company of men led by Lot Smith burns two supply wagon trains for Johnston's army as part of the Saints' effort to slow the army's march.

1907 Because of concerns that his first baptism (which took place in the family bathtub) might not have been performed appropriately, Spencer W. Kimball is baptized a second time, in the Union Canal in Thatcher, Arizona. (He is twelve years and six months old.)

1926 Derek A. Cuthbert, later a member of the First Quorum of the Seventy, is born in Nottingham, England.

1935 Charles Didier, later a member of the Presidency of the Seventy, is born in Ixelles, Belgium.

1947 President J. Reuben Clark of the First Presidency delivers "To Them of the Last Wagon," an important address praising the "meekest and lowliest" members of the Church as symbolized by the faithful pioneers at the end of the wagon train.

1950 Delbert L. Stapley is ordained an Apostle, replacing George F. Richards, who had died.

1958 Enid Greene (Waldhotz), a Utah representative in the U.S. Congress (1995–97), is born in San Rafael, California.

1961 Gordon B. Hinckley is ordained an Apostle, replacing Hugh B. Brown, who had been called to the First Presidency.

1967 Alvin Rulon Dyer is ordained an Apostle but not placed in the Quorum of the Twelve. He acts as an additional Counselor in the First Presidency.

1974 Naomi Maxfield Shumway is called as the sixth general president of the Primary, with Sara Broadbent Paulsen and Colleen Bushman Lemmon as counselors.

1986 The First Presidency releases a statement indicating that the Church is opposed to the legalization of gambling and government-sponsored lotteries.

OCTOBER 6

1849 The Deseret Dramatic Association is organized in Salt Lake City.

1867 The first conference to be held in the newly completed Tabernacle on Temple Square in Salt Lake City opens.

1868 Brigham Young Jr., who had been ordained an Apostle in 1864, is called to the Quorum of the Twelve Apostles, replacing George A. Smith, who would be called the next day as a Counselor in the First Presidency.

1890 During general conference, Church members accept what becomes known as the "Manifesto," a document that announces the end of Church-sanctioned plural marriage in Utah.

1907 Anthony W. Ivins is ordained an Apostle, replacing George Teasdale, who had died.

1925 May Anderson is called as the second general president of the Primary, with Sadie Grant Pack and Isabelle Salmon Ross as counselors.

1939 Dennis B. Neuenschwander, later a member of the First Quorum of the Seventy, is born in Salt Lake City, Utah.

1952 The Presiding Bishopric issues a letter introducing the Senior Aaronic Priesthood program, which places men over twenty-one years of age in a separate Aaronic Priesthood quorum.

Richard G. Scott (see 1988).

1961 President J. Reuben Clark Jr. of the First Presidency dies in Salt Lake City. He is the only Apostle in this dispensation to serve his entire apostolic ministry in the First Presidency.

1975 Beginning on this day, BYU observes its centennial during homecoming week.

1988 Richard G. Scott is ordained an Apostle, replacing Marion G. Romney, who had died.

▶ *The Quorum of the Twelve Apostles with Ezra Taft Benson (standing, left) and Spencer W. Kimball (standing, right) (see 1943).*

1844 Following the death of Joseph Smith, the Prophet's uncle, John Smith, is sustained as the Nauvoo Stake president, replacing William Marks, who refused to accept the leadership of the Twelve Apostles.

1844 George Miller is sustained as Second Bishop of the Church.

1889 Marriner W. Merrill, Anthon H. Lund, and Abraham H. Cannon are ordained Apostles, replacing Albert Carrington, who had been excommunicated; Erastus Snow, who had died; and Wilford Woodruff, who had been called to the First Presidency.

1897 Matthias F. Cowley and Abraham O. Woodruff are ordained Apostles, replacing Abraham H. Cannon, who had died, and Moses Thatcher, who had been dropped from the Quorum for refusing to sustain the Church's policy regarding Church leaders' service in government positions.

1925 Spencer Adams, later a Washington Senators baseball player, becomes the first Latter-day Saint to play in the World Series.

1928 Louise Yates Robison is called as the seventh general president of the Relief Society, with Amy Brown Lyman and Julia Alleman Child as counselors.

1940 Richard Stallings, later an Idaho representative in the U.S. Congress (1985–93), is born in Ogden, Utah.

1943 Spencer W. Kimball and Ezra Taft Benson are ordained Apostles, replacing Sylvester Q. Cannon and Rudger Clawson, who had died.

1989 President Gordon B. Hinckley dedicates four restoration projects in Nauvoo as part of the sesquicentennial celebration of the settling of the city in 1839.

1829 Joseph Smith and Oliver Cowdery purchase a large Bible from E. B. Grandin's bookstore in Palmyra. This book will later be used as the source text for the Joseph Smith Translation of the Bible.

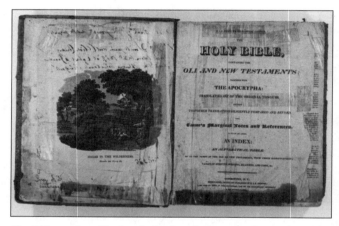

The Bible purchased by Joseph Smith and Oliver Cowdery and used for the Joseph Smith Translation (see 1829).

1833 Outlining the actions of the mob against the Saints in Jackson County, Missouri, William W. Phelps and Orson Hyde present a formal letter to Missouri governor Daniel Dunklin and request that the governor supply troops to help the Saints recover their losses. In subsequent correspondence, Dunklin recommends that the Saints seek redress through the courts.

1847 The last group of the "Big Company" arrives in the Salt Lake Valley. This ends that year's immigration efforts, with over 2,000 Saints having arrived in the valley.

1868 At a historic gathering in Salt Lake City, the entire First Presidency and the Quorum of the Twelve Apostles meet together for the first time in thirty-two years. Charles R. Savage, a Salt Lake photographer, captures the event.

1895 Belle Smith (Spafford), later the ninth general president of the Relief Society, is born in Salt Lake City, Utah.

1903 George Albert Smith is ordained an Apostle, replacing Brigham Young Jr., who had died. He becomes the first son to serve concurrently with his father (Elder John Henry Smith) in the Quorum of the Twelve Apostles.

1928 M. Russell Ballard, later a member of the Quorum of the Twelve Apostles, is born in Salt Lake City, Utah.

1931 Joseph F. Merrill is ordained an Apostle, replacing Orson F. Whitney, who had died.

1942 Heber J. Grant ordains Joseph Fielding Smith, son of Hyrum Mack and Ida E. Bowman Smith, as Church Patriarch.

1953 Richard L. Evans is ordained an Apostle, replacing Albert E. Bowen, who had died.

1961 The Chilean Mission is organized.

1961 LDS military personnel from the United States begin holding Church meetings on the island of Bermuda.

1989 President Gordon B. Hinckley dedicates an addition to the Chicago Illinois Temple.

1992 The East African country of Tanzania grants the Church legal recognition.

❧ ❧ ❧ OCTOBER ❧ ❧ ❧

1843 Joseph Smith speaks at the funeral services of James Adams and remarks, "Could you gaze into heaven five minutes, you would know more than you would by reading all that ever was written on the subject" (*History of the Church*, 6:50).

1846 While encamped on the west bank of the Mississippi River, the last group of Saints to leave Nauvoo (known as the "poor camp") experiences the "miracle of the quail." Hundreds of quail land in the camp and are easily caught, providing meat for the starving company.

1848 Joseph Agnew, an arsonist, sets the abandoned Nauvoo Temple on fire, gutting it.

1875 Elder John Taylor dedicates the Tabernacle in Salt Lake City (the building had been used as early as 1867).

1898 Lorenzo Snow is sustained as the fifth President of the Church, with George Q. Cannon and Joseph F. Smith as Counselors.

1982 The First Presidency announces plans to build the first temple in a communist nation in Freiberg, German Democratic Republic (East Germany).

1986 Joseph B. Wirthlin is ordained an Apostle, replacing Thomas S. Monson, who had been called to the First Presidency.

1993 Ambassadors and others from the Washington, D.C., diplomatic community, representing thirty-three countries, enjoy a western-style picnic sponsored by the Church at the Marriott farm in Hume, Virginia.

President Gordon B. Hinckley breaks ground for the Mount Timpanogos Utah Temple, 9 October 1993.

1993 President Gordon B. Hinckley of the First Presidency breaks ground for the Mount Timpanogos Utah Temple.

1994 President Howard W. Hunter dedicates the Orlando Florida Temple.

1999 Ground is broken for the Birmingham Alabama Temple. Elder Stephen A. West, a member of the Second Quorum of the Seventy and Second Counselor in the North America Southeast Area Presidency, presides over the ceremony.

OCTOBER 10

1842 Missionary Lorenzo Snow presents two copies of the Book of Mormon to British Queen Victoria and Prince Albert. Sir Henry Wheatly accepts the books in behalf of the Queen.

1880 John Taylor is sustained as the third President of the Church, with George Q. Cannon and Joseph F. Smith as Counselors.

1898 Rudger Clawson is ordained an Apostle, replacing Lorenzo Snow, who had been called to the First Presidency.

1901 President Lorenzo Snow dies in Salt Lake City, Utah, at age eighty-seven, after serving for more than fifty-two years as a General Authority.

Army Air Force Lt. Gail Halvorsen preparing treats to drop over Berlin from his plane, 1949 (see 1920).

1919 Belgium's King Albert and Queen Elizabeth attend a recital on Temple Square to hear the Tabernacle organ.

1920 Gail Halvorsen, later known as the "Candy Bomber" for dropping sweets for children during the Berlin airlift (1949), is born in Salt Lake City, Utah.

1953 Paul Alan Cox, later an internationally recognized ethnobiologist and award-winning researcher, is born in Salt Lake City, Utah.

1963 Thomas S. Monson is ordained an Apostle, replacing N. Eldon Tanner, who had been called to the First Presidency.

1975 President N. Eldon Tanner of the First Presidency and Elder Gordon B. Hinckley greet the emperor and empress of Japan in a historic first visit of a Japanese monarch to the United States.

1979 The first Latter-day Saint branch in Papua New Guinea is established, with Athol Pike as president.

1985 M. Russell Ballard is ordained an Apostle, replacing Bruce R. McConkie, who had died.

1987 President Thomas S. Monson of the First Presidency breaks ground for the Toronto Ontario Temple.

Elder M. Russell Ballard with his wife, Barbara, ca. 1986 (see 1985).

1998 Ground is broken for the Detroit Michigan and Spokane Washington Temples. Elder Jay E. Jensen, a member of the First Quorum of the Seventy and President of the North America Northeast Area, and F. Melvin Hammond, a member of the First Quorum of the Seventy and President of the North America Northwest Area, preside over the respective ceremonies.

❧ ❧ ❧ OCTOBER *11* ❧ ❧ ❧

1743 Mary Duty (Smith), a progenitor of four Church Presidents (Joseph Smith, Joseph F. Smith, George Albert Smith, and Joseph Fielding Smith), is born in Rowley, Massachusetts.

1835 Joseph Smith Sr., who had been quite ill, begins to fail quickly. While praying for him, the Prophet Joseph Smith hears the Lord say that his father would recover. Following a blessing that evening, Joseph Sr. is healed.

1838 Following a ten-day siege, the Latter-day Saints living in De Witt, Carroll County, Missouri, surrender and begin the move to Far West in Caldwell County.

1878 Rey L. Pratt, later one of the First Seven Presidents of the Seventy, is born in Salt Lake City, Utah.

1888 Walter Keil Granger, later a Utah representative in the U.S. Congress (1940–52), is born in St. George, Utah.

1930 R. LaVell Edwards, later one of the most successful college football coaches in NCAA history, is born in Provo, Utah.

1934 J. Reuben Clark Jr. and Alonzo Arza Hinckley are ordained Apostles. Alonzo Arza Hinckley replaces David O. McKay, who had been called to the First Presidency; J. Reuben Clark is also called as a Counselor to Heber J. Grant in the First Presidency.

1936 Lowell L. Bennion, an instructor at the institute of religion at the University of Utah, establishes the first chapter of Lambda Delta Sigma, a fraternity/sorority group for young Latter-day Saints.

1945 Matthew Cowley is ordained an Apostle, replacing George Albert Smith, who had been called to the First Presidency.

1951 Marion G. Romney is ordained an Apostle, replacing Stephen L Richards, who had been called to the First Presidency.

San Francisco 49ers quarterback Steve Young, ca. 1995 (see 1961).

1961 Jon Steven "Steve" Young, later a BYU quarterback, San Francisco 49ers quarterback, and a Super Bowl MVP (1994), is born in Salt Lake City, Utah.

1962 Richard Paul Evans, the *New York Times* best-selling author of *The Christmas Box*, is born in Salt Lake City, Utah.

1962 N. Eldon Tanner is ordained an Apostle, replacing George Q. Morris, who had died.

1986 In the first Young Women activity held throughout the Church, an estimated three hundred thousand young women at thousands of sites around the world release helium-filled balloons containing personal messages.

1833 While traveling to upper Canada, Joseph Smith receives Doctrine and Covenants 100 at Perrysburg, New York. Joseph Smith and Sidney Rigdon are assured that their families are well, and Sidney is called to be a spokesman for the Prophet.

1892 Articles of incorporation for the Relief Society are filed, after which the organization is known as the National Women's Relief Societies (the name is changed to Relief Society of The Church of Jesus Christ of Latter-day Saints in 1945).

1932 Jake Garn, later a Utah member of the U.S. Senate (1974–92), is born in Richfield, Utah.

1933 Charles Albert Callis is ordained an Apostle, replacing James E. Talmage, who had died.

1963 President Hugh B. Brown of the First Presidency dedicates the Polynesian Cultural Center, situated near the Church College of Hawaii (later BYU–Hawaii) and the Laie Hawaii Temple.

Polynesian Cultural Center, ca. 1995 (see 1963).

1972 Bruce R. McConkie is ordained an Apostle, replacing Marion G. Romney, who had been called to the First Presidency.

1998 Ground is broken for the Halifax Nova Scotia Temple. Elder Jay E. Jensen, a member of the First Quorum of the Seventy and President of the North America Northeast Area, presides over the ceremony.

1837 Jerusha Barden Smith, the wife of Hyrum Smith and progenitor of several General Authorities, dies in Kirtland, Ohio.

1901 President Lorenzo Snow's funeral is held in the Tabernacle in Salt Lake City, Utah.

1919 Ricks College hosts its first football game.

1921 Marion D. Hanks, later a member of the Presidency of the Seventy, is born in Salt Lake City, Utah.

1959 Marie Osmond, later an entertainer, musician, and member of the famous Osmond family performing group, is born in Ogden, Utah.

1968 The first branch in the Asian country of Singapore is organized, with John McSweeny as president.

1981 The U.S. Tenth Circuit Court of Appeals rules that Utah junior high and high school students may leave school during the day for religious instruction.

1993 President Gordon B. Hinckley of the First Presidency dedicates BYU's new Museum of Art, which opens with a traveling exhibit on the Etruscan civilization, on loan from the Vatican Museums.

BYU's Museum of Art, ca. 1993 (see 1993).

1996 President Gordon B. Hinckley dedicates the Mount Timpanogos Utah Temple.

1834 Joseph Angell Young, later an Apostle, is born in Kirtland, Ohio.

1871 The people of Utah donate $12,000 to help the victims of the Chicago Fire.

1935 Canadians elect Church member John Horne Blackmore to the Canadian Parliament, making him the first Latter-day Saint to serve in that capacity.

1998 The First Presidency announces plans to build a temple in Baton Rouge, Louisiana.

▶ *BYU's fiftieth anniversary celebration, 15 October 1925.*

1857 Martha Horne (Tingey), later the second general president of the Young Women's Mutual Improvement Association (predecessor to the Young Women organization), is born in Salt Lake City, Utah.

1894 George Cole is appointed third president of Ricks College.

1921 Philip Funk Low, later an internationally recognized researcher in soil science and a member of the National Academy of Sciences (1992), is born in Carmangay, Alberta, Canada.

1925 In Provo, former BYU president George H. Brimhall addresses faculty and students to commence a three-day celebration of BYU's fiftieth anniversary.

1956 Samuel F. Cardon, later a composer, arranger, and Emmy Award recipient (1988, 1992), is born in Durango, Colorado.

1959 Howard W. Hunter is ordained an Apostle, replacing Henry D. Moyle, who had been called to the First Presidency.

1963 The first branch of the Church in Yukon Territory, Canada, is created in the town of Whitehorse, with Norman J. Drayton as president.

1974 The Alaska Anchorage Mission is organized.

1989 The Nicaragua Managua Mission is organized.

1996 At a BYU devotional assembly held in the Marriott Center, President Boyd K. Packer of the Twelve counsels Church leaders to emphasize the Atonement of Jesus Christ during funeral services.

1999 The Church announces the sale of department chain store ZCMI to May Department Stores Company.

OCTOBER 16

1792 Salmon Gee, one of the First Seven Presidents of the Seventy, is born in Lyme, Connecticut.

1834 Joseph Smith, Hyrum Smith, David Whitmer, Frederick G. Williams, Oliver Cowdery, and Roger Orton leave Kirtland to visit the Saints living in Pontiac, Michigan.

1875 President Brigham Young deeds lands to and establishes the Brigham Young Academy, which later becomes Brigham Young University.

1882 Heber J. Grant and George Teasdale are ordained Apostles, replacing Orson Pratt, who had died, and Joseph F. Smith, who had been called to the First Presidency.

1943 Hyrum W. Smith, later a well-known business-man, author, and chair of Franklin Quest Company, is born in Centerville, Utah.

1960 The Philadelphia Stake, the first stake in Pennsylvania, is organized, with Bryant F. West as president.

Elder Heber J. and Lucy S. Grant and family, ca. 1887 (see 1882).

1960 The Eastern Atlantic States Mission is organized.

1966 Elder Gordon B. Hinckley dedicates the Taipei Chapel, the first meetinghouse in Taiwan.

1977 The Helsinki Finland Stake, the first stake in Finland, is organized, with Kari Juhani Aslak Haikkola as president.

1999 President Gordon B. Hinckley dedicates the Columbia South Carolina Temple.

1999 Under the direction of Mack Wilberg, the Temple Square Chorale performs its first concert.

▶ *President Joseph F. Smith seated between his Counselors, John R. Winder (left) and Anthon H. Lund (right), ca. 1902 (see 1901).*

1888 The Esselman family, the first converts in Belgium, are baptized.

1901 Joseph F. Smith is ordained and set apart as the sixth President of the Church, with John R. Winder and Anthon H. Lund as Counselors in the First Presidency.

1965 The New York World's Fair concludes. The Mormon Pavilion, with a 127-foot-high replica of the triple east towers of the Salt Lake Temple, was visited by millions during the fair.

1968 Belle S. Spafford, general president of the Relief Society, is named president of the National Council of Women.

1972 The Brazil North Central and the Brazil South Central Missions are organized.

1989 In Budapest, President Thomas S. Monson of the First Presidency dedicates the first LDS meetinghouse in the Eastern European nation of Hungary.

1993 The First Presidency issues a statement reaffirming the Church's right to discipline members of the Church.

1998 Ground is broken for the Bismarck North Dakota Temple. Elder Kenneth Johnson, a member of the First Quorum of the Seventy and the First Counselor in the North America Central Area, presides over the ceremony.

1999 Jerold Ottley, conductor of the Mormon Tabernacle Choir for twenty-five years, conducts his last broadcast of *Music and the Spoken Word*.

1833 Joseph Smith and others arrive in Ontario on a short mission and stay with Freeman A. Nickerson's family in Mount Pleasant.

1846 Captain James Brown leaves Santa Fe, New Mexico, for Pueblo, Colorado, with a detachment of sick Mormon Battalion members.

1861 President Brigham Young sends his first telegram over the overland telegraph lines to J. H. Wade, the president of the telegraph company.

1881 Elder William John McDonald baptizes Ngataki, the first Maori convert in New Zealand.

1992 President Gordon B. Hinckley of the First Presidency rededicates the London England Temple.

Elder Edward Cliff, an early missionary to New Zealand, ca. 1885 (see 1881).

1856 The Martin handcart company encounters its first major winter storm at Red Buttes (located near what would become Casper, Wyoming).

1931 Donald L. Staheli, later a member of the Second Quorum of the Seventy, is born in St. George, Utah.

1940 President David O. McKay of the First Presidency dedicates the site for the Idaho Falls Temple (later the Idaho Falls Idaho Temple).

1947 The South Carolina Stake, the first stake in South Carolina, is organized, with W. Wallace McBride as president.

1971 Elders Gordon B. Hinckley, Thomas S. Monson, and Boyd K. Packer organize the Genesis Branch (also known as the Genesis Group) in the Salt Lake City area, with Ruffin Bridgeforth as president.

1975 For the first time, Latter-day Saint missionaries enter the republic of Kiribati, a nation composed of thirty-six islands in the mid-Pacific.

1984 President Gordon B. Hinckley of the First Presidency dedicates the Dallas Texas Temple.

1991 Elder Marvin J. Ashton dedicates the Central American country of Guatemala for the preaching of the gospel.

1992 During the second day of the rededication of the London England Temple, President Gordon B. Hinckley of the First Presidency announces that the Church will build a temple in Preston, England, the site of the first missionary activity in the country 155 years earlier.

1999 BYU and the Foundation for Ancient Research and Mormon Studies (FARMS) sign an affiliation agreement, officially joining the organizations together.

1834 Joseph Smith and a company of missionaries arrive in Pontiac, Michigan, and preach to the Saints in that area.

1862 Colonel Patrick E. Connor and his "California Volunteers" march into Salt Lake City, Utah. Having received reports from Utah's anti-Mormon governor that the Saints were incapable of guarding the overland mail route through the Intermountain West, President Abraham Lincoln had sent Connor to perform this function in their place. The Saints resent the presence of Connor, an avowed anti-Mormon, and the presence of a federal army, in the territory.

1937 E. Ray Bateman, later a member of the Second Quorum of the Seventy, is born in Sandy, Utah.

1950 Christopher "Chris" B. Cannon, later a Utah representative in the U.S. Congress (1997–), is born in Salt Lake City, Utah.

1979 The first Latter-day Saint branch is organized on the island of Barbados in the Carribean Sea, with John Naime as president.

◄ The Hand-Cart Emigrants in a Storm, *1873 (see 1856)*.

1848 At a conference held at Kanesville, Iowa, Oliver Cowdery recounts his involvement with the Saints in the early years of the Church and bears testimony of the Book of Mormon and of the leadership of the Twelve Apostles following the death of Joseph Smith. This was the first time he had spoken to a Church congregation since his excommunication in April 1838. He is rebaptized nine days later.

1854 Mischa Markow, later an early and tireless missionary to Eastern Europe and the Near East, is born in Szerb-Czernyn, Hungary.

1855 The first branch in Germany is organized in Dresden, with Karl G. Maeser as president.

1878 Rafael Monroy, an early Mexican Church leader who was martyred for refusing to deny his testimony during the Mexican Revolution (1915), is born in Octopam, Mexico.

1905 Franklin S. Forsberg, later a U.S. ambassador to Sweden (1981), is born in Salt Lake City.

1926 Chieko Nishimura (Okazaki), later a well-known speaker, author, and the first non-Caucasian female general Church officer, is born in Kohala, Hawaii.

◀ *Rafael Monroy (left) and family, ca. 1913–14 (see 1878).*

1961 The first branch in New Caledonia, a territory of France in the South Pacific, is organized, with Teahu Manoi as president.

1979 Elizapan and Ebisiba Osaka and their children, the first African converts in Kenya, are baptized.

1805 Jonathan Browning, later a gunsmith and progenitor of several gun inventors who found the internationally famous Browning Company, is born in Brushy Fork, Tennessee.

1880 Lucy Grant (Cannon), later the fourth general president of the Young Women's Mutual Improvement Association (predecessor to the Young Women organization), is born in Salt Lake City, Utah.

1903 The First Presidency authorizes the purchase of twenty-five acres of the original temple lot in Independence, Missouri, preparing the way for the first Latter-day Saint presence in Jackson County since the Saints' expulsion some seventy years earlier.

1905 President J. Wilford Booth of the Near East Mission baptizes Rigas Profantis, Nicholas Malavetis, and three others, the first converts in Greece.

1967 President Hugh B. Brown of the First Presidency dedicates the Salt Lake Temple Annex.

1968 Spain grants the Church official recognition.

1977 T. M. Conrad Mailo and his wife, Nisor Cerly David, the first converts of the Church in Chuuk, Micronesia, are baptized.

1980 The Church organizes the Kingstown Branch, the first branch in the Caribbean islands of the Grenadines, with Edmund Israel as president.

1995 The Port Moresby Papua New Guinea Stake, the first stake in Papua New Guinea, is organized, with Valba Rome as president.

1795 Elias Higbee, later a Caldwell County judge and a friend of Joseph Smith, is born in Galloway, New Jersey.

1820 John Brown, later the leader of the Mississippi Saints who gather to Utah from the South in 1846 and 1847, is born in Sumner County, Tennessee.

1903 The name of the Church academy in Provo is changed from Brigham Young Academy to Brigham Young University (BYU).

1927 President Heber J. Grant dedicates the Arizona Temple (later the Mesa Arizona Temple).

1965 After her work at the Church's pavilion at the New York World's Fair, the First Presidency appoints Irene Edwards Staples as the official hostess of the Church.

1976 On Pohpei Island, Latter-day Saint missionaries enter the South Pacific islands of Micronesia for the first time.

1985 President Gordon B. Hinckley of the First Presidency dedicates the new Genealogical Library in Salt Lake City (later called the Family History Library).

1988 Indra Sukhdeo, the first convert in the South American country of Guyana, is baptized.

1991 Elder James E. Faust dedicates Uganda for the preaching of the gospel.

1992 President Gordon B. Hinckley of the First Presidency rededicates the Swiss Temple (later the Bern Switzerland Temple).

1999 President Gordon B. Hinckley dedicates the Detroit Michigan Temple.

1811 Lyman E. Johnson, later a member of the Quorum of the Twelve Apostles, is born in Pomfret, Vermont.

1841 Elder Orson Hyde ascends the Mount of Olives and dedicates the land of Palestine, praying, "Now, O Lord! Thy servant has been obedient to the heavenly vision which Thou gavest him in his native land . . . to dedicate and consecrate this land unto Thee" (*History of the Church*, 4:456).

1883 Hugh B. Brown, later a member of the Quorum of the Twelve Apostles and a Counselor in the First Presidency, is born in Granger, Utah.

1901 Hyrum Mack Smith, son of President Joseph F. Smith, is ordained an Apostle, replacing Anthon H. Lund, who had been called to the First Presidency.

◄ *Church Hostess Irene Edwards Staples (second from right) and Temple Square visitors, including movie and TV star Telly Savalas (center), 17 November 1974 (see 1965).*

1932 Stephen R. Covey, later a *New York Times* best-selling author, a lecturer, and the founder of the Covey Leadership Center, is born in Salt Lake City, Utah.

1949 In celebration of the Mormon Tabernacle Choir's twentieth year of continuous network broadcasting, Columbia Records releases the choir's first record album, *The Mormon Tabernacle Choir of Salt Lake City, Volume 1.*

Stephen R. Covey, ca. 1998 (see 1932).

1979 President Spencer W. Kimball dedicates the Orson Hyde Memorial Gardens on the Mount of Olives in Jerusalem.

1981 Elder Thomas S. Monson and business and community leaders in Salt Lake City meet with U.S. president Ronald Reagan, who praises the Church welfare program.

1986 President Ezra Taft Benson dedicates the Denver Colorado Temple.

1988 President Thomas S. Monson of the First Presidency meets with officials of the German Democratic Republic (DDR) and asks for permission for the Church to send missionaries to the DDR and to call DDR citizens to serve missions to other countries. Government officials later grant his requests.

1991 Elder James E. Faust dedicates Kenya for the preaching of the gospel.

1999 President Gordon B. Hinckley breaks ground for the reconstruction of the Nauvoo Temple.

OCTOBER 25

1828 Ira N. Hinckley, later a pioneer educator, civil and Church leader, and builder of Cove Fort in central Utah, is born in Leeds County, Ontario, Canada.

1831 Joseph Smith receives Doctrine and Covenants 66, which contains the Lord's instructions to William E. McLellin.

1838 During a battle at Crooked River in Missouri, Elder David W. Patten of the Quorum of the Twelve, Gideon Carter, and Patrick O'Banion are killed.

1890 In the first experiment in weekday religious education for public school students in the United States, the First Presidency directs stake presidents and bishops to hold religion classes after school or on Saturdays in every ward where there is not a Church school.

1893 President Grover Cleveland signs a resolution providing for the return to the Church of some of the property confiscated under the antipolygamy Edmunds-Tucker Act.

1902 Milton R. Hunter, later a member of the First Council of the Seventy, is born in Holden, Utah.

1933 William R. Bradford, later a member of the First Quorum of the Seventy, is born in Springville, Utah.

1991 Elder James E. Faust dedicates Zimbabwe for the preaching of the gospel.

1992 *On the Way Home,* a Church video production depicting a family's joy in finding the gospel, premieres over the Church satellite network as part of missionary open houses held in Church meetinghouses throughout North America.

1911 The first stake mission is organized when sixty-one seventies in the Granite Stake in Salt Lake City, Utah, are called to serve.

1947 The Central Atlantic States Mission is organized.

1979 The Church receives title to the Newel K. Whitney Store in Kirtland, Ohio.

The Newel K. Whitney Store, ca. 1910 (see 1979).

1814 Daniel H. Wells, later a member of the First Presidency, is born in Trenton, New Jersey.

1833 Joseph Smith baptizes twelve converts after preaching to a large congregation in Mt. Pleasant, Ontario, Canada.

1838 Upon receiving word of the encounter between Missouri troops and Mormon militia at Crooked River on 25 October, Missouri governor Lilburn W. Boggs issues the "extermination order," decreeing that the Saints must be driven from the state.

1850 During services in La Tour, Italy, Elder Lorenzo Snow baptizes Jean Antoine Box, the first Italian convert to the Church in Italy.

1854 Augustus Farnham, president of the Australian Mission, and William Cooke arrive in New Zealand as the first LDS missionaries to begin work on this Pacific island chain.

1880 Francis M. Lyman and John Henry Smith are ordained Apostles, replacing John Taylor and George Q. Cannon, who had been called to the First Presidency.

1952 Lynn G. Robbins, later a member of the First Quorum of the Seventy, is born in Payson, Utah.

1977 Elizabeth Jackson, later a five-time BYU all-American in track and field and cross-county and the 1999 national 3,000-meter steeplechase champion, is born in Salt Lake City, Utah.

1980 President Spencer W. Kimball dedicates the Tokyo Temple (later the Tokyo Japan Temple).

1983 President Gordon B. Hinckley of the First Presidency dedicates the Papeete Tahiti Temple.

The Tokyo Temple dedication, 27 October 1980.

1787 Frederick G. Williams, later a member of the First Presidency, is born in Suffield, Connecticut.

1856 Joseph A. Young and his companions, who had been sent from Salt Lake City to help rescue the handcart companies, meet the Martin handcart company in Wyoming, sixteen miles from the Platte Bridge.

1893 Bertha Stone (Reeder), later the fifth general president of the Young Women's Mutual Improvement Association (predecessor to the Young Women organization), is born in Ogden, Utah.

1926 William M. Lawrence, later a member of the Second Quorum of the Seventy, is born in Salt Lake City, Utah.

1938 Anne Perry, later a best-selling Victorian mystery novelist, is born in London, England.

1956 Lewis Field, later a three-time World Champion All-Around Cowboy (1985–87), is born in Salt Lake City, Utah.

Best-selling author Anne Perry, ca. 1985 (see 1938).

1958 Jay Don Blake, later the winner of the 1980 NCAA golf championship and the 1981 College Player of the Year, is born in St. George, Utah.

1961 The Swiss Stake, the first stake in Switzerland, is organized, with Wilhelm Friedrich Lauener as president.

1984 The Ciudad Obregon Mexico Yaqui Stake, the fifteen hundredth stake of the Church, is organized, with Jorge Mendez Ibarra as president.

1993 Members of the Mormon Tabernacle Choir coordinate the performance of Handel's *Messiah* by a Vietnamese choir, accompanied by the National Vietnamese Symphony Orchestra in the Hanoi Opera House.

1998 President Thomas S. Monson of the First Presidency dedicates the BYU Salt Lake Center.

1998 The Church announces that it will play a key role in establishing a new family-history research facility in the Ellis Island Immigration Museum in New York.

▶ *President David O. McKay and U.S. president Lyndon B. Johnson, 29 October 1964.*

❧ ❧ ❧ **OCTOBER** ❧ ❧ ❧
29

1839 Joseph Smith, in company with Sidney Rigdon, Elias Higbee, and Orrin Porter Rockwell, leave Commerce (Nauvoo), Illinois, for Washington, D.C., to petition the federal government for assistance concerning the Missouri persecutions.

1851 Governor Brigham Young establishes Fillmore, Millard County, as the new territorial capital of Utah.

1855 The First Presidency issues the Thirteenth General Epistle, recounting important events in Utah and in the Church's missions and initiating the handcart companies.

1875 Thomas E. McKay, later an Assistant to the Quorum of the Twelve Apostles, is born in Huntsville, Utah.

1950 Richard J. Maynes, later a member of the Second Quorum of the Seventy, is born in Berkeley, California.

1964 U.S. president Lyndon B. Johnson speaks in the Salt Lake Tabernacle.

1999 The Temple Square Chorale, the Orchestra at Temple Square, and the Mormon Tabernacle Choir perform in their first joint concert in the Tabernacle.

OCTOBER 30

1831 In Hiram, Ohio, Joseph Smith receives Doctrine and Covenants 65 (according to the Kirtland Revelation Book), which he designates as a prayer. This is the first of fifteen revelations received by the Prophet in Hiram.

1838 Some two hundred vigilantes attack the isolated Mormon settlement of Haun's Mill, killing seventeen men and boys and wounding fourteen more. The Missouri State Militia, consisting of approximately twenty-five hundred troops, arrives at the outskirts of Far West. Eight or nine hundred Mormons stand ready to defend the community.

1840 Three weeks after their arrival, missionaries organize the first branch of the Church in Wales.

1851 The Australian Mission is organized when Elders John Murdock and Charles Wandell arrive in Sydney from Utah. Missionary work had commenced in 1840.

1926 Laurence J. Burton, later a Utah representative in the U.S. Congress (1963–71), is born in Ogden, Utah.

1940 Bruce C. Hafen, later a member of the First Quorum of the Seventy, is born in St. George, Utah.

1941 Carl B. Pratt, later a member of the First Quorum of the Seventy, is born in Monterrey, Mexico.

1950 John Taylor Doolittle, a California representative in the U.S. Congress (1991–), is born in Glendale, California.

1966 At a meeting in Saigon (Ho Chi Minh City), Elder Gordon B. Hinckley dedicates Vietnam for the preaching of the gospel.

1967 Ty Detmer, later a record-breaking quarterback at BYU, Heisman Trophy winner (1990), and NFL player, is born in San Marcos, Texas.

Haun's Mill, *by C.C.A. Christensen, 1885 (see 1838).*

1978 President Spencer W. Kimball dedicates the São Paulo Temple (later the São Paulo Brazil Temple).

1982 The Church opens a visitors' center at the Grandin printing building, in Palmyra, New York, where the Book of Mormon was first printed in 1830.

1993 President Gordon B. Hinckley breaks ground for the St. Louis Missouri Temple.

1998 The First Presidency announces plans to build new temples in Villahermosa, Mexico, and in Melbourne, Australia.

OCTOBER 31

1833 Violence erupts in Jackson County, Missouri, as local citizens attempt to expel Church members.

1838 Missouri militia officers demand that the Saints give up their arms, pay for the cost of the war, leave the state, and surrender Joseph Smith, Sidney Rigdon, Lyman Wight, Parley P. Pratt, and George W. Robinson. George Hinkle, colonel of the Mormon forces guarding Far West, agrees to the demands and lures Joseph and the others into the mob's camp, where they are immediately taken prisoner.

1847 President Brigham Young of the Twelve returns to Winter Quarters from his pioneer trek to the Salt Lake Valley, having made the return trip in only sixty-seven days.

1875 Albert E. Bowen, later a member of the Quorum of the Twelve Apostles, is born in Henderson Creek, Idaho.

1913 William E. Hall, later a World War II pilot and U.S. Congressional Medal of Honor recipient (1943) for helping sink an enemy aircraft carrier and managing to land his aircraft safely, all while seriously injured, is born in Storrs, Utah.

1918 The First Presidency, the Quorum of the Twelve Apostles, and the Church Patriarch accept and endorse President Joseph F. Smith's Vision of the Redemption of the Dead as the word of the Lord.

1949 The Great Lakes Mission is organized.

1963 Troy Tanner, later an Olympic gold medalist in volleyball at the 1988 Seoul games, is born in Whittier, California.

1979 The first branch of the Church in the Netherlands Antilles (two island groups in the Caribbean Sea) is organized.

1985 Elder Thomas S. Monson dedicates Yugoslavia for the preaching of the gospel.

NOVEMBER 1

1799 Thomas B. Marsh, later a member of the Quorum of the Twelve Apostles, is born in Acton, Massachusetts.

1808 John Taylor, later a member of the Quorum of the Twelve Apostles and the third President of the Church, is born in Milnthorpe, England.

1831 The Prophet Joseph Smith receives the "Lord's Preface," now known as Doctrine and Covenants 1. Historical evidence also indicates that Doctrine and Covenants 67, instructing several elders to try to duplicate a revelation like unto the Prophet's, was also received on this date.

1838 Near midnight General Samuel Lucas holds a hastily organized court martial and orders General Alexander Doniphan to execute Joseph Smith and the other Mormon prisoners. Because Joseph Smith and the other Mormon leaders are not members of the state militia, Doniphan refuses and threatens to charge Lucas with murder if they are killed. Lucas reconsiders, and then lifts the death sentence.

1850 The Italian Mission is organized.

1851 Elder John Taylor begins publication of *Zion's Panier* in Germany.

1853 George D. Watt releases the first issue of the *Journal of Discourses* in England with an introduction by the First Presidency.

1864 The Netherlands Mission is organized.

1924 Malcolm S. Jeppsen, later a member of the Second Quorum of the Seventy, is born in Mantua, Utah.

1959 The Andes Mission is organized.

1960 The Florida and West Mexican Missions are organized.

Jane Clayson and Bryant Gumbel (see 1999).

1969 The Southeast Asia Mission is organized.

1976 The Scotland Glasgow Mission is organized.

1993 Richard A. Searfoss successfully lands the space shuttle *Columbia* after a fourteen-day voyage, the shuttle's longest flight to date.

1997 On or near this date Church membership reaches ten million.

1999 Jane Clayson, a BYU graduate in broadcasting and communications, joins Bryant Gumbel as cohost of the *Early Show* on CBS television.

1836 The Brethren at Kirtland, Ohio, draw up articles of agreement preparatory to organizing a banking institution that will later be known as the Kirtland Safety Society. Oliver Cowdery is sent to Philadelphia, Pennsylvania, to procure plates to engrave the money, and Orson Hyde is sent to Columbus, Ohio, to petition the state legislature for a charter.

1838 At Far West, Missouri, the Saints sign away their property to pay for the cost of the "Mormon War." After a brief visit with their families, Joseph Smith and his fellow prisoners, Sidney Rigdon, Hyrum Smith, Parley P. Pratt, Lyman Wight, Amasa Lyman, and George W. Robinson, begin their journey under guard to Independence for trial.

1851 Elders John Murdock and Charles W. Wandell hold the first Church meeting in Sydney, Australia.

1925 Hans B. Ringger, later a member of the First Quorum of the Seventy, is born in Zurich, Switzerland.

1939 David Daniel (Dan) Marriott, later a Utah representative in the U.S. Congress (1976–84), is born in Bingham, Utah.

Kirtland Safety Society safe (see 1836).

1966 In Bangkok's Lumpini Park, Elder Gordon B. Hinckley dedicates Thailand for the preaching of the gospel.

1996 The Church releases a 160-page book entitled *Our Heritage: A Brief History of The Church of Jesus Christ of Latter-day Saints,* emphasizing "the spiritual legacy of all members."

1996 The Church announces the formation of Latter-day Saint Charities, an entity created to deliver humanitarian aid to individuals and nations throughout the world.

1997 President Hinckley dedicates the Vernal Utah Temple.

1998 The Church sends 240,000 pounds of supplies from the Bishop's Central Storehouse in Salt Lake City to victims of Hurricane Mitch in Central America.

1998 The First Presidency announces plans to build a temple in Montevideo, Uruguay.

NOVEMBER

1772 Joseph Knight Sr., who later assisted Joseph Smith in translating the Book of Mormon by providing provisions and other assistance, is born in Oakham, Massachusetts.

1807 Luke S. Johnson, later a member of the Quorum of the Twelve Apostles, is born in Pomfret, Vermont.

1831 At a conference of the Church held in Hiram, Ohio, Joseph Smith receives Doctrine and Covenants 133, which contains teachings on the Savior's Second Coming. The section was subsequently designated to be the appendix to the 1833 Book of Commandments.

1843 On a mission to the Pacific Islands, Knowlton F. Hanks dies at sea, becoming the first Latter-day Saint missionary buried at sea.

1896 Martha Hughes Cannon wins a seat in the Utah State Senate, becoming the first woman in the United States to be elected to a state senate.

1945 President George Albert Smith meets with U.S. president Harry S. Truman in Washington, D.C., to obtain permission for the Church to send food and supplies to the Saints in war-torn Europe.

President George Albert Smith meets with U.S. president Harry S. Truman, 8 November 1945.

1972 The Mormon Battalion Visitors' Center opens in San Diego, California, overlooking the historic Old Town.

1975 U.S. president Gerald Ford appoints Lieutenant General Brent Scowcroft as his national security affairs (NSA) advisor, replacing Henry Kissinger, who had been both secretary of state and NSA advisor. Scowcroft is the first Latter-day Saint to serve in this top position. He serves again in this position under U.S. president George Bush (1989–93).

1977 Bruce C. Hafen is appointed as the eleventh president of Ricks College.

1992 Olene Walker is elected as lieutenant governor of Utah, the highest state political position obtained by an LDS woman in the United States.

1992 The Mexico Monterrey South Mission is organized.

1996 The Kinshasa Zaire Stake, the first stake in the African Democratic Republic of Congo, is organized, with Mulielegwa Musithi as president.

▶ *BYU professor Paul A. Cox, ca. 1995 (see 1997).*

NOVEMBER 4

1830 Joseph Smith receives Doctrine and Covenants 34, containing instructions and promises to teenager Orson Pratt, who had recently been baptized.

1833 The final major confrontation between the Jackson County citizens and the Saints occurs near the Blue River. As a result of the fighting, three people, including Latter-day Saint Andrew Barber, are killed.

1843 In an effort to prepare the Saints for the election of 1844, Joseph Smith writes letters to U.S. presidential candidates John C. Calhoun, Lewis Cass, Richard M. Johnson, Henry Clay, and Martin Van Buren concerning their position regarding the Latter-day Saints.

1898 John Longden, later an Assistant to the Quorum of the Twelve Apostles, is born in Oldham, England.

1933 U.S. president Franklin D. Roosevelt meets with Presidents Heber J. Grant, Anthony W. Ivins, and J. Reuben Clark.

1948 Mission president Frederick S. Williams baptizes Avelino Juan Rodriguez and his wife, Maria Esther, the first converts in Uruguay.

1959 Lelei Alofa Fonoimoana-Moore, later an Olympic silver medalist in swimming at the 1976 Montreal games, is born in Sterling, Illinois.

1979 Rose Tahi Soui Tchong, the first convert on the Indian Ocean island of Reunion, is baptized.

1997 *Time* magazine features BYU professor Paul Alan Cox, winner of one of the six prestigious Goldman Environmental Prizes for 1997, for his efforts to find plants that will benefit Western medicine.

NOVEMBER 5

1830 Parley P. Pratt baptizes John Murdock, one of the first converts in Ohio and father of the twins later adopted by Joseph and Emma Smith.

1839 Charles O. Card, later a pioneer to Latter-day settlements in Alberta, Canada, is born in Ossian Township, New York.

1882 Emma Lucy Gates (Bowen), later an opera star and promoter of music in Utah, is born in St. George, Utah.

1895 The people of Utah ratify the state constitution, approve statehood, and elect the first Mormon state governor, Heber M. Wells. Utah officially becomes a state on 4 January 1896.

1896 In a formal letter, the First Presidency announces that fast day will be moved from the first Thursday of each month to the first Sunday. Because of increasing industrialization, many members had not been able to attend Thursday meetings.

1903 The Church announces the purchase of Carthage Jail, the site of the martyrdom of the Prophet Joseph Smith and the Patriarch Hyrum Smith; this is the first of many purchases of historic properties by the Church.

1903 William Adams Dawson, later a Utah representative in the U.S. Congress (1947–49, 1953–59), is born in Layton, Utah.

1910 William H. Bennett, later a member of the First Quorum of the Seventy, is born in Taber, Alberta, Canada.

1913 Ground is broken for the Alberta Temple (later the Cardston Alberta Temple), the first temple outside of the United States.

Crowds attending the groundbreaking ceremony for the Alberta Temple, 5 November 1913.

1978 The Saskatoon Saskatchewan Stake, the first stake in Saskatchewan, Canada, is organized, with Noel W. Burt as president.

1985 President Spencer W. Kimball dies in Salt Lake City at age ninety, after serving for more than forty-two years as a General Authority.

1985 The first Latter-day Saint branch in the African kingdom of Swaziland is established, with George Gardner as president.

1988 Serge and Christie Bonuoit, the first converts in French Guiana, are baptized.

❧❧❧ NOVEMBER ❧❧❧

1846 Seraph Young, a niece of Brigham Young and later the first woman to vote in the United States (1870), is born in Winter Quarters.

1913 Calvin L. Rampton, later Utah's three-term governor (1965–77), is born in Bountiful, Utah.

1914 H. Verlan Andersen, later a member of the First Quorum of the Seventy, is born in Logan, Utah.

1937 Lucy Grant Cannon is called to serve as the fourth general president of the Young Women's Mutual Improvement Association (predecessor to the Young Women organization), with Helen Spencer William and Verna Wright Goddard as counselors.

1940 Dieter F. Uchtdorf, later a member of the First Quorum of the Seventy, is born in Ostrava, Czechoslovakia.

A sculpture by Lawrence O. Ehigiator, a Nigerian convert, displayed at the international art exhibit of the Museum of Church History and Art (see 1987).

1945 The temple endowment is presented in Spanish, the first time the sacred ceremonies are presented in a language other than English.

1979 John W. Welch files articles of incorporation for the Foundation for Ancient Research and Mormon Studies (FARMS), a nonprofit organization established to support and publish original research into the Book of Mormon and other Latter-day Saint scripture. FARMS later becomes part of BYU (1999).

1987 The Museum of Church History and Art in Salt Lake City opens its first international art exhibit.

1993 Elder M. Russell Ballard, a descendent of Joseph Smith Sr., presides at a Latter-day Saint worship service held in the Kirtland Temple (owned by the RLDS Church) in connection with an area priesthood leadership training meeting and mission presidents' seminar. The meeting is believed to be the first Latter-day Saint service held in the temple in 140 years.

1998 President Gordon B. Hinckley receives the annual International Executive of the Year Award from BYU's Marriott School of Management. The award was established in 1974 to honor outstanding executives from the public and private sectors.

NOVEMBER 7

1833 Forced at gunpoint to leave their homes and lands, the Jackson County Saints—numbering some 1,200 men, women, and children—cross the Missouri River and enter Clay County.

1837 After the excommunication of Frederick G. Williams, Hyrum Smith is sustained as Second Counselor to Joseph Smith in the First Presidency. This is the only time two brothers have served in the First Presidency together.

1855 Benjamin E. Rich, later a missionary and long-time mission president in the southern United States, is born in Salt Lake City, Utah.

1879 The *SS Arizona,* a ship that carried more than 1,250 Latter-day Saints in nine crossings of the Atlantic, collides with a huge iceberg on its way from New York to Liverpool. Four Mormon missionaries are on board. The damage is extensive, but the ship makes it safely to a port in Newfoundland.

1900 Mark E. Petersen, later a member of the Quorum of the Twelve Apostles, is born in Salt Lake City, Utah.

1911 Local citizens elect Mary Woolley Chamberlain mayor of Kanab, with an all-female town council, the first such political event in U.S. history.

1928 Richard G. Scott, later a member of the Quorum of the Twelve Apostles, is born in Pocatello, Idaho.

1963 Elder James A. Cullimore, later an Assistant to the Quorum of the Twelve Apostles, dedicates the Londonderry chapel, the first meetinghouse in Ireland.

1998 The First Presidency announces that temples will be built in Villahermosa, Mexico; Montevideo, Uruguay; and Melbourne, Australia.

NOVEMBER 8

1832 Brigham Young and Heber C. Kimball arrive in Kirtland after traveling from Mendon, New York, to meet Joseph Smith for the first time. In the evening meeting, Brigham Young speaks in tongues—the first time the Prophet had witnessed the manifestation of the gift.

1841 A wooden baptismal font in the Nauvoo Temple is dedicated by Brigham Young. Later, in 1845, a stone font replaces the wooden font.

◄ SS Arizona *after striking an iceberg fifty miles outside of St. John, Newfoundland (see 1879).*

1851 Elder Parley P. Pratt and his companion Rufus Allen arrive by ship in Valparaiso as the first Latter-day Saint missionaries to Chile.

1869 Work is begun on the gallery in the Salt Lake Tabernacle, providing an additional three thousand seats and improving the building's acoustics.

1912 The First Presidency announces the creation of a Correlation Executive Committee to coordinate scheduling and streamline the functioning of the Church auxiliaries.

Elaine Jack with Saints in India, 1992 (see 1992).

1938 California citizens elect Culbert L. Olson as governor of California, the first Latter-day Saint elected as governor outside of Utah.

1939 Eric B. Shumway, later the eighth president of BYU–Hawaii, is born in St. Johns, Arizona.

1992 President Elaine L. Jack, the general president of the Relief Society, makes the first visit to India by a Church auxiliary president.

1993 The First Presidency announces TempleReady™, a software program designed to speed up the process of clearing names obtained from family history research for temple work. Also, *A Member's Guide to Temple and Family History Work* is introduced to general and local Church officers.

1998 The blessings and sacred nature of family history are discussed in a program transmitted over the Church satellite system. Presentations include those of President Boyd K. Packer of the Quorum of the Twelve and Elder D. Todd Christofferson of the Presidency of the Seventy.

NOVEMBER 9

1818 Erastus Snow, later a member of the Quorum of the Twelve Apostles, is born in St. Johnsbury, Vermont.

1820 John Shark, later known as the "Railroad Bishop" because of his supervision of the construction of portions of the Union Pacific, Utah Central, and Utah Southern Railroad lines, is born in Devon Iron Works, Scotland.

1838 Following Governor Boggs' extermination order and the siege of Far West, General Samuel Lucas arrives in Richmond, Missouri, with Joseph Smith and six other Mormon prisoners for a preliminary hearing in the circuit court of Judge Austin A. King.

1856 Aided by rescuers sent out by Brigham Young, the Willie handcart company arrives in Salt Lake City, the fourth handcart company to have made the trek. More than one hundred people in the company—which had originally numbered some five hundred—had perished from hunger and cold.

1871 President Brigham Young breaks ground for the St. George Temple (later the St. George Utah Temple). President George A. Smith, First Counselor in the First Presidency, offers the site dedicatory prayer.

1952 The Detroit Stake, the first stake in Michigan, is organized, with George W. Romney as president.

1972 The International Mission is organized for members of the Church living in areas where no formal missionary work is being conducted.

1972 Ruth Hardy Funk is called as the president of the Aaronic Priesthood MIA (Young Women), with Hortense Hogan Child and Ardeth Green Kapp as counselors. When this auxiliary was renamed the Young Women organization in 1974, Sister Funk was retained as its president.

Converts in Nigeria, ca. 1978 (see 1978).

1978 Latter-day Saint missionaries enter the African republic of Nigeria for the first time.

1990 Terrence H. Rooney is elected to the British Parliament, becoming the first member of the Church ever elected to that body.

1995 Elder Dallin H. Oaks of the Quorum of the Twelve and Elder Vaughn J. Featherstone of the First Quorum of the Seventy receive awards from the national Freedoms Foundation at Valley Forge and the Utah chapter of the Freedoms Foundation.

NOVEMBER 10

1838 The Saints at Adam-ondi-Ahman surrender to General Moses Wilson of the Missouri militia and are ordered to leave Daviess County within ten days. They are granted permission to live in Caldwell County until spring. Permission is also given for a committee of twelve Saints to travel between Adam-ondi-Ahman and Far West for a period of four weeks to convey their crops from Daviess to Caldwell Counties.

1901 Bathsheba Wilson Smith is sustained as the fourth general president of the Relief Society, with Annie Taylor Hyde and Ida Smoot Dusenberry as counselors.

1923 Relief Societies throughout North America receive a charge to collect and repair clothing and shoes to ease the distress of the Saints in Germany following World War I.

1944 John E. Fowler, later a member of the Second Quorum of the Seventy, is born in Redding, California.

1966 Elder Ezra Taft Benson rededicates Italy for the preaching of the gospel. Elder Lorenzo Snow had dedicated the land first in 1850.

1985 Ezra Taft Benson is ordained and set apart as the thirteenth President of the Church, with Gordon B. Hinckley and Thomas S. Monson as Counselors.

President Ezra Taft Benson, ca. 1986 (see 1985).

1989 Steven D. Bennion is inaugurated as the seventh president of Ricks College.

1994 In the Relief Society Building, President Howard W. Hunter attends a reception commemorating the 125th anniversary of the Young Women organization, organized 28 November 1869.

1996 President Hinckley breaks ground for the Cochabamba Bolivia Temple.

▶ *The St. George Temple (see 1975).*

1872 Maude Ewing Adams, later a popular stage actress in the early twentieth century and particularly noted for her title role in *Peter Pan,* is born in Salt Lake City, Utah.

1921 Terrel H. Bell, later the U.S. secretary of education (1981–84), is born in Lava Hot Springs, Idaho.

1924 Rulon G. Craven, later a member of the Second Quorum of the Seventy, is born in Murray, Utah.

1940 Lance B. Wickman, later a member of the First Quorum of the Seventy, is born in Seattle, Washington.

1948 Belle Smith Spafford, later the general president of the Relief Society, begins service as the vice president of the National Council of Women.

1950 The West Central States Mission is organized.

1950 Terrence Henry Rooney, later the first Latter-day Saint ever elected to the British Parliament, is born in Bradford, Yorkshire, England.

1975 President Spencer W. Kimball rededicates the remodeled St. George Temple (later the St. George Utah Temple).

1979 The Panama City Panama Stake, the first stake in Panama, is organized, with Nelson Altamirano Lopez as president.

1994 *Music and Values,* a Church-produced public affairs radio program, wins the 1994 Gabriel Award in the national-religious category.

1831 Joseph Smith receives Doctrine and Covenants 70, which gives instructions to the members of the newly organized Literary Firm and establishes it in accordance with the law of consecration.

1838 Judge Austin A. King holds a Court of Inquiry on the so-called Mormon War in Missouri, and, following the hearing, some sixty-four Mormon defendants are examined. Five—including Parley P. Pratt—are committed to the Richmond Jail and six—Joseph Smith, Hyrum Smith, Sidney Rigdon, Lyman Wight, Caleb Baldwin, and Alexander McRae—are committed to the Liberty Jail while they await further trial.

1848 Elder Orson Hyde rebaptizes Oliver Cowdery in Mosquito Creek near Council Bluffs, Iowa. Cowdery had been alienated from the Church for over ten years.

1888 Jacob Spori is appointed the first principal (president) of the Fremont or Bannock Stake Academy (the forerunner to Ricks College) in Rexburg, Idaho.

1967 The Montevideo Stake, the first stake in Uruguay, is organized, with Vincente C. Rubio as president.

1978 The Winnipeg Manitoba Stake, the first stake in Manitoba, Canada, is organized, with Lorne Leslie Clapson as president.

1988 Ricks College celebrates its centennial.

1988 The Ricks College women's cross-country team wins its first national title.

1838 Joseph F. Smith, later a member of the Quorum of the Twelve Apostles and the sixth President of the Church, is born in Far West, Missouri.

1894 Elder Franklin D. Richards is appointed president of the newly organized Genealogical Society of Utah.

1898 Wallace F. Bennett, later a Utah member of the U.S. Senate (1951–75), is born in Salt Lake City, Utah.

1994 President Howard W. Hunter speaks at the centennial of the Genealogical Society of Utah (later the Church Family History Department); there he is honored for his service as president of the Genealogical Society (1964–72).

President Joseph F. Smith, by Albert Salzbrenner, 1915 (see 1838).

1995 After meeting with U.S. president Bill Clinton and vice president Al Gore, President Gordon B. Hinckley holds a press conference at the Harvard Club in New York City, New York.

1996 The U.S. Air Force promotes Sharla "Kris" Cook, a BYU graduate and native of Utah, to the rank of brigadier general.

1799 David W. Patten, later a member of the Quorum of the Twelve Apostles and the first apostolic martyr in this dispensation, is born in Theresa, New York.

1843 The Halifax Branch, the first branch of the Church in Nova Scotia, is organized.

1907 Howard W. Hunter, later a member of the Quorum of the Twelve Apostles and the fourteenth President of the Church, is born in Boise, Idaho.

1966 The Andes South Mission is organized.

1998 Ground is broken for the Regina Saskatchewan Temple. Elder Hugh W. Pinnock, a member of the First Quorum of the Seventy and President of the North America Central Area, presides over the ceremony.

President Howard W. Hunter with his Counselors, Gordon B. Hinckley and Thomas S. Monson at the Orlando Florida Temple dedication (see 1907).

1999 President Gordon B. Hinckley dedicates the Halifax Nova Scotia Temple, and President Boyd K. Packer of the Quorum of the Twelve dedicates the Regina Saskatchewan Temple. These ceremonies mark the first time in the Church that two temples have been dedicated on the same day.

1792 William Marks, later Nauvoo's highly influential stake president, is born in Rutland, Vermont.

1831 Oliver Cowdery and John Whitmer leave Kirtland, Ohio, for Independence, Missouri, to publish the Book of Commandments, which contains Joseph Smith's revelations. Because of mob action, however, the volume is never completed.

1845 Eliza R. Snow's poem "My Father in Heaven" is published in the *Times and Seasons* in Nauvoo. It is later put to music as the beloved hymn "O My Father."

1891 Charles N. Watkins is appointed second president of Ricks College.

1950 The First Presidency issues a policy stating that only members of record in a unit should be called to serve as officers of that unit.

1993 After ninety-six years, the statue of Brigham Young is moved from the intersection of South Temple and Main streets in Salt Lake City, Utah, to a location eighty-two feet to the north.

Eliza R. Snow, ca. 1845 (see 1845).

1996 President Gordon B. Hinckley breaks ground for the Recife Brazil Temple.

1853 Ruth May Fox, later the third general president of the Young Women's Mutual Improvement Association (a predecessor to the Young Women organization), is born in Wiltshire, England.

1878 In the Salt Lake Theater some two thousand Latter-day Saint women protest the federal government's interference with religious practice in Utah.

1879 The Mexican Mission is organized.

1920 Champ Bean Tanner, later an internationally recognized research scientist in soil physics, micrometeorology, and plant physiology and a member of the National Academy of Sciences (1981), is born in Idaho Falls, Idaho.

Ruth May Fox, ca. 1880 (see 1853).

1952 The Central American Mission is organized.

1975 The Paris France Stake, the first stake in France, is created, with Gerard Giraud-Carrier as president.

1981 President Marion G. Romney of the First Presidency dedicates the Jordan River Temple (later the Jordan River Utah Temple).

1993 Church leaders applaud the Religious Freedom Restoration Act, passed and signed into law by the U.S. Congress. The U.S. Supreme Court later declares the law unconstitutional.

1993 The First Presidency announces plans to build a temple in Santo Domingo, Dominican Republic.

1846 Led by Captain James Brown, the sick detachment of the Mormon Battalion arrives in Pueblo, Colorado, where it will spend the winter with a group of Saints from Mississippi.

1900 Franklin D. Richards, later a member of the Presidency of the Seventy, is born in Ogden, Utah.

1964 President David O. McKay dedicates the Oakland Temple (later the Oakland California Temple).

1980 President Spencer W. Kimball dedicates the Seattle Washington Temple.

1984 President Gordon B. Hinckley of the First Presidency dedicates the Taipei Taiwan Temple.

1994 The First Presidency announces plans to build a temple in Nashville, Tennessee.

1997 Ground is broken for the Monticello Utah Temple. Elder Ben B. Banks, a member of the First Quorum of the Seventy and President of the Utah South Area, presides over the ceremonies.

The Monticello Utah Temple, ca. 1999 (see 1997).

NOVEMBER 18

1908 Naomi H. Ward (Randall), author of "I Am a Child of God," is born in North Ogden, Utah.

1975 The Church Genealogical Department (later the Family History Department) is reorganized with five divisions.

The Mistolar Branch meetinghouse (made of wooden poles supporting a tin roof) in Paraguay, ca. 1992 (see 1980).

1980 Elders Bruce Blosil and Ricky Loynd baptize 139 Nivacle Indians in the village of Mistolar, Paraguay. Twenty-two more are baptized on Christmas Day and another forty-five in April 1981.

1988 U.S. president Ronald Reagan awards the Church a President's Historical Preservation Award for restoring the Newel K. Whitney Store, in Kirtland, Ohio.

1994 Eric B. Shumway is inaugurated as the eighth president of BYU–Hawaii.

1996 Elder Joseph B. Wirthlin ministers to the Saints in Vladivostok, Russia, as the first Apostle of this dispensation to visit far east Russia.

NOVEMBER 19

1823 Alvin Smith, the eldest brother of Joseph Smith, dies in Manchester, New York, from the effects of "bilious colic" and an overdose of calomel. On his deathbed, he charges Joseph to faithfully keep the commandments of the Lord so that he will be able to obtain the gold plates.

1918 President Joseph F. Smith dies in Salt Lake City, Utah, at age eighty, after serving for more than forty-two years as a General Authority.

1927 Harold A. Lafount is appointed as chair of the Federal Radio Commission, the first Latter-day Saint to hold this position.

Alvin Smith grave marker, Palmyra, New York (see 1823).

1963 Missionaries arrive for the first time in Luxembourg.

1972 The Santiago Chile Stake, the first stake in Chile, is organized, with Carlos A. Cifuentes as president.

1974 President Spencer W. Kimball dedicates the Washington D.C. Temple.

1974 The Portugal Lisbon Mission is organized.

1998 President Gordon B. Hinckley commences a three-day tour of storm-ravaged Nicaragua and Honduras, bringing comfort and humanitarian relief to victims of Hurricane Mitch.

1818 Mary Isabella Hales (Horne), later an original member of the first Relief Society (1842) and a women's leader in Utah, is born in Rainham, England.

1863 The *Union Vidette,* an anti-Mormon newspaper, is issued for the first time at Camp Douglas, Utah, under the direction of Colonel Patrick Connor.

1879 In Mexico City the first branch of the Church in Mexico is organized, with Plotino C. Rhodacanaty as president.

1889 Joseph Anderson, later the secretary to the First Presidency, a member of the First Quorum of the Seventy, and the oldest living General Authority at the time of his death at 102 years of age, is born in Salt Lake City, Utah.

1894 The First Presidency and Quorum of the Twelve Apostles approve the articles of incorporation of the Genealogical Society of Utah.

1960 The Rarotonga Mission is organized.

1966 The Buenos Aires Stake, the first stake in Argentina, is organized, with Angel Abrea as president.

1998 During his visit to storm-stricken Nicaragua and Honduras, President Gordon B. Hinckley speaks to victims of Hurricane Mitch.

1999 President Gordon B. Hinckley dedicates the Billings Montana Temple.

1999 Ground is broken for the Perth Australia Temple. Elder Kenneth Johnson, a member of the First Quorum of the Seventy and the First Counselor in the Australia/New Zealand Area Presidency, presides over the ceremonies.

President Hinckley helping clean up after Hurricane Mitch, ca. November 1998 (see 1998).

1999 The BYU men's soccer team wins the club national title for the fourth year in a row.

NOVEMBER 21

1841 Apostles Brigham Young, Heber C. Kimball, and John Taylor perform baptisms for the dead for some forty individuals in the newly completed Nauvoo Temple baptismal font. This is the first time this ordinance is performed in a temple during this dispensation.

1860 George D. Pyper, later the general Sunday School superintendent (1934–43), a Mormon Tabernacle Choir tour manager, and a composer, is born in Salt Lake City, Utah.

1894 Elder Franklin D. Richards, president of the Genealogical Society of Utah, files the society's articles of incorporation, making it a legal entity.

Rendell Mabey, one of the first official representatives of the Church in West Africa, baptizes a new convert (see 1978).

1910 Hamer Budge, later an Idaho representative in the U.S. Congress (1951–61), is born in Pocatello, Idaho.

1944 Margaret Dyreng (Nadauld), later the eleventh general president of the Young Women, is born in Manti, Utah.

1960 The Vancouver British Columbia Stake, the first stake in British Columbia, Canada, is organized, with Ernest E. Jensen as president.

1960 The Alaskan-Canadian Mission is organized.

1978 Edwin and Janath Cannon and Rendell and Rachel Mabey, the first official representatives of the International Mission in West Africa, witness the fruits of their labors with the baptism of twenty-one Nigerians. Within the year some seventeen hundred Nigerians and Ghanians are baptized.

1992 Young women throughout the Church join in a day of service for the Young Women Worldwide Celebration entitled "Walk in the Light."

1998 President Boyd K. Packer of the Quorum of the Twelve Apostles, Elder Dallin H. Oaks, and Relief Society general president Mary Ellen Smoot make presentations at the Second World Conference on Families, in Salt Lake City, Utah.

NOVEMBER 22

1854 Erastus Snow begins publishing the *St. Louis Luminary,* a Church paper, in St. Louis, Missouri.

1856 Heber J. Grant, later a member of the Quorum of the Twelve Apostles and the seventh President of the Church, is born in Salt Lake City, Utah.

1903 Henry D. Taylor, later a member of the First Quorum of the Seventy, is born in Provo, Utah.

1911 During a service featuring the Mormon Tabernacle Choir, Elder Heber J. Grant dedicates the Oliver Cowdery Monument in Richmond, Missouri.

1918 Heber J. Grant presides at the graveside services held for President Joseph F. Smith. Because of a nationwide influenza epidemic, no public funerals were allowed during this time.

1969 President Hugh B. Brown of the First Presidency dedicates the Mormon Battalion Monument, overlooking Old Town in San Diego, California.

1970 Lan LaJeunesse, later a professional cowboy and the 1999 World Champion Bareback Rider, is born in Bountiful, Utah.

1988 Elder Marvin J. Ashton dedicates the islands of Mauritius and Reunion, located off the eastern coast of Africa, for the preaching of the gospel.

1999 The BYU women's cross-country team wins the NCAA national championship. Having also won the 1997 championship, it becomes the first BYU team to win two national championships.

The BYU women's cross-country team, 22 November 1999.

NOVEMBER 23

1816 Daniel Tyler, later a member of the Mormon Battalion and an author of a history recounting the group's epic journey, is born in Semproneous, New York.

1849 Parley P. Pratt and fifty other men leave the Salt Lake Valley to explore southern Utah. By the first of the year they would reach the site of St. George and collect a wealth of information about central and southern Utah's settlement potential.

1870 Richard R. Lyman, later a member of the Quorum of the Twelve Apostles and the first General Authority to have obtained a Ph.D., is born in Fillmore, Utah.

1872 Abraham O. Woodruff, later a member of the Quorum of the Twelve Apostles, is born in Salt Lake City, Utah.

1914 Rex C. Reeve Sr., later a member of the First Quorum of the Seventy, is born in Hinckley, Utah.

1918 Heber J. Grant becomes the seventh President of the Church, with Anthon H. Lund and Charles W. Penrose as Counselors.

1919 Leonard C. Brostrom, later a World War II army private and U.S. Congressional Medal of Honor recipient (1945 posthumously) for single-handedly taking out several enemy positions while exposed to and mortally wounded by enemy fire, is born in Preston, Idaho.

1958 The Cincinnati Stake, the first stake in Ohio since the Kirtland era, is organized, with Thomas Blair Evans as president.

1993 The First Presidency issues a statement that emphasizes keeping the Sabbath day holy.

NOVEMBER 24

1830 William Bowker Preston, later the fourth Presiding Bishop of the Church, is born in Halifax, Virginia.

1850 The Swiss Mission is organized.

1869 Gas street lamps are used for the first time in Salt Lake City, Utah.

1921 George R. Hill III, later a member of the First Quorum of the Seventy, is born in Ogden, Utah.

1962 The North Scottish Mission is organized.

1964 Missionaries arrive in Bolivia for the first time.

1990 The Gospel Essentials course is made part of the regular Sunday School curriculum.

1990 The first converts in Bulgaria, Emil and Diana Christov and their two sons, Ventizlav and Marela Lazarov, are baptized.

1997 The BYU women's cross-country team wins its first NCAA national championship.

NOVEMBER 25

1794 George Miller, later the second Bishop of the Church (a position akin to Presiding Bishop of the Church), is born in Orange County, Virginia.

1833 Orson Hyde and John Gould arrive in Kirtland and report to the Prophet on the expulsion of the Saints from Jackson County, Missouri.

1834 Joseph Smith receives Doctrine and Covenants 106, which appoints Warren A. Cowdery to preside over the Saints in Freedom, New York.

1848 President Brigham Young, Elder John Taylor, and John Kay create designs and inscriptions for coins to be minted in Utah from California gold. The designs include an all-seeing eye and the motto "Holiness to the Lord."

1883 Paul Haslinger, the first convert in Austria, is baptized.

1925 Russell C. Taylor, later a member of the First Quorum of the Seventy, is born in Red Mesa, Colorado.

1952 U.S. president Dwight D. Eisenhower asks Elder Ezra Taft Benson to serve as the U.S. secretary of agriculture. Acting on the advice of President McKay, Elder Benson accepts and serves in the position for eight years.

1967 Elder Spencer W. Kimball visits northern Brazil on a fact-finding assignment to determine whether to expand or cut back missionary activity in the area. Within a year, a new mission is created, and later, as a result of President Kimball's revelation on priesthood, northern Brazil becomes one of the most successful missionary fields in the Church.

1979 Elder Boyd K. Packer breaks ground and dedicates a site for the Mexico City Temple (later the México City D.F. México Temple), the first temple to be built in Mexico.

Elder Greg Christofferson of the Brazilian Mission and Elder Spencer W. Kimball of the Twelve at Recife, Brazil, during Elder Kimball's fact-finding tour of northeastern Brazil, 25 November 1967.

1981 The first branch of the Church on the Cayman Islands is established.

1989 The First Presidency announces the elimination of stake and ward budget assessments for financing local Church units in the United States and Canada.

1990 Lloyd D. Newell becomes the voice of *Music and the Spoken Word*.

1772 Joseph Knight Sr., later a friend and supporter of Joseph Smith and the progenitor of a large family dedicated to the Church, is born in Oakham, Massachusetts.

1851 The first baptisms in Norway are performed at Osterrisor.

Kresimir Cosic, ca. 1972 (see 1948).

1948 Kresimir Cosic, later an all-American basketball player at BYU, Olympic bronze, silver, and gold medalist in basketball, and a Croatian diplomat, is born in Zagreb, Croatia.

1966 A replica of the *Christus* statue, which had been used at the Mormon Pavilion at the New York World's Fair, is placed in the Bureau of Information (visitors' center) on the Los Angeles Temple (later the Los Angeles California Temple) grounds.

1984 The First Presidency announces that full-time single elders would again serve for twenty-four months, following a period of several years when many had been called to serve for eighteen months.

1999 Lee Groberg's *American Prophet: The Story of Joseph Smith*, narrated by Gregory Peck, makes its national premiere on PBS. (Utah residents saw it on 26 September on KBYU.)

1832 Joseph Smith writes to W. W. Phelps in Jackson County, Missouri, giving him information about the duties of the clerk in Zion. Part of the letter is later canonized as Doctrine and Covenants 85.

1850 President Heber C. Kimball dedicates the Warm Springs bathhouse (located just north of Salt Lake City), a favorite resort for the Saints in early Utah.

1919 President Heber J. Grant dedicates the Laie Hawaii Temple on Thanksgiving Day (U.S.).

1934 During a gunbattle between FBI agents and gangster George "Baby Face" Nelson, Inspector Samuel P. Cowley, the first LDS agent in the FBI and the head of the antigangster unit, is mortally wounded. Cowley continues firing his weapon as he falls to the ground and kills Nelson. Cowley dies the following day.

U.S. president Jimmy Carter speaks in the Tabernacle, 27 November 1978.

1978 U.S. president Jimmy Carter speaks in the Tabernacle in Salt Lake City, Utah.

1982 Elder Marvin J. Ashton breaks ground for the Johannesburg South Africa Temple.

1992 The first branch of the Church in the African country of Burundi is organized, with Egide Nzojibwami as president.

1831 Carl Christian Anton Christensen, later a Danish convert and artist particularly known for his "Mormon Panorama" and murals in the Manti and St. George Temples (later the Manti Utah and St. George Utah Temples), is born in Copenhagen, Denmark.

1841 Joseph Smith informs the Quorum of the Twelve Apostles that "the Book of Mormon was the most correct of any book on earth, and the keystone of our religion, and a man would get nearer to God by abiding by its precepts, than by any other book" (*History of the Church,* 4:461).

1869 President Brigham Young organizes the Young Ladies' Department of the Cooperative Retrenchment Association, which paves the way for the later creation of the Young Women's Mutual Improvement Association in the 1870s.

1921 James H. Langenheim, later an award-winning architect whose works include the master plan for the campus at the University of California, Irvine; the Los Angeles Art Museum; the BYU Museum of Art ; the Prudential Federal Building in Salt Lake City; and the Transamerica Building in San Francisco, is born in Bethlehem, Pennsylvania.

1930 J. Reuben Clark Jr., newly appointed U.S. ambassador to Mexico, presents himself to Mexican president Ortiz Rubio at the National Palace in Mexico City.

1999 Ground is broken for the Winter Quarters Temple. Elder Hugh Pinnock, a member of the First Quorum of the Seventy and President of the North America Central Area, presides over the ceremony.

❧❧❧ NOVEMBER ❧❧❧ 29

1839 Joseph Smith and Elias Higbee have an interview with U.S. president Martin Van Buren concerning the wrongs suffered by the Saints in Missouri and are told, "Gentlemen, your cause is just, but I can do nothing for you. . . . If I take up for you I shall lose the vote of Missouri" (*History of the Church,* 4:80).

1911 The Church forms the first "MIA Scout" troop in Salt Lake City, with Arthur William Sadler, one of Lord Baden-Powell's original British Scouts. Later the Church formally associates with the Boy Scouts of America (1913).

President Spencer W. Kimball (left) with U.S. president Gerald M. Ford and Betty Ford, 29 November 1977.

1947 The First Presidency announces to the Saints in North America that the regular December fast day will be dedicated to relieving the suffering of the people in Europe resulting from World War II. About $210,000 is collected and distributed to Europeans of all faiths by an agency not connected with the Church.

1959 In Los Angeles, California, at the first televised awards show of the National Academy of Recording Arts and Sciences, the Mormon Tabernacle Choir is given a Grammy Award for its recording of "The Battle Hymn of the Republic."

1960 The Minnesota Stake, the first stake in Minnesota, is organized, with Delbert F. Wright as president.

1977 U.S. president Gerald M. Ford visits Church headquarters in Salt Lake City, Utah.

1994 Wilfred Navalta, BYU–Hawaii women's volleyball coach, becomes a member of the National Association of Intercollegiate Athletics Hall of Fame.

1845 President Brigham Young dedicates the attic of the Nauvoo Temple so that the Saints can receive their endowments before abandoning the city for the West.

1856 Aided by rescue teams sent out by President Brigham Young, the Martin handcart company arrives in Salt Lake City. Some 150 men, women, and children—one-fourth of the company—had perished with hunger and cold on the journey.

1973 In response to U.S. president Richard Nixon's request to conserve energy during the energy crisis, the Church announces that Christmas lights on Temple Square will not be turned on this year.

1985 President Gordon B. Hinckley breaks ground for the Las Vegas Nevada Temple.

1990 The government of Ghana gives the Church permission to resume public activities in that country. In June 1989, the government had expelled the Church's missionaries and confined worship services to private homes.

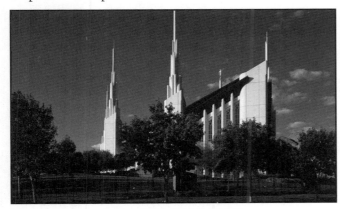

The Las Vegas Nevada Temple, ca. 1995 (see 1985).

1831 Joseph Smith receives Doctrine and Covenants 71, which instructs the Prophet and Sidney Rigdon to temporarily cease working on the translation of the Bible and to spend their time counteracting the teachings of Ezra Booth, who had begun publishing false statements about Joseph Smith and the Church.

1838 Joseph Smith, Hyrum Smith, Sidney Rigdon, Lyman Wight, Caleb Baldwin, and Alexander McRae are incarcerated in Liberty Jail.

1878 John Jacques, a survivor of the Martin handcart company, begins a series of letters to the *Salt Lake Herald* describing the tragic journey of the company.

1937 H. Bruce Stucki, later a member of the Second Quorum of the Seventy, is born in St. George, Utah.

1970 The last issues of five Church magazines, the *Children's Friend* (published by the Primary), the *Relief Society Magazine,* the *Instructor* (published by the Sunday School), the *Improvement Era* (originally published by the MIA but later a general Church magazine), and *Impact* (published by the seminaries and institutes) are released.

1998 The Church announces a proposal to purchase the block of Main Street east of Temple Square and convert it into a plaza uniting Temple Square with the Church Office Building block to the east. The plaza is to feature gardens, walkways, and underground parking.

DECEMBER 2

1834 Jesse N. Smith, later a key colonizer of Arizona, is born in Stockholm, New York.

1856 About sixty wagons and teams leave Salt Lake City to meet the wagon companies led by Captains Hodgett and Hunt that had accompanied the Martin and Willie handcart companies.

1886 Adam Samuel Bennion, later a member of the Quorum of the Twelve Apostles, is born in Taylorsville, Utah.

1902 President Joseph F. Smith issues a public report to the Associated Press supporting Reed Smoot's election to the U.S. Senate and indicates that charges against Smoot are unfounded.

1929 Eran A. Call, later a member of the Second Quorum of the Seventy, is born in Colonia Dublán, Mexico.

1939 Harry Reid, a Nevada representative in the U.S. Congress (1983–87) and a U.S. Senator (1987–), is born in Searchlight, Nevada.

1971 Marvin J. Ashton is ordained an Apostle, replacing Richard L. Evans, who had died.

1975 Hugh B. Brown of the First Presidency dies in Salt Lake City on the same day as Elder ElRay L. Christiansen, Assistant to the Quorum of the Twelve Apostles, dies. This is the first time two General Authorities have died on the same day since the deaths of Joseph and Hyrum Smith.

1982 Making medical history, Dr. William DeVries implants the first artificial heart into a human, Barney Clark. Both doctor and patient are LDS.

1983 President Gordon B. Hinckley of the First Presidency dedicates the Mexico City Temple (later the México City D.F. México Temple).

1989 Church membership reaches seven million.

1995 The BYU–Hawaii women's volleyball team claims the National Association of Intercollegiate Athletics championship for the second year in a row.

1998 Li Zhaoxing, China's ambassador to the United States, joins Elder John K. Carmack in turning on the three hundred thousand Christmas lights at the Washington D.C. Temple grounds.

Los Angeles Times *article announcing Dr. William DeVries's success in implanting an artificial heart, 2 December 1982.*

DECEMBER 3

1851 The first baptisms in New South Wales, Australia, take place at Sydney.

1898 The first issue of the *Latter-day Saints' Southern Star,* a weekly Church periodical, is published in Chattanooga, Tennessee.

1940 Jeffrey R. Holland, later BYU president and a member of the Quorum of the Twelve Apostles, is born in St. George, Utah.

1962 The Mexico Stake, the first Spanish-speaking stake, is organized in Mexico City, with Harold Brown as president.

1998 L. Jay Silvester, the world discus champion and Olympic medalist, is inducted into the National Track and Field Hall of Fame.

1999 The First Presidency announces that Craig D. Jessop has been appointed music director of the Mormon Tabernacle Choir, replacing Jerold D. Ottley, who later retires after leading the choir for twenty-five years.

L. Jay Silvester at the national championship in Sacramento, 1968 (see 1998).

DECEMBER 4

1831 Joseph Smith receives Doctrine and Covenants 72, which appoints Newel K. Whitney to be a bishop of the Church in Kirtland and sets forth various responsibilities of bishops in the Church.

1842 Having been divided into four political areas called wards since 1 March 1841, Nauvoo is redivided into ten wards. A bishop is assigned to each ward and is given the responsibility of providing for the temporal needs of the poor in his respective ward.

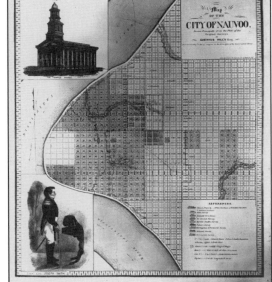

1933 C. Max Caldwell, later a member of the

Map of Nauvoo (see 1842).

Second Quorum of the Seventy, is born in Salt Lake City, Utah.

1961 The first twenty-nine missionaries enter the Missionary Language Institute (MLI), the forerunner of the Language Training Mission (LTM), and the Missionary Training Center (MTC), in Provo, Utah.

❧ ❧ ❧ DECEMBER 5 ❧ ❧ ❧

1833 Joseph Smith writes a letter from Kirtland to Bishop Edward Partridge in Missouri, advising the Missouri Saints, who had recently been driven from Jackson County, against selling their lands even though they no longer possessed them. He counsels them to seek every lawful means for redress.

1834 Joseph Smith ordains Oliver Cowdery to the office of Assistant President of the Church.

1847 At a council meeting of the Quorum of the Twelve Apostles held in Hyde Park (near Council Bluffs), Iowa, the assembled Apostles reorganize the First Presidency, with Brigham Young as President of the Church; he later names Heber C. Kimball and Willard Richards as Counselors.

1903 *Harper's Weekly,* a U.S. national newspaper, defends Elder Reed Smoot during the Senate hearings on his worthiness to be seated following his election to the U.S. Senate.

1990 Ty Detmer, a BYU quarterback, receives the Heisman Trophy from the New York Downtown Athletic Club, recognizing him as the best college football player in America.

1993 With the creation of the São Leopoldo Brazil Stake, Brazil becomes the second country outside the United States to have one hundred stakes. Valmir Severo Dutra is called as president of the new stake.

1998 Ground is broken for the Columbia South Carolina Temple. Elder Gordon T. Watts, a member of the Second Quorum of the Seventy and First Counselor in the North America Southeast Area Presidency, presides over the ceremony.

BYU quarterback Ty Detmer, ca. 1990 (see 1990).

1832 Joseph Smith receives Doctrine and Covenants 86, which contains additional scriptural application to the parable of the wheat and tares.

1925 In Buenos Aires, Argentina, Elder Melvin J. Ballard organizes the South American Mission, the first mission in South America.

Elder J. Vernon Sharp near Macchu Picchu, Peru, just two years after South America had been dedicated for the preaching of the gospel, 1927 (see 1925).

1981 Elder Gene R. Cook organizes the Otavalo Ecuador Stake, the first all-Indian stake in South America, with Luis Alfonso Morales C. as president.

1992 With the creation of the Harvest Park Ward in the Salt Lake Granger South Stake, the Church reaches the milestone of having twenty thousand wards and branches.

1842 Elder Orson Hyde returns to Nauvoo from his historic mission to the Holy Land, during which he blessed the land and visited international capitals throughout Europe and the Middle East.

1883 Clifford E. Young, later an Assistant to the Quorum of the Twelve Apostles, is born in Salt Lake City, Utah.

1920 Elder David O. McKay of the Twelve and Hugh J. Cannon, editor of the *Improvement Era,* board the *Empress of Japan* at Vancouver British Columbia, beginning their approximately 60,000-mile tour of missions throughout the world.

1941 Captain Mervyn S. Bennion, son-in-law of President J. Reuben Clark, is mortally wounded during the Japanese attack on Pearl Harbor as he stands at the bridge of his ship, the *USS West Virginia.* For his bravery he is later posthumously awarded the Congressional Medal of Honor.

1953 The West German government grants the Church *Koerperschaft des Oeffentlichen Rechts* (Corporation under Public Law), giving it equal rights with the established churches in Germany. This is the first time in German history that a foreign church has been so honored.

1968 President Hugh B. Brown of the First Presidency conducts the site dedication and groundbreaking for the Washington D.C. Temple, the first temple in the eastern United States.

1991 The *Church News* announces the release of the five-volume *Encyclopedia of Mormonism.* Published by Macmillan in New York City, it contains some twelve hundred articles by 738 writers and is considered to be the most comprehensive reference work ever published about the Church.

1992 Elder Russell M. Nelson dedicates Belize for the preaching of the gospel. This completes the dedication of all seven nations in Central America.

1996 The BYU–Hawaii women's volleyball team wins the U.S. National Association of Intercollegiate Athletics Division II volleyball championship in San Diego, California.

The Washington D.C. Temple (see 1968).

DECEMBER 8

1831 George Teasdale, later a member of the Quorum of the Twelve Apostles, is born in London, England.

1876 A central committee of the Young Men's Mutual Improvement Association (predecessor to the Young Men organization) is created, with Junius F. Wells as president.

1911 James E. Talmage is ordained an Apostle, replacing Charles W. Penrose, who had been called to the First Presidency.

1931 John R. Lasater, later a member of the First Quorum of the Seventy, is born in Farmington, Utah.

Junius F. Wells, ca. 1872 (see 1876).

1975 The Wilmington Delaware Stake, the first stake in Delaware, is organized, with Rulon Edward Johnson Jr. as president.

1999 Commemorating the sesquicentennial of the organization of the Sunday School, President Gordon B. Hinckley presides over the sealing of a time capsule to be opened in 2049.

 DECEMBER *9*

1849 Some fifty children meet at the Salt Lake City home of Richard Ballantyne for the first Church-sponsored Sunday School.

1850 Marsena Cannon, the first photographer in Utah, begins advertising his services to execute "Daguerreotype Likenesses" in Salt Lake City. His images preserve our earliest views of the Latter-day Saints and their community in the Rocky Mountains.

1852 George H. Brimhall, later a progressive educator and president of BYU, is born in Salt Lake City, Utah.

1867 President Brigham Young reorganizes the School of the Prophets in Salt Lake City as a means of helping Church members in the Great Basin successfully meet the challenges posed by the coming of the transcontinental railroad (which is completed in 1869) and other facets of modernization. Branches of the school are eventually established in many other Latter-day Saint settlements.

1895 The Colonia Juárez Mexico Stake, the first stake in Mexico, is organized, with Anthony W. Ivins as president.

1907 Wallace F. Toronto, later a pioneering missionary and mission president in Czechoslovakia, is born in Salt Lake City, Utah.

1922 For the first time, Church leaders ask prospective missionaries to have a medical exam before sending in their names for assignments.

1928 The East Central States Mission is organized.

1934 The New York Stake, the first stake in New York, is organized, with Fred G. Taylor as president.

1978 Missionary couples Rendell N. and Rachel Mabey and Edwin and Janath Cannon, the first missionaries to Ghana, arrive in that country and soon baptize eighty-nine people who have been waiting for the missionaries, some of them for many years. Within a year, more than four hundred people are baptized.

Richard Ballantyne Organizes the First Sunday School, *by Arnold Friberg, ca. 1949 (see 1849).*

DECEMBER 10

1830 At the Joseph Smith Sr. home near Waterloo, New York, Sidney Rigdon and Edward Partridge meet Joseph Smith for the first time.

1833 Joseph Smith writes a letter to the Saints in Missouri, who had recently been driven from their lands in Jackson County, expressing his love and concern for them and offering his encouragement.

1845 President Brigham Young of the Quorum of the Twelve Apostles and Elder Heber C. Kimball begin administering the endowment to the members of the Church in the Nauvoo Temple for the first time.

1856 The First Presidency issues the Fourteenth General Epistle to the Church, reviewing missionary efforts throughout the world, immigration to Utah by handcarts, and the state of developing industries in the Great Basin.

1938 Han In Sang, later the translator of the Book of Mormon into Korean, a pioneer Church leader in Korea, and member of the Second Quorum of the Seventy, is born in Seoul, Korea.

1952 LDS missionaries enter Honduras for the first time.

1967 The Texas South Mission is organized.

1971 Henry B. Eyring is inaugurated as the ninth president of Ricks College.

1972 The Rapid City Stake, the first stake in South Dakota, is organized, with Briant LeRoy Davis as president.

DECEMBER 11

1821 John R. Winder, later a member of the First Presidency, is born in Biddenham, England.

1830 Joseph Smith baptizes Edward Partridge, later the first bishop of the Church, in the Seneca River. The Prophet receives Doctrine and Covenants 35 and 36 in behalf of Sidney Rigdon and Edward Partridge.

1846 The Mormon Battalion is forced to fight a herd of wild bulls near the San Pedro River, resulting in the death of about ten to fifteen bulls and the wounding of three men.

1850 Andrew Jenson, later an assistant Church historian and chronologist, is born in Torsler, Hjörring amt, Denmark.

1885 J. Wyley Sessions, later director of the first institute of religion in the Church (Moscow, Idaho), is born in Marion, Idaho.

1896 Delbert L. Stapley, later a member of the Quorum of the Twelve Apostles, is born in Mesa, Arizona.

1960 The Winter Quarters Stake, the first stake in Nebraska, is organized, with William D. Hardy as president.

1982 Dr. Thomas E. and Donna Bauman, the first full-time missionaries to the Bahamas arrive in that island country.

1994 President Howard W. Hunter presides at the creation of the Mexico City Mexico Conreras Stake, the two thousandth stake in the Church, with Victor Manuel Salinas G. as president.

1999 President Gordon B. Hinckley of the First Presidency dedicates the Edmonton Alberta Temple.

DECEMBER 12

1850 The Hawaiian (Sandwich Islands) Mission is organized.

1889 The First Presidency of the Church issues an important manifesto regarding the Church's view on the relationship between Church and civil courts.

1942 The LDS book publisher Bookcraft is established. Its first publication is *The Gospel Kingdom: Selections from the Writings and Discourses of John Taylor,* selected, arranged, and annotated by G. Homer Durham.

1995 BYU President Rex E. Lee, forced to retire because of his battle with cancer, bids the faculty, administration, staff, and students good-bye in a farewell devotional.

◄ *The Moscow Idaho Institute of Religion Building. J. Wyley Sessions was the first director at the Institute of Religion in Moscow, Idaho (see 1885).*

DECEMBER 13

1875 Lucy Jane Brimhall (Knight), later one of the first single sister missionaries, is born in Spanish Fork, Utah. She and Amanda Inez Knight (Allen) are set apart on 1 April 1898 to serve in the British Mission.

1902 Professor James H. Linford becomes the first president of the Brigham Young College Society of American Archaeology in Logan. The society's mission is to study the Book of Mormon from a scientific perspective.

1926 Truman G. Madsen, later a popular lecturer, educator, philosopher, and author, is born in Salt Lake City, Utah.

1952 The state of Nebraska opens the Mormon Pioneer Memorial Bridge in Florence, Nebraska.

1959 Johnny "John" Whitaker, later a child actor and costar of such TV series and motion pictures as *Family Affair* (1966–71) and *Tom Sawyer* (1973), is born in Van Nuys, California.

1964 Tresa Spaulding (Hamson), later a four-time all-American on BYU's women's basketball team (1983–87) and the 1986–87 NCAA leading scorer, is born in Dallas, Texas.

1907 In a letter to the Saints in the Netherlands, the First Presidency for the first time urges European members not to immigrate to the United States. Prior to this time, new converts from other countries had been encouraged to gather with the rest of the Saints in Latter-day Saint communities in the western United States.

1980 The San Juan Puerto Rico Stake, the first stake in Puerto Rico, is organized, with Herminio De Jesus as president.

1984 President Gordon B. Hinckley of the First Presidency dedicates the Guatemala City Temple (later the Guatemala City Guatemala Temple).

1985 President Gordon B. Hinckley of the First Presidency dedicates the Seoul Korea Temple (later the Seoul South Korea Temple), the first temple on mainland Asia.

1996 In Tucson, Arizona, President Gordon B. Hinckley dedicates a monument honoring the Mormon Battalion.

1833 William W. Phelps writes to Church leaders in Kirtland, informing them that Governor Dunklin of Missouri is willing to assist the Saints in reclaiming their lands and to help restore the Saints in the county but that he has no power to guard and protect them once they return.

1845 The Welsh Mission is organized.

1896 The Colorado Mission is organized.

1979 In preparation for the 1980 Winter Olympics, a temporary LDS visitors' center is opened at Lake Placid, New York.

1992 The First Presidency announces an effort sponsored by the Relief Society to raise literacy rates in the Church worldwide.

1992 The Dar es Salaam Branch, the first branch of the Church in Tanzania, is organized, with Robert Muhile as president.

1833 Joseph Smith receives Doctrine and Covenants 101, outlining some of the causes for the sufferings of the Missouri Saints and comforting them over their losses.

1840 Governor Thomas Carlin of Illinois signs the act chartering the city of Nauvoo. Effective 1 February 1841, the Nauvoo charter delineates the rights and privileges of the residents of Nauvoo and of the city government.

1866 President Brigham Young asks the bishops in Salt Lake City to organize Relief Societies in every ward. By the end of the month, Eliza R. Snow is called as the second general president of the Relief Society, the first to be called since the society was disbanded in March 1844.

1902 The U.S. Justice Department promises the Church that it will protect LDS missionaries in the southern states against mob attacks, which had been common up to that time.

1939 The Church announces that membership has reached 750,000.

1957 The Saints in Japan receive the first copies of the Doctrine and Covenants and Pearl of Great Price in Japanese.

1989 President Gordon B. Hinckley of the First Presidency dedicates the Las Vegas Nevada Temple.

1995 The *Church News* becomes available on the Internet.

1872 President George A. Smith of the First Presidency visits Versailles, France, and meets with M. Thiers, president of the French Republic.

1922 Robert Edward Sackley, later a member of the First Quorum of the Seventy, is born in Lismore, Australia.

1934 Joseph W. B. Johnson, later one of the first converts in Ghana and the first branch president and the first stake patriarch in Ghana, is born in Lagos, Nigeria.

1958 President David O. McKay dedicates the Church College of Hawaii campus (later known as BYU–Hawaii), in Laie, Hawaii.

1989 The first converts in the countries of Estonia (eastern Europe) and Lesotho (southern Africa) are baptized.

The Church College of Hawaii, ca. 1958 (see 1958).

DECEMBER 18

1833 The Prophet Joseph Smith ordains his father, Joseph Smith Sr., as the first Patriarch of the Church.

1836 Brigham Young Jr., later a member of the Quorum of the Twelve Apostles and First Presidency, is born in Kirtland, Ohio.

1886 Arthur V. Watkins, later a U.S. senator from Utah (1946–58), is born in Midway, Utah.

1904 John H. Vandenberg, later a member of the First Quorum of the Seventy and the ninth Presiding Bishop of the Church, is born in Ogden, Utah.

1936 Ronald T. Halverson, later a member of the Second Quorum of the Seventy, is born in Ogden, Utah.

1939 Adhemar Damiani, later a member of the Second Quorum of the Seventy, is born in São Paulo, Brazil.

1982 Elder Mark E. Petersen of the Quorum of the Twelve Apostles breaks ground for the Boise Idaho Temple.

1995 Reporter Mike Wallace interviews President Gordon B. Hinckley for an episode of the popular weekly program *60 Minutes* to be aired on CBS in April 1996.

1999 President Gordon B. Hinckley dedicates the Raleigh North Carolina Temple.

President Gordon B. Hinckley showing Mike Wallace Temple Square (see 1995).

DECEMBER 19

1831 The Church purchases nearly sixty-four acres of the temple lot in Independence, Missouri, from Jones H. Flournoy at a cost of $130.

1838 John E. Page and John Taylor are ordained Apostles, replacing John F. Boynton and Lyman E. Johnson, who had apostatized.

1933 F. Melvin Hammond, later a member of the First Quorum of the Seventy, is born in Blackfoot, Idaho.

1980 The BYU football team wins the 1980 Holiday Bowl, the team's first bowl victory, over Southern Methodist University. In the final minutes, the Cougars make an impressive comeback capped by quarterback Jim McMahon's forty-six yard "hail Mary" touchdown pass to tight end Clay Brown in the closing seconds of the game. The game is later called the "Miracle Bowl."

1988 Teresa Hughes from Kingsport, Tennessee, becomes the four millionth visitor to Temple Square.

1993 A choir of missionaries from the Italy Rome Mission sings carols for the Vatican Radio Christmas Mass in St. Peter's Basilica.

1996 Charles Osgood, anchor of the CBS television program *Sunday Morning* and of CBS Radio's *The Osgood File,* joins the Mormon Tabernacle Choir for its annual Christmas concert. Portions of the program are aired on *Sunday Morning* on 22 December.

DECEMBER 20

1838 Emma Smith visits her husband, Joseph, in Liberty Jail, Missouri, and spends two days confined with him in the jail.

1839 Alexander Wright and Samuel Mulliner, the first missionaries to Scotland, begin preaching the gospel in that country.

1842 Elder Lorenzo D. Barnes dies at Bradford, England. He is the first missionary to die while serving a foreign mission.

1873 Peter O. Thomassen issues the first foreign-language paper (Danish and Norwegian) published in Utah, the *Utah Posten.*

1885 Stayner Richards, later an Assistant to the Quorum of the Twelve Apostles, is born in Salt Lake City, Utah.

1917 Julia N. Mavimbela, later the organizer of Women for Peace, an organization dedicated to helping in the peaceful transition from apartheid to majority rule in South Africa, and a recipient of a BYU presidential citation and medallion, is born in Standerton, South Africa.

1921 After a year-long tour of Church missions throughout the world, Elder David O. McKay arrives back in the United States at New York City.

1948 Angela "Bay" Buchanan, later the U.S. treasurer (1981–83), is born in Washington, D.C.

1972 The Church organizes the Church Music Department, with O. Leslie Stone as managing director.

1998 President Gordon B. Hinckley ends his travel for the year, having logged some 77,000 miles and having met with an estimated 372,000 members in 16 countries.

DECEMBER 21

1852 In Washington, D.C., Elder Orson Pratt publishes the first issue of *The Seer,* a Church newspaper.

1896 Leroy J. Robertson, later the composer of eight hymns found in the 1985 hymnal and the *Oratorio from the Book of Mormon,* is born in Fountain Green, Utah.

1913 Arnold Friberg, later an internationally acclaimed artist, whose works include artistic renderings for Cecil B. DeMille's *The Ten Commandments,* a series of Book of Mormon paintings, and *Prayer at Valley Forge,* is born in Winnetka, Illinois.

1955 Ground is broken for the Auckland New Zealand Temple. Local leaders Ariel Ballif, Wendell B. Mendenhall, and George R. Biesinger preside at the ceremony.

1969 The Summerside Branch, the first branch of the Church on Prince Edward Island, Canada, is organized, with Ralph Waugh as president.

1984 The BYU football team wins the Holiday Bowl over the University of Michigan, 24–17, capping an undefeated season (13–0). The team later receives the number one ranking and the NCAA national championship.

1995 The First Presidency announces plans to build the Monterrey México Temple.

The BYU football team—NCAA national champions—21 December 1984.

1918 The Church holds a special fast to petition the Lord to end a worldwide influenza epidemic that had killed over twenty-one million people in four months.

1930 Alexander B. Morrison, later a member of the First Quorum of the Seventy, is born in Edmonton, Alberta, Canada.

1945 Having received permission from U.S. president Harry S. Truman to send aid to the Saints in war-torn Europe, the First Presidency assigns Elder Ezra Taft Benson of the Quorum of the Twelve Apostles to go immediately to Europe to assess the spiritual and temporal needs of the thirty thousand members of the Church there.

Elder Ezra Taft Benson (left) with a former prisoner at a concentration camp in Germany, ca. 1946 (see 1945).

1805 Joseph Smith, later the first prophet and President of the restored Church, is born in Sharon, Vermont.

1816 Thomas Bullock, later a diarist and clerk for Joseph Smith and Brigham Young, is born in Leek, England.

1838 Joseph Smith spends his thirty-third birthday confined in Liberty Jail, Missouri.

1905 President Joseph F. Smith dedicates the Joseph Smith Memorial Cottage and Monument in Sharon, Vermont, on the one hundredth anniversary of the birth of the Prophet Joseph Smith.

1991 The African country of Congo grants the Church formal recognition.

1995 The Church announces a new logo for the name of the Church, focusing the design more prominently on the name of Jesus Christ.

The Prophet Joseph Smith, by Danquart A. Weggelund, ca. 1875 (see 1805).

1905 Children of the Church gather on Christmas Eve at the Tabernacle on Temple Square to commemorate the one hundredth anniversary of the birth of the Prophet Joseph Smith.

1920 The First Presidency announces the release of a new edition of the Book of Mormon with footnotes and new chapter introductions. The text of this version is set in two columns on each page rather than one.

1938 Emmanuel A. Kissi, later a doctor, philanthropist, and Church leader in Ghana, is born in Abomosu, Ghana.

1961 The CBS Radio program *Faith in Action* highlights the Church's activities in Brazil.

1998 China radio airs a Mormon Tabernacle Choir broadcast during prime time.

1999 President Gordon B. Hinckley appears on CNN's *Larry King Live,* which is broadcast from the Tabernacle. Also appearing on the program are Reverend Robert Schuller, who was in Bethlehem, and South African Archbishop Desmond Tutu, who was at the National Cathedral in Washington, D.C.

Talk show host Larry King and President Gordon B. Hinckley, 24 December 1999.

1832 Joseph Smith receives Doctrine and Covenants 87, which contains a prophecy on war.

Temple Square at Christmastime.

1843 Orrin Porter Rockwell, after nearly ten months of imprisonment in Missouri, arrives at the home of Joseph Smith in the midst of a Christmas party. The overwhelmed Prophet joyfully receives his old friend.

1914 The First Presidency asks members of the Church to donate money to relieve suffering of victims of the "Great War" (World War I), being waged in Europe.

1925 Nineteen days after organizing the South American Mission in Buenos Aires, Argentina, Elder Melvin J. Ballard dedicates South America for the preaching of the gospel.

1936 Robert S. Wood, later a member of the Second Quorum of the Seventy, is born in Idaho Falls, Idaho.

1835 Joseph Smith receives Doctrine and Covenants 108, which contains instructions and promises to Lyman Sherman.

Harold B. Lee, ca. 1972 (see 1973).

1895 Sidney B. Sperry, later an author, professor, and BYU Religious Education administrator, is born in Salt Lake City, Utah.

1973 President Harold B. Lee dies in Salt Lake City, Utah, at age seventy-four, after serving for more than thirty-two years as a General Authority.

1992 The Mormon Tabernacle Choir embarks on a historic tour of Israel, with concerts to be held in Jerusalem, Tel Aviv, and Haifa.

1832 Joseph Smith begins to receive the revelation contained in Doctrine and Covenants 88, known as the "Olive Leaf." It commands the Saints to build a temple in Kirtland and offers insights associated with the light of Christ and the laws governing the celestial, terrestrial, and telestial kingdoms.

1847 In the Kanesville Log Tabernacle (located at what would later become Council Bluffs, Iowa), President Brigham Young is unanimously sustained as the second President of the Church, with Heber C. Kimball and Willard Richards as Counselors.

1929 Clinton L. Cutler, later a member of the Second Quorum of the Seventy, is born in Salt Lake City, Utah.

1955 The Presiding Bishopric announces that students at BYU will be organized into campus wards and stakes, setting a pattern for other colleges with a large number of Latter-day Saint students.

Brigham Young a few years after being sustained as President of the Church, 12 December 1850 (see 1847).

1964 The British South Mission is organized.

DECEMBER 28

1789 Algernon Sidney Gilbert, later business partner of Newel K. Whitney and a merchant in Jackson County, Missouri, is born in New Haven, Connecticut.

1927 Robert E. Wells, later a member of the First Quorum of the Seventy, is born in Las Vegas, Nevada.

1946 Francisco J. Vinas, later a member of the First Quorum of the Seventy, is born in Montevideo, Uruguay.

1998 A major revision of the *Church Handbook of Instructions* is completed, bringing priesthood and auxiliary leader guides together for the first time in a two-volume handbook, replacing thirty earlier handbooks and publications.

DECEMBER 29

1818 Sarah Granger (Kimball), later the Relief Society general secretary for twelve years and a women's rights leader, is born in Phelps, New York.

1833 Wilford Woodruff begins recording early Latter-day Saint history in his diary for the first time. In these diaries he would record the daily events of the Church for some sixty-five years.

Actors rehearsing a scene for the Hill Cumorah Pageant, which was composed by Crawford Gates (see 1921).

1921 Crawford Gates, later a music educator and the composer of the productions *Promised Valley* (1947), the Hill Cumorah Pageant (1957 and 1988), and *Visions of Eternity* (1993), is born.

1930 Richard E. Turley Sr., later a member of the Second Quorum of the Seventy, is born in El Paso, Texas.

1934 The Church announces a new schedule for Aaronic Priesthood advancement.

❧❧❧ DECEMBER 30 ❧❧❧

1854 Colonel Edward Steptoe and other prominent non-Mormons in Utah draw up and sign a petition asking U.S. president Franklin Pierce to retain Brigham Young as governor of the territory of Utah. Steptoe had been sent by Pierce to replace Brigham as governor, but he refused to do so when he saw how well the territory was being run.

1884 The Turkish Mission is organized.

1933 J. Kent Jolley, later a member of the Second Quorum of the Seventy, is born in Rexburg, Idaho.

1973 Spencer W. Kimball is ordained and set apart as the twelfth President of the Church, with N. Eldon Tanner and Marion G. Romney as Counselors.

1979 The Church organizes the first branch on La Reunion, a volcanic island in the Indian Ocean.

President Spencer W. Kimball, by Judith Mehr, 1983 (see 1973).

❧❧❧ DECEMBER 31 ❧❧❧

1833 Wilford Woodruff is baptized in an icy stream near Richland, New York. (He is twenty-six years and ten months old.)

1887 Because of government actions during the federal antipolygamy persecutions, the Church is forced to stop work on the Salt Lake Temple.

1900 At the end of the nineteenth century the Church has 283,765 members, 43 stakes, 20 missions, 967 branches and wards, and 4 operating temples.

Jerold Ottley and the Mormon Tabernacle Choir (see 1999).

1940 The First Presidency releases a statement on the military, indicating that the Church will not knowingly call young men on missions to have them avoid the draft established in the United States.

1946 The Church's missionary force rises from an average of 477 serving during 1945 to an average of 2,244 during 1946.

1948 A report indicates that the total value of relief supplies sent to the Saints in Europe after World War II amounts to $1,736,000.

1950 Church membership reaches 1.1 million.

1952 The First Presidency announces that the Primary will sponsor Cub Scout groups (part of the Boy Scouts of America).

1970 The *Millennial Star,* the oldest continuous Church publication, having been published in England since 1840, ends publication. The British Saints are to receive the *Ensign* magazine.

1999 Jerold Ottley retires from the Mormon Tabernacle Choir after a long and distinguished career as director. He is replaced by Craig Jessop, who had been an assistant director since 5 June 1995.

SELECTED BIBLIOGRAPHY

Allen, James B., and others. *Men with a Mission, 1837–1841: The Quorum of the Twelve Apostles in the British Isles.* Salt Lake City: Deseret Book Company, 1992.

Anderson, Richard Lloyd. *Investigating the Book of Mormon Witnesses.* Salt Lake City: Deseret Book Company, 1981.

Andrus, Hyrum L. *Doctrinal Commentary on the Pearl of Great Price.* Salt Lake City: Deseret Book Company, 1998.

Arrington, Leonard J. *Brigham Young: American Moses.* New York: Knopf, 1985.

Backman, Milton V. Jr. *The Heavens Resound: A History of the Latter-day Saints in Ohio, 1830–1838.* Salt Lake City: Deseret Book Company, 1983.

Bennett, Richard E. *Mormons at the Missouri, 1846–1852: "And Should We Die—"* Norman, Oklahoma: University of Oklahoma Press, 1987.

_____. *We'll Find the Place: The Mormon Exodus, 1846–1848.* Salt Lake City: Deseret Book Company, 1997.

Britsch, R. Lanier. *From the East: The History of the Latter-day Saints in Asia, 1851–1996.* Salt Lake City: Deseret Book Company, 1998.

Bushman, Richard L. *Joseph Smith and the Beginnings of Mormonism.* Urbana and Chicago: University of Illinois Press, 1984.

Cannon, Donald Q., and Lyndon W. Cook, *Far West Record: Minutes of The Church of Jesus Christ of Latter-day Saints, 1830–1844.* Salt Lake City: Deseret Book Company, 1983.

Church History in the Fulness of Times: Religion 341–43. Salt Lake City: The Church of Jesus Christ of Latter-day Saints, 1989.

Clark, James R., comp. *Messages of the First Presidency of The Church of Jesus Christ of Latter-day Saints.* 6 vols. Salt Lake City: Bookcraft, 1965–75.

Clayton, William. *William Clayton's Journal: A Daily Record of the Journey of the Original Company of 'Mormon' Pioneers from Nauvoo, Illinois, to the Valley of the Great Salt Lake.* Salt Lake City: Deseret News, 1921.

Cook, Lyndon W. *The Revelations of the Prophet Joseph Smith.* Salt Lake City: Deseret Book Company, 1985.

Cooke, Phillip St. George, and others. *Exploring Southwestern Trails 1846–1854.* Ed. Ralph P. Bieber and Averam B. Bender. Glendale: Arthur H. Clark Company, 1938.

Cowan, Richard O., and William E. Homer. *California Saints: A 150-Year Legacy in the Golden State.* Provo: Religious Studies Center, 1996.

Crockett, David R. *Saints Find the Place: A Day-by-Day Pioneer Experience.* Tucson: LDS-Gems Press, 1997.

_____. *Saints in Exile: A Day-by-Day Pioneer Experience.* Tucson: LDS-Gems Press, 1996.

_____. *Saints in the Wilderness: A Day-by-Day Pioneer Experience.* Tucson: LDS-Gems Press, 1996.

Deseret News Church Almanac. Salt Lake City: Deseret News, 1973–1998.

Evening and Morning Star. Independence, Missouri and Kirtland, Ohio.

Hancock, Levi W. "The Life of Levi Ward Hancock." Typescript, Brigham Young University Archives.

Hill, Donna. *Joseph Smith, the First Mormon.* Garden City: Doubleday, 1977.

Jenson, Andrew, comp. *Church Chronology: A Record of Important Events Pertaining to the History of the Church of Jesus Christ of Latter-day Saints,* 2d ed. rev. Salt Lake City: Deseret News, 1914.

Jessee, Dean C., comp. and ed. *The Personal Writings of Joseph Smith.* Salt Lake City: Deseret Book Company, 1984.

Journal History of The Church of Jesus Christ of Latter-day Saints, LDS Church Archives, Salt Lake City, Utah.

Launius, Roger D. *Zion's Camp: Expedition to Missouri, 1834.* Independence, Missouri: Herald Publishing House, 1984.

LDS Church News. Salt Lake City, Utah.

Ludlow, Daniel H., ed. *Encyclopedia of Mormonism.* 4 vols. New York: Macmillan Publishing Company, 1992.

Matthews, Robert J. *"A Plainer Translation": Joseph Smith's Translation of the Bible, a History and a Commentary.* Provo, Utah: Brigham Young University Press, 1975.

Newell, Linda Kind, and Valeen Tippents Avery. *Mormon Enigma: Emma Hale Smith.* Garden City: Doubleday, 1984.

Oaks, Dallin H., and Marvin S. Hill. *The Carthage Conspiracy: The Trial of the Accused Assassins of Joseph Smith.* Urbana: University of Illinois Press, 1981.

Pratt, Parley P. *Autobiography of Parley P. Pratt.* Salt Lake City: Deseret Book

Company, 1985.

Quincy, Josiah. *Figures of the Past from the Leaves of Old Journals.* Boston: Roberts Brothers, 1883.

Quinn, D. Michael. *The Mormon Hierarchy: Extensions of Power.* Salt Lake City: Signature Books, 1997.

_____. *The Mormon Hierarchy: Origins of Power.* Salt Lake City: Signature Books, 1994.

Roberts, B. H. *A Comprehensive History of the Church of Jesus Christ of Latter-day Saints,* 6 vols. Provo, Utah: Brigham Young University Press, 1965.

Shipps, Jan, and John W. Welch, eds. *The Journals of William E. McLellin, 1831–1836.* Provo, Utah: Brigham Young University Studies and Urbana: University of Chicago, 1994.

Smith, Joseph Jr. *History of The Church of Jesus Christ of Latter-day Saints,* ed. B. H. Roberts, 2d ed. rev., 7 vols. Salt Lake City: Deseret Book Company, 1971.

Smith, Lucy Mack. *Biographical Sketches of Joseph Smith, the Prophet, and His Progenitors for Many Generations.* Liverpool: S. W. Richards, 1853.

Watson, Eldon J. *Manuscript History of Brigham Young, 1846–1847.* Salt Lake City: Eldon J. Watson, 1971.

PHOTO AND ILLUSTRATION CREDITS

Page 68—Courtesy of LDS Church Archives, Salt Lake City, Utah

Page 70—Courtesy of LDS Church Archives, Salt Lake City, Utah

Page 71 (left)—Courtesy of LDS Church Archives, Salt Lake City, Utah

Page 71 (right)—Courtesy of LDS Church Archives, Salt Lake City, Utah

Page 72—Courtesy of LDS Church Visual Resource Library, Salt Lake City, Utah; copyright Intellectual Reserve, all rights reserved

Page 73—Courtesy of LDS Church Visual Resource Library, Salt Lake City, Utah; copyright Intellectual Reserve, all rights reserved

Page 74—Courtesy of Richard Neitzel Holzapfel

Page 75—Courtesy of Gary L. and Carol B. Bunker

Page 76—Courtesy of LDS Church Visual Resource Library, Salt Lake City, Utah; copyright Intellectual Reserve, all rights reserved

Page 77 (left)—Courtesy of Utah State Historical Society, Salt Lake City, Utah

Page 77 (right)—*Deseret News* photo, Salt Lake City, Utah

Page 78—Courtesy of LDS Church Archives, Salt Lake City, Utah

Page 79—Courtesy of Nebraska State Historical Society, Lincoln, Nebraska

Page 81—Courtesy of Stephen H. Smoot

Page 82—Courtesy of LDS Church Visual Resource Library, Salt Lake City, Utah; copyright Intellectual Reserve, all rights reserved

Page 84—*Deseret News* photo, Salt Lake City, Utah

Page 85—Photo by Thales Haskell Smith, courtesy of LDS Church Archives, Salt Lake City, Utah

Page 86 (left)—Courtesy of LDS Church Archives, Salt Lake City, Utah

Page 86 (right)—Courtesy of Darrel Chamberlain

Page 87—Courtesy of Photo Archives, Marriott Library, University of Utah, Salt Lake City, Utah

Page 88 (left)—Courtesy of H. Von Packard

Page 88 (right)—Courtesy of Utah State Historical Society, Salt Lake City, Utah

Page 89—Courtesy of Photo Archives, Marriott Library, University of Utah, Salt Lake City, Utah

Page 90—Courtesy of LDS Church Archives, Salt Lake City, Utah

Page 91—Photo by Mark A. Philbrick, courtesy of University Communications, Brigham Young University, Provo, Utah

Page 92—Courtesy of R. Q. Shupe

Page 93—Photo by Charles R. Savage, courtesy of Richard Neitzel Holzapfel

Page 94 (left)—Courtesy of LDS Church Archives, Salt Lake City, Utah

Page 94 (right)—Courtesy of LDS Church Archives, Salt Lake City, Utah

Page 95—Painting by C. J. Fox, courtesy of LDS Museum of Church History and Art, Salt Lake City, Utah

Page 96—Photo by Robert Wilson Stum, courtesy of LDS Church Archives, Salt Lake City, Utah

Page 97—Photo by Mark A. Philbrick, courtesy of University Communications, Brigham Young University, Provo, Utah

Page 98—Painting by Christian Eisele, courtesy of LDS Museum of Church History and Art, Salt Lake City, Utah

Page 99 (top)—Photo by Albert Wilkes, courtesy of LDS Church Archives, Salt Lake City, Utah

Page 99 (bottom)—Courtesy of LDS Church Archives, Salt Lake City, Utah

Page 100—Courtesy of Utah State Historical Society, Salt Lake City, Utah

Page 101—Courtesy of LDS Church Archives, Salt Lake City, Utah

Page 102 (left)—Courtesy of LDS Church Archives, Salt Lake City, Utah

Page 102 (right)—Cartoon by Jonathon Brown, *Deseret News* photo, Salt Lake City, Utah

Page 103 (left)—Courtesy of Richard Neitzel Holzapfel

Page 103 (right)—Courtesy of LDS Church Archives, Salt Lake City, Utah

Page 104—Courtesy of LDS Church Archives, Salt Lake City, Utah

Page 105—Courtesy of LDS Church Archives, Salt Lake City, Utah

Page 106—Courtesy of Robert Harmon

Page 107—Courtesy of Photo Archives, Harold B. Lee Library, Brigham Young University, Provo, Utah

Page 109 (left)—Photo by Marsena Cannon, courtesy of LDS Church Archives, Salt Lake City, Utah

Page 109 (right)—Courtesy of Utah State Historical Society, Salt Lake City, Utah

Page 110—Mariner's Museum, Newport News, Virginia

Page 111—Photo by Charles W. Carter, courtesy of LDS Church Archives, Salt Lake City, Utah

Page 112—Courtesy of LDS Church Archives, Salt Lake City, Utah

Page 113—Photo by George Edward Anderson, courtesy of LDS Church Archives, Salt Lake City, Utah

Page 114—Courtesy of LDS Church Visual Resource Library, Salt Lake City, Utah; copyright Intellectual Reserve, all rights reserved

Page 115—Photo by Robert Wilson Stum, courtesy of LDS Church Archives, Salt Lake City, Utah

Page 116—Photo by Charles W. Carter, courtesy of R. Q. Shupe

Page 117—Courtesy of LDS Church Archives, Salt Lake City, Utah

Page 118—Painting by Paul Clowes, courtesy of *Deseret News*, Salt Lake City, Utah

Page 119—Courtesy of Mark H. Willes

Page 120—Courtesy of Alexander L. Baugh

Page 121 (left)—Photo by Mark A. Philbrick, courtesy of University Communications, Brigham Young University, Provo, Utah

Page 121 (right)—Courtesy of LDS Church Archives, Salt Lake City, Utah

Page 122—Courtesy of Susannah Broberg Langenheim

Page 123—*Deseret News* photo, Salt Lake City, Utah

Page 124 (left)—Courtesy of LDS Church Visual Resource Library, Salt Lake City, Utah; copyright Intellectual Reserve, all rights reserved

Page 124 (right)—Photo by Lucian Foster, courtesy of LDS Church Archives, Salt Lake City, Utah

Page 125—Courtesy of LDS Museum of Church History and Art, Salt Lake City, Utah

Page 126—Courtesy of LDS Church Archives, Salt Lake City, Utah

Page 127—Painting by Gary Smith, courtesy of LDS Museum of Church History and Art, Salt Lake City, Utah

Page 128—Courtesy of LDS Museum of Church History and Art, Salt Lake City, Utah

Page 130—Photo by Mark A. Philbrick, courtesy of University Communications, Brigham Young University, Provo, Utah

Page 131—Courtesy of Alexander L. Baugh

Page 133—Courtesy of Richard Neitzel Holzapfel

Page 134—Courtesy of LDS Church Archives, Salt Lake City, Utah

Page 135—Courtesy of Photo Archives, Harold B. Lee Library, Brigham Young University, Provo, Utah

Page 136—Courtesy of Utah State Historical Society, Salt Lake City, Utah

Page 137 (left)—Courtesy of LDS Church Archives, Salt Lake City Utah

Page 137 (right)—Courtesy of Elaine Cannon

Page 138 (left)—Courtesy of R. Q. Shupe

Page 138 (right)—Courtesy of Cynthia Doxey

Page 140 (left)—Courtesy of Utah State Historical Society, Salt Lake City, Utah

Page 140 (right)—Courtesy of Janet Lee

Page 141—Courtesy of LDS Museum of Church History and Art, Salt Lake City, Utah

Page 142—Courtesy of Don Busath

Page 143—Courtesy of LDS Museum of Church History and Art, Salt Lake City, Utah

Page 144 (left)—Photo by P. Cardinell Vincent Company, courtesy of LDS Church Archives, Salt Lake City, Utah

Page 144 (right)—*Deseret News* photo

Page 145—Courtesy of Kenneth L. Cannon II

Page 146—Painting by A. Westwood, courtesy of LDS Museum of Church History and Art, Salt Lake City, Utah

Page 147 (left)—Courtesy of LDS Church Archives, Salt Lake City, Utah

Page 147 (right)—Courtesy of LDS Church Archives, Salt Lake City, Utah

Page 148—Courtesy of Cory Maxwell

Page 149—Photo by Charles W. Carter, courtesy of LDS Church Archives, Salt Lake City, Utah

Page 150—Painting by Knud Ebsberg, courtesy of LDS Museum of Church History and Art, Salt Lake City, Utah

Page 151—Courtesy of LDS Church Visual Resource Library, Salt Lake City, Utah; copyright Intellectual Reserve, all rights reserved

Page 152 (left)—Courtesy of Glen L. Rudd

Page 152 (right)—Courtesy of Alexander L. Baugh

Page 153 (top)—Courtesy of BYU Sports Information

Page 153 (bottom)—Photo by Charles W. Carter, courtesy of LDS Church Archives, Salt Lake City, Utah

Page 154—Courtesy of Floyd Holdman

Page 155—Photo by Robert Wilson Stum, courtesy of LDS Church Archives, Salt Lake City, Utah

Page 156—Courtesy of Associated Press, World Wide Photo

Page 158 (left)—Courtesy of Photo Archives, Harold B. Lee Library, Brigham Young University, Provo, Utah

Page 158 (right)—Courtesy of LDS Church Visual Resource Library, Salt Lake City, Utah; copyright Intellectual Reserve, all rights reserved

Page 159—Photo by George Edward Anderson, courtesy of LDS Church Archives, Salt Lake City, Utah

Page 160—Courtesy of LDS Church Archives, Salt Lake City, Utah

Page 161 (left)—Photo by Charles R. Savage, courtesy of Nelson B. Wadsworth

Page 161 (right)—Courtesy of LDS Church Visual Resource Library, Salt Lake City, Utah; copyright Intellectual Reserve, all rights reserved

Page 163 (left)—Courtesy of LDS Church Visual Resource Library, Salt Lake City, Utah; copyright Intellectual Reserve, all rights reserved

Page 163 (right)—Painting by Knud Ebsberg, courtesy of LDS Museum of Church History and Art, Salt Lake City, Utah

Page 164 (left)—Courtesy of LDS Church Archives, Salt Lake City, Utah

Page 164 (right)—Courtesy of Photo Archives, Harold B. Lee Library, Brigham Young University, Provo, Utah

Page 165 (left)—Courtesy of LDS Church Visual Resource Library, Salt Lake City, Utah; copyright Intellectual Reserve, all rights reserved

Page 165 (right)—Painting by Lynn Fausett, courtesy of LDS Museum of Church History and Art, Salt Lake City, Utah

Page 166 (left)—Courtesy of LDS Church Archives, Salt Lake City, Utah

Page 166 (right)—Courtesy of LDS Church Visual Resource Library, Salt Lake City, Utah; copyright Intellectual Reserve, all rights reserved

Page 168—Courtesy of Utah State Historical Society, Salt Lake City, Utah

Page 169 (left)—Painting by George M. Ottinger, courtesy of LDS Museum of Church History and Art, Salt Lake City, Utah

Page 169 (right)—Courtesy of Photo Archives, Marriott Library, University of Utah, Salt Lake City, Utah

Page 170—Painting by H. E. Petersen, courtesy of LDS Museum of Church History and Art, Salt Lake City, Utah

Page 171—Courtesy of Utah State Historical Society, Salt Lake City, Utah

Page 172—Photo by Mark A. Philbrick, courtesy of University Communications, Brigham Young University, Provo, Utah

Page 173—Photo by James H. Crockwell, courtesy of Nelson B. Wadsworth

Page 174—Courtesy of LDS Church Archives, Salt Lake City, Utah

Page 175—Painting by Knud Ebsberg, courtesy of LDS Museum of Church History and Art, Salt Lake City, Utah

Page 176—Courtesy of RLDS Church Archives, Independence, Missouri

Page 177—Courtesy of LDS Church Archives, Salt Lake City, Utah

Page 178—Painting by Lewis A. Ramsey, courtesy of LDS Museum of Church History and Art, Salt Lake City, Utah

Page 179 (left)—Courtesy of Richard Neitzel Holzapfel

Page 179 (right)—Courtesy of Larry B. Nicholson

Page 180—Deseret Book Company photo

Page 181—Courtesy of LDS Church Archives, Salt Lake City, Utah

Page 182—International Daughters of Utah Pioneers, Salt Lake City, Utah

Page 183—Courtesy of Photo Archives, Harold B. Lee Library, Brigham Young University, Provo, Utah

Page 184 (left)—Painting by Tom Lovell, courtesy of LDS Church Visual Resource Library, Salt Lake City, Utah; copyright Intellectual Reserve, all rights reserved

Page 184 (right)—Photo by Craig Diamond, courtesy of LDS Church Visual Resource Library, Salt Lake City, Utah; copyright Intellectual Reserve, all rights reserved

Page 185—Courtesy of Darrel Chamberlain

Page 186 (left)—Photo by Christensen N. LaVeal, courtesy of Photo Archives, Harold B. Lee Library, Brigham Young University, Provo, Utah

Page 186 (right)—Photo by Floyd Holdman, courtesy of LDS Church Archives, Salt Lake City, Utah

Page 187 (left)—Courtesy of LDS Church Visual Resource Library, Salt Lake City, Utah; copyright Intellectual Reserve, all rights reserved

Page 187 (right)—Deseret Book Company photo

Page 188—Courtesy of BYU Physical Plant Department

Page 189—Courtesy of LDS Church Archives, Salt Lake City, Utah

Page 191 (left)—Courtesy of Vance A. Law

Page 191 (right)—Photo by George Edward Anderson, courtesy of Photo Archives, Harold B. Lee Library, Brigham Young University, Provo, Utah

Page 192—Courtesy of Richard Neitzel Holzapfel

Page 193—Courtesy of LDS Church Visual Resource Library, Salt Lake City, Utah; copyright Intellectual Reserve, all rights reserved

Page 194—Courtesy of LDS Church Visual Resource Library, Salt Lake City, Utah; copyright Intellectual Reserve, all rights reserved

Page 195—Courtesy of Utah State Historical Society, Salt Lake City, Utah

Page 196—Courtesy of RLDS Church Archives, Independence, Missouri

Page 197—Courtesy of Bill Cox Photography

Page 198 (left)—Courtesy of Gail S. Halvorsen

Page 198 (right)—Courtesy of LDS Church Visual Resource Library, Salt Lake City, Utah; copyright Intellectual Reserve, all rights reserved

Page 199—Courtesy of Forever Young, Inc.

Page 200 (left)—Photo by Mark A. Philbrick, courtesy of University Communications, Brigham Young University, Provo, Utah

Page 200 (right)—Courtesy of Museum of Art, Brigham Young University, Provo, Utah

Page 201—Photo by George Edward Anderson, courtesy of LDS Church Archives, Salt Lake City, Utah

Page 202 (left)—Courtesy of LDS Church Archives, Salt Lake City, Utah

Page 202 (right)—Courtesy of LDS Church Archives, Salt Lake City, Utah

Page 203—Courtesy of LDS Church Archives, Salt Lake City, Utah

Page 204—Courtesy of LDS Museum of Church History and Art, Salt Lake City, Utah

Page 205—Courtesy of LDS Church Archives, Salt Lake City, Utah

Page 206—Courtesy of Richard Staples

Page 207—Courtesy of Stephen R. Covey

Page 208—Courtesy of LDS Church Archives, Salt Lake City, Utah

Page 209 (left)—Deseret Book Company photo

Page 209 (right)—*Deseret News* photo, Salt Lake City, Utah

Page 210—Courtesy of LDS Church Archives, Salt Lake City, Utah

Page 211—Painting by C.C.A. Christensen, courtesy of Museum of Art, Brigham Young University, Provo, Utah

Page 213 (left)—Courtesy of Craig B. Blankenhorn, CBS News

Page 213 (right)—Courtesy of Western Reserve Historical Society

Page 214—*Deseret News* photo

Page 215—Photo by Mark A. Philbrick, courtesy of University Communications, Brigham Young University, Provo, Utah

Page 216—Courtesy of LDS Church Archives, Salt Lake City, Utah

Page 217—Sculpture by Lawrence O. Ehigiator, courtesy of LDS Museum of Church History and Art, Salt Lake City, Utah

Page 218—U.S. Naval Historical Center, Washington, D.C.

Page 219—Courtesy of Elaine L. Jack

Page 220 (left)—*Deseret News* photo

Page 220 (right)—Courtesy of Busath Photography

Page 221—Courtesy of Darrel Chamberlain

Page 222—Painting by Albert Salzbrenner, courtesy of LDS Museum of Church History and Art, Salt Lake City, Utah

Page 223 (left)—*Deseret News* photo

Page 223 (right)—Photo by Lucian Foster, courtesy of LDS Church Archives, Salt Lake City, Utah

Page 224 (left)—Courtesy of Utah State Historical Society, Salt Lake City, Utah

Page 224 (right)—Courtesy of LDS Church Archives, Salt Lake City, Utah

Page 225 (left)—Courtesy of LDS Church Archives, Salt Lake City, Utah

Page 225 (right)—Courtesy of LDS Church Archives, Salt Lake City, Utah

Page 226—*Deseret News* photo

Page 227—Deseret Book Company photo

Page 228—Photo by Mark A. Philbrick, courtesy of University Communications, Brigham Young University, Provo, Utah

Page 230 (left)—Courtesy of Greg Christofferson

Page 230 (right)—Courtesy of Photo Archives, Harold B. Lee Library, Brigham Young University, Provo, Utah

Page 231—Courtesy of LDS Church Archives, Salt Lake City, Utah

Page 232—Courtesy of LDS Church Archives, Salt Lake City, Utah

Page 233—Courtesy of Darrel Chamberlain

Page 234—Courtesy of Robert L. Freeman

Page 235 (left)—Courtesy of L. Jay Silvester

Page 235 (right)—Courtesy of Nelson B. Wadsworth

Page 236—Photo by Mark A. Philbrick, courtesy of University Communications, Brigham Young University, Provo, Utah

Page 237—Courtesy of LDS Church Archives, Salt Lake City, Utah

Page 238 (left)—Courtesy of Darrel Chamberlain

Page 238 (right)—Courtesy of LDS Church Archives, Salt Lake City, Utah

INDEX

261